Digital Diasporas

Digital Diasporas

Labor and Affect in Gendered Indian Digital Publics

Radhika Gajjala

ROWMAN & LITTLEFIELD
INTERNATIONAL

London • New York

Published by Rowman & Littlefield International, Ltd.
6 Tinworth Street, London SE11 5AL
www.rowmaninternational.com

Rowman & Littlefield International, Ltd. is an affiliate of
Rowman & Littlefield
4501 Forbes Boulevard, Suite 200, Lanham, Maryland 20706, USA
With additional offices in Boulder, New York, Toronto (Canada), and London
(UK)
www.rowman.com

British Library Cataloguing in Publication Information
A catalogue record for this book is available from the British Library

ISBN: HB 978-1-7834-8115-6
ISBN: PB 978-1-7834-8116-3

Library of Congress Cataloging-in-Publication Data

Name: Gajjala, Radhika, 1960- author
Title: Digital diasporas : Labor and affect in gendered Indian digital publics /
    Radhika Gajjala.
Description: London ; New York : Rowman & Littlefield International, Ltd., 2019. / Includes
    bibliographical references and index.
Identifiers: LCCN 2019002455 / ISBN 9781783481156 (cloth) / ISBN
    9781783481163 (pbk.) / ISBN 9781783481170 (electronic)
Subjects: LCSH: Information society--India. / Digital divide--India. / Computers and women-
    -India. / Women--India--Social conditions.
Classification: LCC HM 851.G335 2019 / DDC 302.230954--dc23
LC record available at https://lccn.loc.gov/2019002455

Digital Diasporas

Labor and Affect in Gendered Indian Digital Publics

Radhika Gajjala

R O W M A N *&*
L I T T L E F I E L D
——————————— INTERNATIONAL

London • New York

Published by Rowman & Littlefield International, Ltd.
6 Tinworth Street, London SE11 5AL
www.rowmaninternational.com

Rowman & Littlefield International, Ltd. is an affiliate of
Rowman & Littlefield
4501 Forbes Boulevard, Suite 200, Lanham, Maryland 20706, USA
With additional offices in Boulder, New York, Toronto (Canada), and London
(UK)
www.rowman.com

British Library Cataloguing in Publication Information
A catalogue record for this book is available from the British Library

ISBN: HB 978-1-7834-8115-6
ISBN: PB 978-1-7834-8116-3

Library of Congress Cataloging-in-Publication Data

Name: Gajjala, Radhika, 1960- author
Title: Digital diasporas : Labor and affect in gendered Indian digital publics /
    Radhika Gajjala.
Description: London ; New York : Rowman & Littlefield International, Ltd., 2019. / Includes
    bibliographical references and index.
Identifiers: LCCN 2019002455 / ISBN 9781783481156 (cloth) / ISBN
    9781783481163 (pbk.) / ISBN 9781783481170 (electronic)
Subjects: LCSH: Information society--India. / Digital divide--India. / Computers and women-
    -India. / Women--India--Social conditions.
Classification: LCC HM 851.G335 2019 / DDC 302.230954--dc23
LC record available at htps://lccn.loc.gov/2019002455

In conversation with

Sarada Nori Akella
Varsha Ayyar
Sohni Chakrabarti
Arpita Chakraborty
Sriya Chattopadhyay
Christina Thomas Dhanaraj
Mirna Guha
Pallavi Guha
Nithila Kanagasabai
Divya Kandukuri
Sukhnidh Kaur
Damini Kulkarni
Inji Pennu
Shilpa Phadke
Debipreeta Rahut
Pallavi Rao
Raya Sarkar
Riddhima Sharma
Puthiya Purayil Sneha
Shobha SV
Noopur Tiwari
Smita Vanniyar
Ayesha Vemuri
Tarishi Verma
Kaitlyn Wauthier

Contents

Acknowledgments

This book is dedicated to my mother, who passed away in June 2017 at the age of ninety-three, and who, in her span of life, saw many firsts in communication and media technologies—telegram, radio, telephone, cinema, television, the internet, smartphones . . . (my last memories of her are from a few days before she passed away, speaking to me on Skype).

The introduction and conclusion of this book—as well as other chapters—contain many acknowledgments, as I tell the story of collaborations, so I will not reiterate those here. I thank all the coauthors of the dialogue interludes.

Fulbright-Norway and the University of Bergen provided me opportunity to travel and interview migrants from South Asia in Norway. I am thankful also to Bowling Green State University for the Faculty Improvement Leave granted to me in order to take advantage of my Fulbright award and to reside in Norway while also travelling in Europe during the 2015–2016 academic year. Physically moving through various South Asian and other immigrant spaces in Europe and UK during this period – taking ethnographic field notes and interviewing some of the South Asians – gave an even more nuanced understanding of how complex and layered the histories of migration from the South Asian region are. Teaching topics related to digital labor and social media as well as postcolonial theory to undergraduate and graduate students at the University of Bergen was very productive to the process of understanding global digital mediation. Thanks especially to Jill

Walker Rettberg, Hilde Corneliussen, and Gilda Seddighi for conversations of relevance to this project. Thanks also to Sandra Ponzanezi, Koen Leurs, and their "Dream Team" (Claudia Minchilli, Laura Candidatu, Donya Alinejad, Mel Mevsimler) working on issues around digital migrants in the ERC-funded Connecting Europe project. Madhuri Prabhakar, whom I met through this team, also was helpful and generously shared her experience of studying Surinamese Indians living in Netherlands.

In 2016, I was invited to the DigiNaka symposium, at TISS, Mumbai, where I met several of those whom I later interviewed and some who contributed to the interludes. The Girls at Dhabas group from Pakistan also needs to be acknowledged—we had several sessions of conversations via Skype along with Shilpa Phadke while I was in Norway and also when I was in Bowling Green. In fact my initial understandings of contemporary "digital streets" activisms in South Asia came from conversations with Jasmeen Patheja, Shilpa Phadke, and Girls at Dhabas.

I did not include the writing and conversations with them in the final manuscript because the book narrowed to a nation orientation as "Indian" digital diasporas. The dialogue interlude I started with Jasmeen also did not end up in the final book manuscript because of time and other logistics. But I have several interviews with her, and she was one of the first few Indian feminist activists (in digital space post-2003) that I interviewed for this project as well. She and I have had many engaging conversations (even in person in "Coconut Grove" over Kerala food and at her home in Bangalore over tea and cookies). I hope to have the opportunity to write with them or use their interview data in other writing projects. In summer 2018 I was invited to IIIT Bangalore by Preeti Mudliar—I had extensive discussions with her as well that fed into some of my writing in this book. During my visit to the Center for Internet and Society in Bangalore, I had extremely productive discussions with Sumandro Chattapadhyay, P. P. Sneha, Padmini Ray Murray, Pooja Sagar, and Chinar Shah.

I would be remiss if I did not mention early connectors and supporters of this project including Namita Aavriti, Shakuntala Banaji, Maitreyi Basu, Sujatha Subramanian and so many others. These were some my early contacts who connected me to several interviewees. I know I've missed many names here.

Thanks also to participants of the GIAN Programme: Studying Gender, Digital Labor and Globalization: Theory and Method (August

2018) at Savithribai Phule Pune University, and to Professor Saroj Ghaskadbi and Professor Madhavi Reddy, who made the seminar possible. All the participants of this group had valuable inputs for me. Consider yourselves named and thanked! Of this group, I especially want to thank Damini Kulkarni for volunteering to do more than I asked of most of the dialogue interlude coauthors and for talking me through issues around what might be trigger points in interludes, helping with the editing, and giving me support and advice in the final stages of the manuscript preparation. Sai Amulya and Devina Sarwatay – thanks for the cheering on and suggesting literature to consult via instagram and facebook! I also want to thank Usha Raman and Elizabeth Losh for their encouragement of this project and Andre Brock for periodically cheering on via twitter.

The "South Asian Twitterverse" group deserves mention as well— Srila Roy, Sonja Thomas, Debarati Sen, Pallavi Guha, Sohni C, Arpita Chakraborti, Ayesha Vemuri, Padmini Ray Murray, and all the others who wove in and out of our conversations. I am also grateful for conversations on various Facebook timelines (mine and Srila Roy's especially)—publicly shared—with all of these folks and with Nandini Deo, Inderpal Grewal, Trish Mitra-Kahn, and several of those already named and acknowledged. And thank you to the National Women's Studies Association South Asia Caucus colleagues from 2017 and 2018 NWSA meetings such as Sobia Khan, Archana Bhat, Nandini Iyer, Archana Pathak, Dhanashree Thorat, Charu Charusheela, Priya Jha, and Prathim-Maya Dora-Laskey (the latter three who connect back to my SAWnet days from the 1990s). And of course thank you to my fellow panelists from 2018 NWSA—Sanjam Ahluwalia, Karolina Kulicka, Devaleena Das, and also several others in the audience. Also thank you to Archana Bhat and Ashwini Tambe for conversations and insights.

The Dalit feminist Twitterverse is an amazing resource for Savarna women trying to understand where the Indian feminist movement went wrong and why the class ("economic") argument should not be made to discount Dalit voices. Special thanks to Varsha Ayyar, Christina Thomas Dhanraj, Divya Kandukuri, Swati Kamble, and a couple of anonymous Twitter users from this Twitterverse for the excellent work they do—but also for being willing to engage in conversation with me and putting up with my many emails, WhatsApp messages, and DMs.

Contact with Tarishi Verma and Riddhima Sharma began when they agreed to be interviewees and then later to do dialogue interludes. They continue now to educate me about their generation of Indian feminists here in Bowling Green as my doctoral advisees. In the Spring semester of 2019, Shamika Dixit (who was a participant the GIAN seminar at Pune) came for her foreign immersion to Bowling Green State University, and conversations with her also contributed to some last minute tweaks in the manuscript. Zehui Dai, Alyssa Fisher, Shane Snyder, and David Stephens directly and indirectly helped me get past some moments when I was "stuck." Discussions with one of my colleagues, Michaela Walsh, were key in helping me get unstuck as did repeated in-person meetings and WhatsApp messages with Sriya, and Skypes, WhatsApp messages, and phone calls with Sarada and Sneha. Similarly, several other of my co-authors were also willing to talk, write, and edit with me—whatever time zone I happened to be in (Bergen, Bowling Green, or Hyderabad) when I had repeated concerns about whether what I was writing was a "plausible account" based on interviews and conversations that I had had with them.

My research assistant from 2017–2018 (Kaitlyn Wauthier), whose main job was to work with me on Fembot Collective and *Ada* journal work, contributed her time and effort to proofreading during times when *Ada*/Fembot work was a little slower. She also continued to be my sounding board after she was no longer my paid research assistant. I also want to thank the many interviewees who gave of their time—in compliance with the internal review board guidelines, I cannot reveal their names here—as well as my Bowling Green State University colleagues and students.

Thanks to all my Facebook, Twitter, and Instagram cheerer-on-ers and to good friends and colleagues from Fembot Collective and from various academic and social spaces for their encouragement (especially Carol Stabile). Finally, I'd like to thank all the staff at Rowman & Littlefield International (even those working behind the scenes) who worked with me on various stages of this project: Martina O'Sullivan worked with me to get my contract approved in 2014. Most of my communication in regard to what was the final manuscript was with Natalie Linh Bolderston, Elaine McGarraugh, and Gurdeep Mattu, and I appreciate their willingness to work with the format of writing I adopted. Thanks also to the very insightful feedback on a related essay by Nandini Dhar and Peerzada Raouf, which allowed me to see some gaps regarding explanations of the class and caste nexus and the relationship between the digital streets and physical streets—both problematic binaries—that needed to be engaged and addressed. I aim to address these further in a future book that is being written even as this one goes to press.

Thanks also to blind peer reviewers of the proposal between late 2013 and January 2014 and of the first completed draft of the manuscript between March and June 2018. The project has changed from 2013 to 2018, but a lot of the original review suggestions were relevant and taken into account as well.

To all my siblings, nieces, nephews, nephews-in-law, grandnieces, grandnephews, grandnephew-in-law—even as infrequently as I've been able to see them in person or on social media (whether they think they know me or I know them).

As always, thanks to my spouse, Venkat Gajjala, and my son, Pratap Gajjala, for understanding and tolerating my writing obsessions. Also much appreciation for Durga, my muse. She's a feisty, huggable, large dog who woke up to sit with me—and also occasionally typed and drooled over my laptop as early as 4 a.m. on some days when I would sneak in the darkness to write (she belongs to my son, in case you were wondering).

Finally, if I have overlooked someone (I'm sure I have), my sincerest apologies! All faults and mistakes in this manuscript are mine.

Introduction

A key point of entry for the research in this book is the "South Asian (digital) diaspora" as narrated through histories of internet use/digital connectivity of South Asians worldwide. There are several possible ways to conceptualize a research project that studies how South Asians become part of digital diasporas. In a binary framing of user research versus the study of textual/visual representations, for instance, we can think of South Asian digital diasporas by privileging the examination of access to informational communication technologies for various people of South Asian descent—where their spatio-temporal everyday experience shifts their subjectivities and corporeal existence through immersion in global digital environments; the other way is to look at texts (including audio, visual, interactive, and so on) online as manifestations of subject positions from particular geographical, sociocultural, and/or religious locations that are considered to be of the South Asian region. These are not mutually exclusive approaches—one informs the other—and most research projects use a mix of both approaches and engage methods for data collection that allow us to see the interdependence. In the case of the former, where the focus begins with questions of access from the geographical region from which the access to digital is taking place, we think through (dominant regional/national/cultural) histories that privilege where and when a body is in a certain place and how that impacts the accessing of and participation in the digital. The temporal register here is the location of the body within a timeline of geographical and economic access (again narrated through dominant national/regional/cultural frameworks) to particular "new" technologies. In the case of the latter, where we privilege texts as publics in emphasizing texts and formats, we generally think in terms of affordances of technological platforms, mobile applications, and associated gadgets. Our temporal register—narrative—is seen as a linear progression of technological innovation that is supposedly always moving us toward a self-empowered and egalitarian society.

In talking of geographical/national/regional access, we talk of policy shifts, literacy, education, culture, and opportunities for upward mobility through connectivity. We also tend to think of empowerment and access in terms of "voice"—as direct (unmediated by power hierarchies) speech coming from a corporeal body on the other end of the gadget/computer. In a public imaginary of such empowerment, the gadgets and computers are releasing the body from its shackles through digital connectivity. In examinations of representations as well we can fall into the trap of looking at the disembodied text as representing freedom and agency, even as we know that negotiation of speech and agency is a much more complex negotiation—and that being able to connect outward does not completely and by itself guarantee the extraction of a person from within oppressive infrastructures.

However, we can think critically and use a nuanced approach to how we examine the emergence of online subjects from both these entry points. In thinking of issues of access from various geographical locations, we can ask questions about which populations have access and how they are positioned through their access points. Do the affordances of the gadget and/or platform for engaging the digital provide access, misinformation, or surveillance, for example? Under what conditions is access liberating and empowering? In discussing diasporas as represented through the textual—where we start with thinking through who is represented, how, and why—we look at how the digital publics as texts and the forms of a variety of texts are internet mediated. We observe how they shape the South Asian presence based on who feels invited, oppressed, marginalized, or silenced—and who is simply not even there in these spaces, even as any sort of a discursive presence.

Both of these approaches are necessary to think in terms of histories of online presences (and absences) of South Asians and of representative community formations through digital publics. Thus we have to acknowledge that the history of South Asian digital publics started even before a large number of people from the region of South Asia had direct access to these spaces. South Asian immigrants to (mostly) the Global North had already formed South Asian communities online before those from the region began to join these digital diasporas. Therefore, even the digital subjectivities of the South Asians connecting from the region of South Asia encounter this ethos as they come into digital global publics—even as they may have started their access in digitally local publics with tools that were not as widespread in the Global North, such as Orkut or regional language texting for instance. The larger South Asian digital diasporas, which have been shaped by a combination of existing technological design, invisible algorithmic logics, and platform rules and guidelines, in addition to the sociocultural and political discourses put out by South Asians in diaspora, collide and clash with digital subjects that come directly from the region. Yet these temporally previous South Asian digital diasporas that predate those that I describe in this book are also complex. They never were homogenous. Neither were they comprised of just the post 1960s immigrants to the global north. Rather they were perceived as homogenous - more so than the post 2005 forms of South Asian digital diasporas. Currently, the number of available platforms, their access points and affordances, contribute to the visibility of the diversity of voices in South Asian digital diasporas driven by what Appadurai (1996) would characterize as technoscapes shaped by "complex relationships among money flows, political possibilities, and the availability of both un- and highly skilled labor."[1] Thus, for instance, on the one hand we have young women from different social groups in India connecting to the internet, but on the other we also have young women with histories of travel and family migration out of the region of South Asia that date back to the 1800 when indentured laborers were being brought to the Caribbean Islands[2] who in contemporary times also connect to the internet and identify as part of an "Indian" diaspora. Thus an examination of south Asian digital diasporas through a deep hanging out in online spaces and through indepth and semi-structured interviews potentially takes us through a complex layered journey into histories of labor, (re)connectivity and affective bonds, as well as into protest movements in digital publics around issues of caste and race. Thus we see an emerging transnational Dalit Twitter[3] for instance and we also see racial coalitions connecting Black, Indigenous, People of Color (BIPOC)[4] where South Asians who share common histories of labor migration and oppression connect with Black and Indigenous activists online. In addition to these internet mediated transnational activist connections, there is also a visibilizing of networks formed through historical connections between Dalit diasporas and Black communities which pre-date social media publics. For instance, as far back as the 1970s, NRI Dalit formations such as the "Volunteers in Service to India's Oppressed and Neglected" (VISION) and they

> aligned with the Black Panther movement in the US and 114 Economic and Political Weekly January 3, 2004 highlighted their plight, which became the symbol of dalit and black unity. According to a VODI report, 2000 the Ambedkar centre for Justice and Peace was established in Canada a decade before issues of dalits were highlighted at different International forums.[5]

Dalit feminists in contemporary social media space reach for Black feminists such as Audre Lorde and bell hooks for inspiration.

Histories of South Asians in diaspora who become digital also includes the splitting up and layering of South Asian diasporas into (imagined) nation-state-based digital diasporas—where the digital presences of Indians in diaspora for instance produce "India online." In looking for and finding an India online that predates access from diverse regions and from diverse identity categories (defined through linguistics, religious backgrounds, caste, class, etc.), one finds that the certain groups are already treated as implicitly not Indian based in diasporic Indian imaginaries and a reenvisioning of Indianness through an "idea of the nation—not the nation as a bounded geographical unit but the nation as an ideological force."[6]

Since the early 1990s, a time that coincides with global access to the internet in the form of the World Wide Web, there have been certain rearticulations of categories of diasporas from the South Asian region through techno-mediation. Such rearticulations are based in the naming of diasporas alternatively through the politics of nation-state and through transnational linkages along the lines of struggle for nation-state (as in the case of Tamil Eelam diasporas). Digitally produced and circulated media play a significant role in such South Asian diasporas. They cut across South Asian nation-state-based identities sometimes, but the nation-state distinctions are implicit in the interactions oftentimes as well.

Thus, for instance, in the case of the Indian nation-state, online interaction and sharing of media and information among transnationally located Indian diasporic communities from various generations contributes to nostalgia for an imagined homeland for non-resident Indian (NRI) populations. At the same time, a particular section of the NRI population—particularly the upper-class, dominant-caste, and the post-1960s wave of immigrants to Western counties—started to be encouraged to "return home" to establish transnational industry and business in India in a post-1990s neoliberal economic era.[7] The term "diaspora," in turn, has been mobilized by the Indian government and industries to build particular types of transnational connections. In this context, the phrase "digital diaspora" becomes a way to build networks of consumer citizens, networks of care, networks of activisms, religious networks, upper caste networks and so on through circuits of transnational capital and labor.

The argument emerging from research examining diasporic Indians in internet spaces is that "Indian diasporas" have formed in these digital publics. These have come to be shaped by implicitly and explicitly "Hindu" majoritarian ideologies—with mostly dominant-caste[8] participation in such publics. Thus, for instance, in the 1990s, scholars such as Amit Rai and Vinay Lal noted how Hindu fundamentalist discourses emerged and began to dominate Indian internet spaces corresponding to how Indian diasporic communal spaces were forming in physical locations, particularly in response to the Ayodhya and Babri Masjid events of 1992.[9] Such a history and interweaving of Indian diasporas and internet publics sets up an already existing ethos for newer users of social media to enter into—either to feel at "home" within or to contest from the "outside" such a culture and discourse. This internet-mediated "Indianness" then becomes the stage that even users geographically located in India—whatever their caste, class, or religious location—must enter and disrupt or merge with. Further, as Madhavi Mallapragada notes, this version of Indian digital publics relies on the implicit privileging of a particular masculine subject position.[10]

Such an idealization of Indian masculinity in this specific mold of the Kshatriya male, who is closest to the ideal of Western masculinity, not only is reinforced in film and television but also made the basis for how Indian masculinity online must be performed.[11] This in turn has complemented a particular notion of Hindu-dominant, heteronormative, caste/class-specific portrayal and performance of femininity. Even though Mallapragada's argument was made about Indian diasporic internet cultures before 2005, when social networks and social media tools became the dominant mode of being connected, this is true even in 2018. The Silicon Valley concept of masculinity (reinforced through a Gamergate ethos), from which a majority of Indian men in the IT sector take their cues regarding success and upward mobility, further enhances these ideals.

The production of an ideal (modern) Indian female identity, therefore, still has its roots in the subcontinent's colonial encounters with Western masculinity and a rearticulation of Indian masculinity in response to the British male officers' perception of the Indian Brahmin male as "effeminate." As Uma Chakravorty notes, the specific historic encounter with the British notions of masculinity led to a "dramatically reconstituted [past], bringing into sharp focus the need of a people for a different self-image from the one that they hold of themselves."[12]

In such a context of Indian transnational diasporas, members of the Dalit, Bahujan and other "backward" castes in general are marginalized in a way that makes them invisible to next generations of diasporic Indians.[13] Much of the writing on Indian digital diasporas does not unpack the layered labor histories of diasporas from the South Asian/ Indian region. This is perhaps partly because in digital social spaces it is mostly the professional classes who seem to have been most outspoken. Labor movements from the region of South Asia historically were based in either forced mobility through indentured labor, economic migration on the one hand and migration of the professional classes on other.

In March 2018, Equality Labs put out a report on "Caste in the United States" that helps examine this invisibilizing.[14] Key findings in the report revealed, for instance, that 25 percent of the Dalits in the United States "who responded said they faced verbal or physical assault based on their Caste," and 40 percent of Dalits who responded "were made to feel unwelcome at their place of worship because of their Caste."[15]

Social formations in these physical spaces reproduce and reorient notions of "Indian" (often reinforcing and conflating Hindu and dominant-caste identities and cultural practices as "truly" Indian) and online diasporic networks reproduce digital publics routed through renewed identifications and rememberings, while they actively, even intentionally, contribute to processes of transnationalization of labor and business through recoded online and offline subjectivities. Byte-sized representations and authentications of Indianness travel and flow through digital circuits, circulating and remixing into formations that articulate global identities. What this also means is that Dalit women have been doubly marginalized discursively since the 1990s—they are not included in descriptions or analyses of Indian digital diasporas—even when they are in digital space. Thus, on the one hand Dalit women exist in "Indian" spaces through an erasure of their caste identity and history and on the other, it would seem, Indian digital diasporas are implicitly assumed to be made up of upper caste NRIs. The cultural characteristics of food, music and so described as "Indian" are situated yet assumed to be representative of national identity.

These identities are produced within sociocultural digital places constructed by computer software and hardware. Such sociocultural and technically produced time-space compressions enable Indian diasporas to be globally networked and to coproduce their identities both from the actual geographical nation-states in South Asia and through the diasporas. These sociocultural contexts are coproduced by inhabitants who access them. The sociocultural literacies of these inhabitants determine the kinds of free labor they contribute toward the building of these spaces. The continued inhabiting of these spaces leads to a reorganization of social space and everyday practice similar to that experienced by call center workers from India who are tuned in to time-zones and cultural practices in the Western worlds. People from the geographical location of South Asia and digital diasporic inhabitants alike experience varying degrees of social, affective transformations that orient them toward life in global multicultural communities.

Not only are distinctions of nation-state implicit but the online Indian formations are implicitly viewed as "Hindu." Thus, in writing about Indian digital diasporas, even existing research (including my past research), has also erased the Indian Muslim figure.

In early years of my research on South Asian Women—when I was researching the listproc "SAWnet"—I started by focusing on a US-born Muslim woman lawyer of Indian origin. We had much more reasonable (and some very unreasonable) debates around the Babri Masjid episode of December 1992 in the gendered digital space than were visible in online bulletin boards such as soc.culture.india and so on. The Indian digital space—which in the 1990s consisted of internet mediations of Indians mostly in diaspora—showed evidence of Muslim voices and of contestation. Through such contestation it was evident that Indian Muslims, Indian Christians, Indian Sikhs, Indian Parsis—are all Indians. Yet, in later research on gendered Indian digital spaces, whether by me or others—such as Hegde's book *Mediating Migration*, where she has chapters on food blogs and Carnatic music blogs by Indian women, and Mallapragada's work *Virtual Homelands: Indian Immigrants and Online Cultures in the United States*—there is a glossing over of the issue of the Muslim woman as Indian.[16] In Hegde's book, for example, she writes of the Muslim identity in the United States in a manner that implicitly distinguishes this identity from "Indian." In Hegde's, Mallapragada's, and my work on South Asian digital spaces, the Muslim identity in digital space is referred to—but usually as part of larger "South Asian" or of "Desi" formations, not as instances of "Indian" formations online. This is not fully a fault in our analysis so much as a symptom of how discursive spaces and the writing about "Indians" tend to appear. In *Second Life* ethnographies, I met several Muslim-identified avatars who were in South Asian and Indian spaces, but they often came together through the Bollywoodization of the dance clubs in that space. But it is also an epistemic issue—so perhaps it is a fault in the analysis after all.

Similarly, the absence of work on the Dalit presence in Indian digital diasporas is the result of how articulations of modern (post-1960s) Indian diasporas is the focus of much current policy and even postcolonial studies research. Vivek Kumar describes how "Indian dalits were not only taken to different countries as indentured labourers by colonial masters, but they also migrated."[17] Brij Lal has noted, for instance that of those indentured labor migrants that travelled to Fiji between 1879 and 1916, 26.2 percent were of, "low menial castes" while 3.7 percent were Brahmins and 10 percent were Kshatriyas.[18] Caste distinctions and discrimination continued even within migrant South Asian communities where people from different caste backgrounds were moved as part of the indentured labor movement from colonial India. This history of migration from India would no doubt ensure that along with the diasporas of upper caste and middle caste Indians, a large part of south Asian diaspora is also part of a Dalit diaspora.

Further, the use of communication networks and tools in Dalit diasporas is really not "new." It is the seemingly sudden visibility of Dalit activists to researchers of upper caste locations and to western news outlets and academics through mainstream and global hashtag publics[19] that is "new." It is the mainstream awareness of Dalit social movements globally that is new. Dalit social/protest movements and their use of new media for connectivity have a longer history. As P. Thirumal observes, "the Dalits are not inscribed in a particular place or territory, they constitute perhaps the only community other than the Brahmins to display an eagerness to share a pan-Indian identity. This eagerness can be realized through the use of and familiarity with the new media by the nascent Dalit middle class."[20] Gorringe on the other hand points to how the combination of availability of the internet, the role of internationalization of human rights and international Dalit networks have contributed to transnationalization of Dalit movements and mobilized resources for consciousness raising and continued support through "appeal to a higher authority than the state, and to draw parallels with civil rights movements around the world."[21]

Further, existing work on South Asian or Indian diasporas rarely unpacks the existence of Dalit diaspora in connection with histories of labor migration from the region of South Asia both before and after Indian and Pakistani independence from the British. Thus we see that the narration of Indianness in diaspora and the unevenness of how these layered histories are told, combined with contemporary attempts to maintain a "casteless" nationalist ethos, leads to the erasure of caste in digital domesticity as well. Dalit women socially exist in digitally such "Indian" spaces through an erasure of their caste identity and history. Yet their voices and protest movements have recently become visibilized through contemporary hashtag publics—mostly via twitter, facebook and instagram. We thus now see an increasing awareness of caste amongst feminist (and not so feminist) researchers of new media across as we try to make sense of this emergence of a digital Dalit (hashtag) public sphere. However, what is referred to as Dalit twitter is comparatively recent and the subjectivities visible through such publics are generational. I would caution researchers jumping on this bandwagon of writing about the Dalit feminists (whether writing about visible writer/activist presences such as that of Meena Kandaswami or about less high profile Dalit activists using online tools) to first examine the complex regional and historical configurations of offline sociopolitical formations fighting against caste discrimination and how caste and labor movements have shaped South Asian diasporas in pre and postcolonial times have produced such possibilities for the emergence of Dalit feminist digital publics. We must research the histories and work in conversation with these activists as we proceed with this work. Allyship and self-reflexivity of any sort is difficult and fraught with contradictions. Those of us from histories of caste privilege who have become people of color with the associated marginalizations and oppressions in the western world and those of us with histories of oppression and marginalization within western societies as long-term immigrants—we have some unlearning and rethinking to do in if we plan on researching these issues, because our communities have perpetuated caste discrimination for centuries even in diasporic South Asian communities.

In the present book, therefore, as I was researching to write, I was struggling with the complex dynamics around trying to research online/offline intersections yet again (as I did in past research) but also with how to articulate the diversity in South Asian digital diasporas—across region, caste, class and generation. For this current book, I interviewed many of the respondents starting in 2014 and am still continuing these conversations. My interviews with several social media influencers in gendered Indian online spaces that I refer to as "digital streets" activists predates the 2017 #LoSHA are referenced in many of the dialogue interludes. I started conceptualizing this book a little after the Nirbhaya social media activisms[22] and also the online protests following Rohit Vemula's death[23]. I proposed this book in 2013 soon after I was done with my book *Cyberculture and the Subaltern* and several years of emotional and physical immersions in rural India and in Second Life. The work building up to the actual formal writing has been very time consuming in terms of extensive interviewing, and I went back to some interviewees for several follow-up interviews.

Out of the seventy-five or more interviews, at least a third of the interviewees were Muslim Indians. Yet they spoke to me of their families, their use of social media, and their mostly metropolitan lives in ways that were similar to how those who did not self-identity as followers of any particular religion did (or whose names did not clearly identify them as Muslim, Christian, Parsi, or Sikh). Thus, in all these interviews, class, common media consumption, and use of digital tools was what clustered them together. They all spoke as "Indians" or as women of "Indian origin." In other words, my interviews revealed the "Muslim" identity of an interviewee only when the person spoke of using an app (as in the case of one of the seventy-five interviewees) that helped to keep track of dawn and dusk when fasting.

In another instance, while I was discussing WhatsApp and fake news and political propaganda, I started to use examples of how Hindutva messages get interwoven in the everyday use of WhatsApp by mothers trying to foster Indian culture in adult children who have moved out of India for graduate studies or jobs. I was trying to think through the role of digital mothering from a distance—where the mother is performing emotional labor and invoking a sense of home culture through the use of WhatsApp (reproducing home atmosphere through "digital ghar" bytes). I observed that political and religiously fanatic messages are forwarded and political messages are circulated inadvertently. My interviewee then pointed out to me that she saw this sort of behavior even among Catholic mothers. So the point here was about how religion as a part of domestic life and a mother's emotional labor through digital means often includes circulating religious messages. Yet, until religious practices and food habits other than those of dominant-caste Hindus are named, the conversations would gloss over the specificity while talking of "Indian" uses of digital technology. The lack of development into this inquiry probably is due to the way I was interviewing (I discuss the process further in the research method section of this introduction)—perhaps I was too reluctant to start the interview with a question about the interviewee's religious or caste location. I also did not ask if my interviewees identified as cisgender. Of all the people I interviewed, only a few self-identified as either queer or nonbinary. How will I conduct interviews in future? I might have to revisit my interviewing methods and interrogate my discomfort and reluctance to select interviewees based on religion, caste, or sexuality.

Thus, while interviewing, the main common identity that surfaced across a majority of the interviews was one of class and of having had some form of English medium education. In all, there were three interviewees who were not comfortable speaking and writing in English, although they too had reading and writing skills in English. But this characteristic—of not being comfortable speaking and writing in English—was a more obviously visible characteristic than religion, sexuality, or caste.

Overall in this book, I extend existing work that examines how technologically mediated diasporas occur at online/offline intersections, specifically in relation to the conceptualizations of "Indian," "digital," and "diasporic." There are very specific circumstances that allow us to think in terms of digital diaspora, as it encompasses globalized markets as well as the interactive nature of online technologies. At the same time, we also need to take into account the layered and nuanced ways in which such digitally immersed subjectivities are produced if we are to understand how the global/local continuum plays out in specific situations in present cultures and economies.

The term "digital diaspora" is easily used to talk about how diasporic populations around the world use the internet to connect to each other. Digital media used for digital diaspora formations are interactive and potentially allow people all over the world with similar interests and similar missions to feel located in one "place" and able to gather in common space. Online networks formed through digitally mediated communicative media—whether accessed via desktop computers, Xboxes, or iPhones—permit the local to exist within the global and vice versa.

When print media became mass media, it allowed the imagining of the commonplace through what Benedict Anderson called the convergence of capitalism and print technology. The diversity of human language created the possibility of a new form of imagined community, which in its basic morphology sets the stage for the modern nation. Thus, as print media were made accessible—actually or potentially—to "the masses," the world experienced the growth of modern capitalism, as well as the emergence of modern nations and internationalism. [24]

In the case of interactive online technologies, they go hand in hand with trans-nationalism based on global flows of capital and labor. The interactivity of the online technologies in current forms—as they arc made available to "the masses"—is a logical extension for digital financial infrastructures. As Dan Schiller writes, "The architects of digital capitalism have pursued one major objective: to develop an economy-wide network that can support an ever-growing range of intracorporate and intercorporate business processes." [25]

Anderson's work has also formed the basis of a lot of the arguments being made in regard to digital diasporas and virtual communities. The combined logic of digital transnationalism with globalized markets and interactive online technologies allows the emergence of digital diasporas.

The larger South Asian digital diaspora already formed a context into which Indians from India entered global spaces of leisure and work through the digital. Yet there were more localized digital networks within the Global South and within India that were also shaping the contexts. The wave of information technology outsourcing that hit the young population of India in the early 2000s contributed to such local networks that also interwove with more global networks as the offshore technology worker and customer service worker worked according to Global North time zones by staying awake at night and needing to find ways to rest and recover during the day. Their embodied physical lives got rerouted through their digital lives so that they became "digitally diasporic," even though they were not Indians in diaspora through physical border crossings and legal migration.

Thus the born-digital generation inhabiting a range of social media and appified spaces, [26] as well as older generations coming in as new users (some of them as grandmothers)—and also the first generations born into what I might refer to as "a world of iPads and smart phones"—encountered all these previous generations and the digital cultures they had coproduced simultaneously. The entry of these waves of users into the digital through Twitter, Facebook, Instagram, Snapchat, and WhatsApp, among other platforms—as well as through dating apps—led to the emergence of digital formations in both an entrepreneurial neoliberal mode and an activist neoliberal mode. We see different forms of remediation and re-gadgetization at play.[27]

RESEARCH METHODS: ITERATIVE ENGAGEMENT AND IMMERSION IN DIGITAL CONTEXTS, OFFLINE TRAVEL, AND COLLABORATIVE WRITING

I conducted over seventy-five semi-structured interviews with South Asians (mostly women and mostly from India) living in various parts of the world—with at least half of them living in India—over a span of two years. During the two years in which I conducted these interviews I traveled several times to India and a couple times to the Netherlands and the UK, once to Germany, Spain, Rome, and Scotland, and also lived for close to a year in Norway (while on my Faculty Improvement Leave as a Fulbright Professor at the University of Bergen). I mention these travels because during each of these journeys and stays away from the United States, I learned about South Asians and their use of digital tools from different angles, so to speak. There were people of South Asian descent in all these places, and whether I traveled to these places for two days or eleven months, I was able to gain insight into how integral digital connectivity has become to creating common cultural publics and affective networks for South Asian migrants worldwide—regardless of the length of time between their migration away from India or whether they were first-generation, second-generation, or later-generation migrants from South Asia. Most of these women live in a pervasive, overall contemporary ethos of entrepreneurial agency and neoliberal empowerment that centers women's autonomy.

The actual interviews that form the main data set for this book were conducted in person when possible, but a majority of the interviews were conducted via Skype, Facetime, WhatsApp calls, Facebook messenger video, or Google hangout. Even when the interviews were done in person, I did several follow-up interviews with several of the respondents using digital tools. The key central question posed to start off the discussion was: "How do you use technology in your daily life?" I deliberately kept this question broad—and yes while a majority of the respondents assumed I meant digital technology, some did talk about refrigerators, microwaves, and vacuum cleaners, but very few. I followed this with questions like "How do you stay connected with family?" "Do you use these tools for dating?" and so on, but mostly I let them tell their stories. I did not start with questions of how they identified in terms of gender and sexuality—nor did I ask their religion or caste. In conversation, a few of them revealed these directly or indirectly. If I felt the interviewees were outing themselves without realizing, I later alerted them to that and asked if they were okay with revealing these points if necessary. In truth, since I haven't revealed names—unless they coauthored with me or they are public figures—this issue was moot. After I had written up drafts of chapters 1, 2, 5, and 6, I invited interviewees to read and challenge my conceptualizations and descriptions. Several of them took up the challenge to begin the dialogues—most are included in Section II—especially in the final chapter of the book, "Dialogue Interludes." The interlude with Shilpa Phadke follows chapter 2 as an independent chapter. The chapter containing my dialogues with Varsha Ayyar, Divya Kandukuri, and Nithila Kanagasabai is placed strategically after the dialogue in chapters 2 and 3 to provide a contrast in terms of feminist issues and concerns that are shaped through class, caste, and geographical location, even as they all occur through access to digital publics and are "Indian" identified. The interlude with Debapreeta Rahut and Damini Kulkarni in Section II of the book further pushes on the conceptualization in chapter 1.

The dialogues included are written with interviewees and colleagues who are engaged in these spaces and who agreed to write with me by answering questions and developing the arguments put forth.[28] While any misrepresentations of anyone or of anything described and discussed in this book are my fault, obviously, the opinions in the interludes expressed by those in the dialogue interludes are not necessarily the same as mine.

Collaborative writing through humanities frameworks is also a pedagogic exercise of co-transformation and takes more time and work for me as the organizer and the overall conceptual leader of the work than perhaps if I had taken up the themes that emerged and wrote them up myself without having to explain or justify my conceptual frameworks of social and academic location to my informants-turned-coauthors. The coauthors listed are therefore those who struggled through the arduous process of writing and making academic connections and stayed with me to the final end of the writing of this book.

In the collaborative writing for this book, the writing and the discussions happened together and through various venues. In our case, these happened through Twitter, Facebook, WhatsApp, Google Docs, Instant Messenger, Skype, Facetime, phone conversations, and even through in-person meetings if we happened to be in the same physical location at any time. Each of these tools comes with a set of affordances; therefore, I am by no means suggesting there was "convenience" in these forms of writing, even as they provided me access to more diverse writing collaborators than I might have had access to were I to rely purely on encounters through physical travel. Also—because of how we travel in and out of digital nooks and crannies—there are several Google Docs, Facebook messenger, and WhatsApp conversations, for instance, that have been left "hanging" as conversations that I cannot move into publication since they are incomplete and would misrepresent the conversation and the coauthor standpoints as they "hang." These incomplete conversations, however, also contribute to my understanding, and where possible I have acknowledged them in my preface and other places in this book. Most of my previous writing has also taken collaborative initiatives in various ways.

This very process resonates with a feminist methodology of trying to disrupt the idea of a single authoritarian voice. This feminist iterative process of building theory and gathering evidence through dialogue necessitates the inclusion of the last (large) chapter of dialogue interludes. I continue to be inspired by radical collaborations such as that of the Sangtin Writers as they confidently proceed to work together. They describe their experience "as political, intellectual, and emotional labor; a close reading of their stories and the formulation of theory growing out of collective analysis and dialogue points to the epistemological contributions of [the] text," and note that, "throughout three years of writing and rewriting, the Sangtins focus on building structures of accountability and transparency in recalling the autobiographers' own stories and on analyzing them within the larger context of development politics."[29]

My coauthors and I did not become as fused together in voice and in writing as the Sangtin Writers with Richa Nagar. Nor do we use a blended "we." This is mostly because the present book project also needs to make clear the multiple locations of each individual collaborator to a certain extent and because none of us truly and fully represents any particular aspect of the Indian digital diasporas we write about. The technologies for writing and connecting and the affordances—as noted in the previous paragraphs—simultaneously enable and constrain a consensual formation of a "we" for this writing project. I have not spent time extensively and offline with my cowriters—we have actually not co-researched this topic. We have coproduced meaning at particular moments through our intermittent, scattered, and sometimes disjointed encounters through various online tools. Some of these moments of coproduction of meaning are represented through our dialogue interludes. Further, there are clear differences in location of each of the writers/co-authors and informants in this book along caste, class, sexuality, race, religion, and histories of migration. For our project, a blended "we" would be as problematic as my speaking for all the participants and the interviewees that contribute to my conceptualization of contemporary gendered Indian digital diasporas.

The book as a whole draws on conversations across a selection of contemporary Indian and South Asian networks online with a focus on formations of contemporary Indian women in social media space and "appified" space whether these formations are characterized as "digitally domestic," or as "activist." These include (trans)women entrepreneurs; (trans)women-centered bloggers; and digital feminists engaged in debate, dialogue, dissemination of feminist messages or activism through the blogosphere or through Twitter, Tumblr, Instagram, WhatsApp, and Facebook. Histories of technology access and access to dominant modes of expression in these spaces, however, are shaped through neocolonial hierarchies. Arguments to this effect that I have made since the 1990s still hold.[30]

In past work I have noted how postcolonial/marginal subjectivities in digitally mediated environments are produced through individual negotiation of connectivity and within the constraints of hegemonic structures of power. Online interaction still occurs within ontological and epistemological hierarchies shaped by histories of colonialism. In the context of mobile digital connectivity this neocolonial hierarchy reemerges through varied access to gadgets—but also through a global ethos that privileges the gadget user and the connected citizen. Thus, what Ila Nagar points out in relation to Indian queer digital activisms applies to all digital street activisms. The "digital" is indeed seemingly "freely accessible and visibilises queer bodies in India and it should be celebrated as a space for activism and protest, [but] it is not the utopian space that it is framed as."[31]

DIGITAL PUBLICS?

The notion of digital publics[32] is pivotal to discussions in all chapters, whether I refer to privatized digital publics, digitally domestic publics, or activist publics. Yet the definition of the terms "public"—whether digital or not—has a long history of debate and discussion in Western philosophy and politics. In terms of non-Anglo and non-Western theorizing of the term "public," it might be argued that reaching for Sanskrit texts, Japanese texts, Mandarin texts, Arabic texts, anthropological descriptions of indigenous peoples worldwide—or translations of these—might give some insights into particular contexts through which "public" was defined. However, even these definitions are still filtered through a neocolonial and Eurocentric orientation. Further, the excavation of these definitions does not necessarily produce organic understandings of "public" in marginalized communities of the world. Thus, my definition of publics starts from a thinking-through of Jürgen Habermas's defining of public sphere[33] by scholars such as Nancy Fraser,[34] Amit Rai,[35] and Michael Warner.[36] Then I move on to engaging the conceptualizations of "ghar" and "bahir" (home and the world) coming through nineteenth-century Indian literature mostly from elite social spaces of Bengal and the overall Indian nationalist movement's rearticulation of the "woman" and her role in society. As Michael Warner notes about publics, they "have become an essential fact of the social landscape, and yet it would tax our understanding to say exactly what they are"[37]

In the context of social media publics, I do not posit a mutually exclusive binary between public and counterpublic; rather, I see digital publics as spaces simultaneously of contestation and of reinforcement—but framed through dominant technological infrastructures. The counterpublics coexist and interweave on Facebook, Instagram, and Twitter, for instance, in even the current #metooIndia movement of October 2018, where anti-caste feminist counterpublics are formed around the continual reminder that the same mainstream feminists from India who are celebrating #metooIndia are also erasing the fact of #LoSHA, which in fact (as is evident even from the interview of Raya Sarkar that Ayesha Vemuri and I conducted via Skype) had a more careful process for inclusion of names on the crowdsourced list. These counterpublics can be thought of through Nancy Fraser's articulation of "subaltern counterpublic" (although we may not choose to call them

"subaltern counterpublics" out of respect for many of the Dalit feminists who have refused the label of "subaltern"[38]):

> The concept of a counterpublic militates in the long run against separa-
> tism because it assumes an orientation that is publicist. Insofar as these
> arenas are publics they are by definition not enclaves—which is not to
> deny that they are often involuntarily enclaved. After all, to interact
> discursively as a member of a public—subaltern or otherwise—is to
> disseminate one's discourse into ever widening arenas.[39]

Social media space offered by global tools such as Facebook and
Twitter therefore resurface the struggle for common heterogeneous Indian digital publics that had become flattened in spaces of "digital
domesticity"[40] and other Indian digital diasporas such as blog spaces
where there are niche publics rather than counterpublics. Thus, in a
sense, we return to "heterogeneous strands" of Indian publics through
these contestations around feminisms and around #metooIndia reminis-
cent of a time before "Indian diaspora" was easily conflated with "Hindu diaspora"—similar to "the dynamics of this diasporic public sphere
in the context of the events in Ayodhya, India, on 6 December 1992."[41]
Although Rai makes no claim to producing a theory of public sphere or
of counterpublics, that 1995 article examining how "Hindu diaspora is
being written through the lines—the techno-informational lines of electronic bulletin boards" shows how in early internet publics what we
now take for granted as a Hindu India emerged through debates structured by the encounter between offline actual events happening in India
at the time (the demolition of the Babri Masjid in 1992) and the mum-
mified notion of Indian culture fostered through the nostalgia of dominant-caste Hindu Indians in diaspora and conflated as essentially Indian. Integral to these internet publics of the 1990s was the obsession
with the production of Hindu masculinities that then carried over into
the discourse around the "IT boom" of the late 1990s. Heteronormative, aggressive, violent masculinity and a retelling of Hinduism
through a temporally situated diasporic nostalgia that connects with and
homogenizes layered Hindu identified migrants worldwide while erasing the complex intersections and layered histories feed into a Indian
techno-utopianism. Such discursive formations contributed to the
homogenized recasting of Indianness at the same time as the Indian
government was more openly endorsing neoliberal market economy
practices. Rai's description of Indian internet publics and the competing discourses of the 1990s serves as a prehistory to the post 2012

Indian digital publics in which Dalit activisms, Queer activisms, #Lo-SHA, #repeal377, #justiceforAsifa, and #metooIndia became visible to the world outside of the Indian continent. We therefore see that the "punctual time of circulation is crucial to the sense that discussion is currently unfolding in a sphere of activity."[42]

ACTIVISTS?

The idea of the public sphere fuels a lot of the research. The question of whether a public sphere is democratic, egalitarian, and inclusive is not just a question for feminist movements. This is a question for a lot of the world: What sort of public sphere is this we have in today's world? Populist? Elitist? Empowered? Datafied? Constantly surveilled? Paranoid? Why do we assume that digital publics will somehow lead to democratic interactions and empowerment? What's hidden and what's visible? How is this refiguring our social spaces for posterity? In the dialogue interludes in this book, we discuss these issues, but here in the introduction I will rely on some literature review to touch upon some of these questions.

Jodi Dean, in her work on blog theory, notes that:

> Networked media in the society of control amplify the challenge post-fordism poses to collective identity. Yes, they enable people to sign petitions. Yes, they enable people to give money. Yes, they enable people to express their opinions. Yes, *Obama had like a million Facebook friends*. But these particular motions of clicking and linking do not produce symbolic identities: they are ways that I express myself—just like shopping, checking my friends' updates, or following tabloid news at TMZ.com. I may imagine others like me, a virtual local, but this local remains one of those like me, my link list or followers, those who fit my demographic profile, my user habits. I don't have to posit a collective of others, others with whom I might need to cooperate or struggle, to whom I might be obliged, others who might place demands on me. The instant connection of networked association allows me to move on as soon as I am a little uncomfortable, a little put out. Petitions, social network groups (the one on Facebook that aims to get a million people to say they oppose capitalism has 24,672 members), blogs—they are the political equivalent of just in time production, quick responses circulating as contributions to the flows of communicative capitalism.[43]

Dean's point is well taken—and indeed we do see modes of "brand activism." As Sarah Banet-Weiser aptly noted, we live in a time when "feminism" has become "hot take" and so has the label "activist."[44] In chapter 7, Sukhnidh Kaur presents her opinions in relation to the com-modification of feminism. Several of those I interviewed in regard to the "digital streets" and feminism theme in this book either hinted at being activists or openly claimed the identity of "activist." Also, there is much mudslinging that occurs in the process of authenticating who counts as an activist. Social media posts are used to record evidence through proclamations made in tones of accusation against those who are not activist enough or to document the work that the social media user is doing offline (which corroborates their claims to being an acti-vist). Debates around who is an activist and who is not have existed through history. In the context of social media there has been an ongo-ing slactivism/activism discussion. Yet, as Lynn Schoffield Clark points out, even though in some academic literature there is a question-ing of

> casual online and largely observation-only participation [which] might be dismissed as merely a form of "slactivism" . . . such casual observa-tion may serve an important role as a form of early participation that is made possible through digitally networked communication, even as the opportunities to observe those artifacts are increasingly limited as the structures of commercial social network sites continue to shift. . . . [Studying] the role of social media in early political participation among minoritized communities across a variety of social media platforms are necessary to enrich our theories of the role of social media usage in long term political change.[45]

The question of who is an activist particularly resurfaced in the Indian feminist space in October 2017 soon after the crowdsourced list of sexual harassers in the academy (#LoSHA) surfaced via a Facebook post on Raya Sarkar's profile in October 2017. Then, in October 2018, the question of what it means to be intersectional in one's activism and not marginalize Dalit voices emerged for Raya and others who saw the erasure of #LoSHA from the 2018 celebration of #metooIndia by the same renowned feminists who demanded the removal of the list in statements such as the Kafila online statement. Some of this is noted in the dialogue interlude with Sohni Chakrabarti and referred to by inter-ludes with a couple others.

The irony of the contemporary moment of activisms is that capital, branding, and resistance are all interwoven. Some of my interviewees did note a discomfort at the fact that their prolific use of the social media and networking tools was in fact benefiting corporations—be they Twitter, Facebook, or the makers of the gadgets they use. What Maria Elena Martinez-Torres observes in writing about the Zapatistas and their use of the internet still holds true.

> A paradox has emerged from the revolution in communications: the same technology that has taken world capitalism to a new stage of development—corporate globalization—has also provided a significant boost for anticorporate and anti-globalization movements.[46]

While as I noted earlier there is an increasing individualization of activism through social media in the contemporary moment—that is different from the 1990s—at the same time there is an emphasis on individual participation. There is also an affective politics evident—both online and offline—as these precarious activist subjects work to connect with each other—sometimes across geographical distances—to work to make a social movement through this affective contagion. Naisargi Dave examines the meaning of activism and the role of affect in contemporary activism in her work drawing on ethnographies (offline) among queer communities in India. She points out that activism itself is aspirational—a reaching for the virtual, so to speak.

Activism begins, then, precisely as the virtual in the actual world, the previously unthinkable that is now a flickering possibility, just on the verge of entering upon the world of norms. To study activism is to study the relationship between the virtual and the actual, the as-yet-inassimilable and the assimilated.[47]

The process of mediation produces affective responses: the encounter is shaped by the design, the tool, the offline space where we connect from, and the time it takes for the mediation to gain momentum. Whereas Tarrow described the diffusion of the mediated activism of the mid-1990s that was not intensely relational while also pointing out that transnational activism predates internet connectivity and was facilitated by acts like "immigrants bringing remittances home to their families," Dave examines how "affect becomes experience" when social actors (activists) "come to experience the world as a series of different limits, limits that serve as the norms against which new critiques and problematizations arise, and within which dreams of possibility are variously kindled and assimilated."[48] Thus, in thinking through transnational transmissions, travel, and connectivity alongside sociopolitical, legal, and cultural limits placed on dreams of possibility, we see that digital publics become a space for aspirational reaching out—in the hopes that calling out might then lead to connection, community, and collective action through a generation of transnational affects.

The years 2012, 2017, and 2018 provided some recent moments of high visibility and debate in Indian feminist spaces online. The "digital streets" became real to a larger transnational Indian feminist space in a way that some earlier social media–based feminist campaigns such as Blank Noise, Pink Chaddi, Why Loiter?, and Girls at Dhabas did not. Part of the reason for the broader reach of this movement, of course, has to do with it being viewed in the context of the more Global North–centered #metoo movement that has been visible via social media in the recent past. Questions about whether or not this was an activist intervention were raised in debates and discussions among Indian feminists themselves. Several of the dialogue interludes engage this tension in different ways.

Yet as this book manuscript was being completed and being made ready to be sent to the publisher in December 2018—a year after #LoSHA—there was yet another #metoo movement taking over the Indian digital streets. Few of the interludes take this one into consideration because it is happening after we have finished most of the writing in the book. However, we hope to raise some concerns over the implicit and explicit claims that India has only now joined the #metoo movement in 2018. This move to celebrate the current wave of #metoo from the Indian context as the #metoo to be noted and recognized globally once again has to do with who legitimizes what sorts of protests (and hashtags) as activism.

In a series of tweets on October 7, 2018, the Twitter user with the handle of "Makepeace Sitlhou" suggests reasons for why the #metooIndia of 2018 is more visible to the world and is being more easily celebrated than #LoSHA :

> We are so much more receptive to this now becoz a spark was already ignited. So kindly, can Savarna feminists please put their petty politics aside on such things? Unless this is what their politics is.

> LoSHA also was the first of this kind to come out and didn't break on Twitter, a more organised space that makes news faster. In spirit and action, both are the same. In fact, there's less doubt over this becoz due process debate was done with LoSHA.

But let's not forget that LoSHA was reported by a lot of survivors who came from academia, not journalism. Their methodology of outing may not have been perfect, neither is this. It's desperate and that's what alarmed us all.

There are feminist journalists amongst us who are giving this #MeToo movement more credence than the LoSHA list. Why? Because of "context"

Thus, while some Twitter activists acknowledge Raya Sarkar's role (now Steier) in #LoSHA as a first wave of India-oriented #metoo—others have erased this implicitly.

The implicit erasure of #LoSHA as an initiator of the #metoo movement in India is being viewed as a caste issue. Divya Kandukuri's Instagram post calls this out polemically (publicly shared via her Facebook account as well):

You all uppercaste women . . . you are getting to name your abusers! We are not. Can't. Because you wont pat our backs like you're doing [to] your sisters now. We have seen what you did during LoSHA. . . . Your sisterhood is selective, your sisterhood is exclusive.[49]

HISTORICIZING INTERNET ACTIVISM

As noted by Makepeace Sitlou in the quotes above, context is important. To understand the context of digital activism, it is important to know and understand that there is a broader and longer background to transnational activism and the history of intervention into local politics by routing messages transnationally. In other words, calling out to global audiences for support precedes contemporary social media calling out. Different forms of travel, media circulation, and networking contributed to the practices of soliciting transnational support for national and local struggles. As Tarrow notes, transnational activism is indeed transformative because "even prosaic activities, like immigrants bringing remittances home to their families, take on broader meanings when ordinary people cross transnational space."[50] Further, we see as early as the 1990s successful Internet use by activist groups such as the Zapatistas, which in turn led to the understanding that this kind of networking had the potential to help in the formation of solidarity networks through "mediated diffusion" that was not always directly relational.[51] The Zapatista social movement (by the Chiapas of Mexico) in 1994 was amplified into transnational and global space not only because the start of their rebellion coincided with the start of NAFTA, but also because an important sympathizer, Harry Cleaver, began to filter e-mail messages about the insurgency to progressive groups around the United States, and soon a number of listservs and websites appeared that were dedicated to the insurgency. This transformed the Zapatista National Liberation Army (EZLN) "from a conventional to an informational guerrilla movement."[52]

In contemporary access to digital spaces, activist subjectivities that emerge online include young people who, on the one hand, live in a pervasive, overall contemporary ethos of entrepreneurial agency and neoliberal empowerment that centers women's autonomy, but on the other hand are shaped by a techno-mediated precarity. Thus, the emphasis is on an activist who speaks for herself and for a cause where she herself is personally impacted—rather than depending on a savior activist to connect her to the internet. In movements like #metoo the precarious individual is both the activist and also the victim. The participation and involvement of the individual become important. Unlike the 1990s when the Zapatistas as a community relied on a spokesperson (Subcomandante Marcos) and a benevolent internet connector (Harry Cleaver) to represent them—gender activism in the social media world increasingly privileges direct connectivity. Dalit feminists will not be "represented" by Savarna women; rather, they will speak for themselves. They are not "sub" to anyone.

Yet this precarity[53] is different from the precarity experienced in lives of the poor in that this is precarity that strikes at the middle and upper classes—especially the youth. This means that "a double precarity" impacts the digital citizens engaged in everyday sociality and activism in digital diasporas. Looking at precarity through a heuristic of double precarity allows us to see how the digital plays into the everyday performance of precarity in these contexts. As Kergel and Heidkamp note:

> On one hand, precarity can be understood as an unstable employment relationship and analyzed as an effect of neoliberal roll-back processes. Precarity and other societal power structures manifest in the digital age and are re-produced by the way, digital media are used. On the other hand the media change effects a stable instability or precarity. Due to the media change social practices throughout the diverse societal fields are questioned: new social spaces emerge which require new social practices and effect a stable instability of the media use.[54]

In the case of Indian women connecting to online spaces from these conditions of precarity on the one hand and older generations connecting through more comfortable-seeming domesticity or financial security on the other hand, the digital becomes an important gateway to the outside world. Even as it enables them to uncover new personas within themselves that, according to their own accounts in interviews I conducted, are freer and more expressive, they are also simultaneously entering an ethos in which they work to "brand" themselves. There is a self-commodification process that is activated through the very logics of the platform and the dominant ethos of social media use. Thus, "[i]n an increasingly precarious and unstable work environment, individuals work to self-promote and brand themselves online with the hope of possibly cashing in down the line."[55]

Where the digital gap is massive, with 71 percent of the male population using the internet, but only 29 percent of women constituting the space, for instance, access to WhatsApp allows them an interesting negotiation of private to public. The app allows private conversations and allows them to perform the persona they like, very unlike Facebook, which requires a very public persona that has to conform to societal standards.

MY POINT OF ENTRY

Over the years my subjectivity has undergone various transformations in encounters with various sociocultural and economic contexts and experiences. The chapters in this book refer to my location in relation to specific groups of people and contexts: spaciotemporal, geographical, cultural, and so on. I am a dominant-caste and upper-class cis woman with US citizenship, and a person of color in the Western context. My skin color, sexual orientation, and gender or my caste and class status have not changed over my lifespan so far. I have cultural capital and come from a materially comfortable background. Still, my personal location and subjectivity has not remained static, unchanging, and unaffected by things around me. True, like most people, I haven't transformed as much as I probably should have in directions where my empathy/sympathy might lead me as I become aware of various uneven power relations among the people that surround me. Thus I do hail from what has come to be named as a "Savarna" (i.e., dominant caste and class) location,[56] but my feminist location as it is now is that of a transnational cis woman of color in the United States. This location is clearly not aligned *experientially* and historically with Black feminists, Chicana feminists, Dalit feminists, queer feminists, trans feminists, or disabled feminists. These conversations and dialogues are therefore difficult, laden with discomfort and even accusations. Some of those I approached decided to talk with me and write with me. Still others, rightfully, rejected the idea of dialogue across barriers of caste—given that however this might be enacted it will seem to some like it's an appropriation.

I have no claims to being an activist myself: I am first and foremost a learner, teacher, mentor, and researcher. The feminist approach to learning, teaching, mentoring, and researching certainly puts me in spaces of activism and in locations where I might possibly create change that will open up spaces for the marginalized, but these are my micro everyday practices and insertions through teaching and writing. I have no activist credentials to tout or to lose. In what follows in this book, therefore, I look primarily at the *how* of empowerment and activism where these emerge. I also observe the labor issues and affective networking formations that surface around the idea of empowerment and activism through the digital. Each of the examples I discuss in the book follows different trajectories of labor, digital cultures, and global circulation. Each one has successfully—for the moment at least—become transnationalized by routing through Indian-based locations or origin and circulation.

Through particular conversations (in depth, semi-structured interviews, social media–based exchanges/dialogues) and journeys (both through online immersion and repeated travel to offline contexts) and by linking back to personal, South Asian—and more specifically Indian—histories of internet mediation, my coauthors and I reveal how affect and gendered digital labor combine in the formation of global socioeconomic environments.

What Christina Thomas Dhanaraj (with whom I have a dialogue interlude in chapter 8) notes in her *FirstPost* article on November 13, 2018, must be taken seriously, and the issues she raises are indeed true. In her article, she notes the Savarna framework of mainstream Indian feminism that continues even in the context of the #metooIndia movement. She lists seven talking points, including the problems with research that seeks performative ally-ship and collaboration:

6. Marginalised women are treated as study subjects in the name of collaboration: Savarna feminists that do this [performative ally-ship] are usually those that have research or writing careers. Yet it doesn't occur to them they could, in fact, focus on their lives instead of Dalit women's experiences.

Ideally, we Dalit women should write our stories, sans the fear of appropriation. The only reason that's not already happening is because savarna women are occupying media, publishing and academic spaces, thanks to their social and monetary capital.

7. Savarna feminists engage in performative ally-ship in anti-caste movements: At the heart of solidarity lies action. Anything else done for sake of proving one's ally-ship amounts to performative behaviour. Savarna feminists often call themselves anti-caste or casteless. Yet, the readiness with which they offer support to savarna women survivors, is practically zero when it comes to DBA women. Where are these lawyers when DBA women are being murdered and raped?[57]

Thus once again I am faced with the dilemma and problem of representation and speaking about the Other. And I return here to the dilemmas posed by Alcoff in her 1993 essay "The Problem of Speaking for Others":

> Our ability to assess the effects of a given discursive event is limited; our ability to predict these effects is even more difficult. When meaning is plural and deferred, we can never hope to know the totality of effects. Still, we can know some of the effects our speech generates: I can find out, for example, that the people I spoke for are angry that I did so or appreciative. By learning as much as possible about the context of reception I can increase my ability to discern at least some of the possible effects. This mandates incorporating a more dialogic approach to speaking, that would include learning from and about the domains of discourse my words will affect.[58]

ORGANIZATION OF THE BOOK

The book is organized into two sections, excluding the introduction and conclusion. Each section begins with a chapter titled "Gendered Digital Indian Publics." Section I has four chapters and Section II contains five chapters. Needless to say, this is a productively messy project. Complexity and nuance cannot be conveyed in linear timelines—and the way the chapters were (co)written and repeatedly reorganized reflect this complexity. Chapter 2, for instance, was written way before any of the other chapters. Thus it was written way before I encountered the flurry of activity on the Indian digital feminist streets. I was plodding along interviewing women who worked from home or were stay-at-home nonresident mothers—women with H-4 visas, for instance, of the generation that Amy Bhatt writes about, who are re-domesticated upon being restricted by visa status from being employed, and who "create new channels for personal development and self-expression, while also grappling with deep challenges to their identities as educated, modern women with potential for launching careers of their own."[59]

The conceptualization of "digital streets" in Section II has its origins in email exchanges with Sujatha Subramanian in early 2015, when she requested feedback and suggestions for a literature review to help respond to a reviewer on a draft of her very important article later published as "From the Streets to the Web: Looking at Feminist Activism on Social Media."[60] Sujatha and I hoped to have an interlude in this book as well, but, of course, life intervened, and we were unable to coordinate our schedules to write together in time. Several of those I did do interludes with are from a network of scholars and activists that Sujatha is also connected to. Shilpa Phadke (who did a dialogue interlude with me in chapter 3) later connected me to several others as well, including Tarishi Verma and Riddhima Sharma, who first started out as interviewees and then wrote interludes, but also then came to Bowling Green State University to work on their respective PhDs (Tarishi in fall 2017 and Riddhima in fall 2018).

The chapter with Smita Vanniyar was written in early 2017, and the rest of the chapters were written in fall 2017. The review process gave me time to think, and I began revisions in fall 2018. By that time I had had a great deal of input from further interviews and dialogues during my trips to Hyderabad, Pune, and Bangalore.

Finally in the concluding chapter of this book, my research assistant, Kaitlyn Wauthier (2017–2018), writes with me in thinking through the process of collaborative writing engaged in during this project.

NOTES

1. Arjun Appadurai. Modernity At Large: Cultural Dimensions of Globalization (p. 34). University Press of Minnesota Press, 1996.
2. https://en.wikipedia.org/wiki/Indentured_servitude#Indian_indenture_system
3. Rama Laksmi "The new 140-character war on India's caste system," 2016
4. BIPOC is distinct from "POC" (people of color) since it is felt by several activists that in "POC" has become depoliticized and also lends itself to tokenism as well as erasure of Black and Indigenous peoples.

5. Vivek Kumar. "Understanding Dalit Diaspora." *Economic and Political Weekly* 39, no. 1 (2004): pgs 114-15.

6. Anannya Bhattacharjee, "The Habit of Ex-Nomination: Nation, Woman and the Indian Immigrant Bourgeoisie," *Public Culture* 5, no. 1 (1992): 19, doi: 10.1215/08992363-5-1-19.

7. Madhavi Mallapragada, "The Indian Diaspora in the USA and around the Web," in *Web Studies: Rewiring Media Studies for the Digital Age*, ed. David Gauntlett (London: Arnold & Oxford University Press, 2000), 179–85.

8. The concept of dominant caste as it has developed in Indian sociology has been to construct it in gender-neutral terms. It hides the fact that the threat to use violence is exercised by men. In the public sphere the assertion of caste domination is essentially a patriarchal mode of exercising power. Chakravarti, Uma, *Gendering Caste: Through a Feminist Lens* (Sage India, 2003), p. 23.

9. Amit Rai, "India On-Line: Electronic Bulletin Boards and the Construction of a Diasporic Hindu Identity," *Diaspora: A Journal of Transnational Studies* 4, no. 1 (1995): 31–57, doi: 10.1353/dsp.1995.0021; Vinay Lal, "The Politics of History on the Internet: Cyber-diasporic Hinduism and the North American Hindu Diaspora," *Diaspora: A Journal of Transnational Studies* 8, no. 2 (1999): 137–72, doi: 10.1353/dsp.1999.0000.

10. Mallapragada, "The Indian Diaspora."

11. Radhika Gajjala, *Cyber Selves: Feminist Ethnographies of South Asian Women* (Walnut Creek, CA: AltaMira Press, 2004).

12. Uma Chakravorty, "Whatever Happened to the Vedic Dasi? Orientalism, Nationalism, and Script for the Past," in *Recasting Women: Essays in Colonial History*, ed. Kumkum Sangari and Sudesh Vaid (New Brunswick, NJ: Rutgers, 1990), 27.

13. Here, I'd like to note that these next generations of diasporic Indians are not always made aware of contemporary manifestations of caste-ism either in diasporas or in India as they grow up: the diasporas are often positioned in opposition to the host country's dominant cultures and the constructedness and mummification—a freezing of time and particular hierarchies of culture—that result in the fetishizing of dominant caste Hindu-ness as "Indian" in post-1965 migration of Indians to the United States, for instance. Therefore, the awareness of caste discrimination even among next-generation Indians comes through encounters that are both confusing and misinformed. Such encounters again do nothing to include Dalit communities in the Indian diasporic fold.

14. Maari Zwick-Maitreyi, Thenmozhi Soundararajan, Natasha Dar, Ralph F. Bheel, and Prathap Balakrishnan, *Caste in the United States: A Survey of Caste among South Asian Americans* (Equality Labs, 2018).

15. Ibid., 28.

16. See Radha Sarma Hegde, *Mediating Migration*, Global Media and Communication (Cambridge, UK: Polity, 2016); Madhavi Mallapragada, *Virtual Homelands: Indian Immigrants and Online Cultures in the United States* (Champaign: University of Illinois Press, 2014), Kindle.

17. Vivek Kumar. "Understanding Dalit Diaspora." *Economic and Political Weekly* 39, no. 1 (2004): 114-16.

18. Brij V. Lal Labouring Men And Nothing More Some Problems Of Indian Indenture, p. 130.

19. Bruns, A., and Burgess, J. (2015). Twitter hashtags from ad hoc to calculated publics. In N. Rambukkana (Ed.), Hashtag publics (pp. 13–28). New York: Peter Lang.

20. See P. Thirumal, "Situating the New Media: Reformulating the Dalit Question" in Gajjala and Gajjala, *South Asian Technospaces* (New York: Peter Lang, 2008) pg 103

21. Hugo Gorringe. Untouchable Citizens: Dalit Movements and Democratization in Tamil Nadu (Cultural Subordination and the Dalit Challenge) (p. 52).

22. See https://en.wikipedia.org/wiki/2012_Delhi_gang_rape

23. See https://en.wikipedia.org/wiki/Suicide_of_Rohith_Vemula.

24. See Benedict Anderson, *Imagined Communities* (London: Verso, 1983).

25. Dan Schiller, *Digital Capitalism: Networking the Global Market System* (Cambridge, MA: MIT Press, 1999), 1.

26. Jeremy Wade Morris and Sarah Murray, introduction to *Appified: Culture in the Age of Apps* (Ann Arbor: University of Michigan Press, 2018), 1–20.

27. Jay Bolter and Richard Grusin, *Remediation: Understanding New Media* (Cambridge, MA: MIT Press, 1998).

28. The dialogue interludes use the collaborators' initials as a system of identification that indicates which coauthor is writing at any given moment throughout the chapters.

29. Sangtin Writers Collective and Richa Nagar, *Playing with Fire: Feminist Thought and Activism through Seven Lives in India* (Minneapolis: University of Minnesota Press, 2006), Locations 93–96, Kindle.

30. See for instance, Radhika Gajjala, "Studying Feminist E-spaces: Introducing Transnational/Postcolonial Concerns," in *Technospaces*, ed. Sally Munt (London: Continuum International, 2001), 113–26.

31. Ila Nagar, "Digitally Untouched: Janana (In)Visibility and the Digital Divide," in *Queering Digital India: Activisms, Identities, Subjectivities*, ed. Rohit K. Dasgupta and Debanuj DasGupta (Edinburgh: Edinburgh University Press, 2018).

32. Rai, "India On-Line."

33. Habermas—*The Structural Transformation of the Public Sphere: An Inquiry into a Category of Bourgeois Society* (Cambridge, MA: MIT Press, 1989).

34. Nancy Fraser, "Rethinking the Public Sphere," *Social Text* nos. 25–26 (1990): 56–80.

35. Rai, "India On-Line."

36. Michael Warner, *Publics and Counterpublics* (Cambridge, MA: Zone Books, 2002).

37. Michael Warner, "Publics and Counterpublics (abbreviated version)," *Quarterly Journal of Speech* 88, no. 4 (2002): 413–25.

38. https://twitter.com/dalitdiva/status/1001899355471671296.

39. Nancy Fraser, "Rethinking the Public Sphere: A Contribution to the Critique of Actually Existing Democracy," *Social Text*, nos. 25–26 (1990): 56–80.

40. Gina Masullo Chen, "Don't Call Me That: A Techno-Feminist Critique of the Term *Mommy Blogger*," *Mass Communication and Society* 16, no. 4 (2013): 510–32, https://doi.org/10.1080/15205436.2012.737888.

41. Rai, "India On-Line," 31.

42. Warner, *Publics and Counterpublics*, 97.

43. Jodi Dean, *Blog Theory: Feedback and Capture in the Circuits of Drive* (Malden, MA: Polity, 2010), 79–80.

44. Sarah Banet-Weiser presentation on Roundtable at CAMEo 2018, Leicester.

45. L. S. Clark, "Participants on the Margins: #BlackLivesMatter and the Role That Shared Artifacts of Engagement Played among Minoritized Political Newcomers on Snapchat, Facebook, and Twitter," *International Journal of Communication* 10, no. 1 (2016): 235–53.

46. Maria Elena Martinez-Torres, "Civil Society, the Internet, and the Zapatistas," *Peace Review* 13, no. 3 (2001): 347

47. Naisargi N. Dave, *Queer Activism in India: A Story in the Anthropology of Ethics* (Durham, NC: Duke University Press), 10.

48. Dave, *Queer Activism in India*, 10.

49. Divya Kandukuri on her public feed on Facebook, shared by her on October 7, 2018. https://www.facebook.com/20921597/posts/10106075163206240/

50. Sidney Tarrow, *The New Transnational Activism* (Cambridge Studies in Contentious Politics) (Cambridge, UK: Cambridge University Press, 2005), 2.

51. Ibid., 113.

52. Maria Elena Martinez-Torres, "Civil Society, the Internet, and the Zapatistas," 347.

53. The term "is most often used as shorthand for the condition of social and economic insecurity associated with post-Fordist employment and neoliberal governance, which not only gives employers leeway to hire and fire workers at will, but also glorifies part-time contingent work as 'free agency,' liberated from the stifling constraints of contractual regulations." Andrew Ross, *Nice Work If You Can Get It: Life and Labor in Precarious Times* (NYU Series in Social and Cultural Analysis) (New York: New York University Press, 2009), 34.

54. David Kergel and Birte Heidkamp, introduction, in *Precarity within the Digital Age: Media Change and Social Insecurity*, ed. Birte Heidkamp and David Kergel [Prekarisierung und soziale Entkopplung—transdisziplinäre Studien] (Wiesbaden: Springer Fachmedien, 2017), 3.

55. Alison Hearn, "Commodification," in *Keywords for Media Studies*, ed. Laurie Oullette and Jonathan Gray (New York: New York University Press, 2017), 46; Banet-Weiser 2018.

56. Explained in an annotation to "The Annihilation of Caste," Savarna refers to, "in Sanskrit, literally 'those with Varna.' Thus, the term refers to members of the Caste System, and especially those in the three higher-ranking Varnas." B. R. Ambedkar, "The Annihilation of Caste," in *Dr. Babasaheb Ambedkar: Writings and Speeches*, vol. 1 (Bombay: Education Department, Government of Maharashtra, 1979), 25–96. Citation available online at The Annihilation of Caste Multimedia Study Environment (New York: Columbia University, 2004).

57. Christina Thomas Dhanaraj, "MeToo and Savarna Feminism: Revolutions Cannot Start with the Privileged, Feminist Future Must Be Equal for All," *First Post*, November 18, 2018, https://www.firstpost.com/india/metoo-and-savarna-feminism-revolutions-cannot-start-with-the-privileged-feminist-future-must-be-equal-for-all-5534711.html.

58. Linda Alcoff, "The Problem of Speaking for Others," *Cultural Critique* 20 (Winter 1991/92): 26, http://www.jstor.org/stable/1354221.

59. Amy Bhatt, *High-Tech Housewives: Indian IT Workers, Gendered Labor and Transmigration* (Seattle: University of Washington Press, 2018), 21.

60. Sujatha Subramanian, "From the Streets to the Web: Looking at Feminist Activism on Social Media." *Review of Women's Studies, Economic & Political Weekly* 50, no. 17 (April 25, 2015): 71–78, https://www.genderit.org/sites/default/upload/from_the_streets_to_the_web.pdf.

Section I

Chapter One

Gendered Indian Digital Publics

Digital and Domestic

Radhika Gajjala

The connection between the digital and the domestic seems obvious. Clearly we all are in digital and domestic spaces simultaneously a lot of the time regardless of gender. Yet this connection between the digital and the domestic has particular significance in relation to gendered labor in the home space and in relation to care work for the elderly, the disabled, the chronically ill, and for the very young who spend most of their time at home. Thus, even though the connection between the digital and the domestic seems self-evident and commonplace, it is important to think through this connection by highlighting concerns around women's/reproductive labor that mostly happens in the home space, and how such concerns are projected into online space. "Digital domesticity" is something that is produced in relation to feminized reproductive work and tends to be mostly gendered female. This digital domesticity is produced both through prosumerism and through a marketplace offering domestic and related care services and products.

Consumer-oriented digitally domestic texts include websites and mobile apps that offer home cleaning services, at-home caretaking services, and so on. Prosumer[1] -created digital spaces of digital domesticity include food and parenting blogs, home décor and recipe Pinterest boards, fashion and knitting/crafting podcasts, and/or YouTube videos on various aspects of domestic life. The "consumer has instant access [to the online economic marketplace] . . . the processes and structures within which messages are constituted and multiply mediated remain invisible to the consumer."[2] Thus, the digital and the domestic connect up to produce women simultaneously as consumer subjects and laboring subjects framed through a neoliberal entrepreneurial ethos. For instance, many contemporary immigrant and diasporic women from India/South Asia form online communities around domesticity, but they also exert their autonomy by forming such communities. They are also in pursuit of entrepreneurial opportunities through networking.

Thus, it is important to keep in mind that when I use broader terms like digitally domestic or digitally activist in this book I am making a broad generalization based on the discursive spaces left as archives. I am not making assessments about the individuals, who tend to move in and out of and through digital publics and multiple social worlds as they leave behind discursive archives with their posts and other forms of participation

> frozen in time and "space," dead and outside of their [spacio]temporal contexts. But this "death" is not like the disappearance of a spoken word. A word when spoken in a verbal exchange disappears once the people who heard it spoken no longer retain it in their memory. Internet exchanges are stored in computer memory. Contrary to how many people imagine "cyberspace," cyberspace exists in computer chips and is possible because of a modem that connects networks of computers across great distances. The messages online are thus both texts and subjects.[3]

In the case of gendered Indian digital diasporas, this sociality contributes to the formation of digital publics through a variety of offline geographic locations where women of Indian descent connect online through various gadgets.

Activist subjects who emerge in digital publics also negotiate multiple social worlds. In the case of activist voices emerging through social media, the negotiation of home and the world through different nuances resurfaces. Activist subjects sometimes access digital publics from the domestic space in secrecy, but they may also access digital publics from outside of the home space *because* being out of doors allows them more privacy, in an interesting move that can be said to privatize/individualize physical public space. Their moment of engagement in digital publics is treated as a private or secret moment as they engage the digital streets using pseudonyms (such as a Twitter or Instagram handle that may not directly identify who they are offline) or text friends and family within the privacy of a password-locked mobile phone. As observed by Rahul Gairola, mobile phones can serve also as "digital closets." In "Digital Closets: Post-millenial Representations of Queerness in *Kapoor & Sons* and *Aligarh*," he observes how the two movies construct digital closets around queer protagonists.[4] Gairola observes that

> these are in-between spaces that interface with material spaces which are shaped and informed by Section 377's colonial afterlife. Digital closets are the pivot points upon which hinge public disclosure of one's queer lifestyle practices, and the protective shadows of life online that obscure gender and sexuality identities. Such closets, which are distinct from those described by Eve Kosfsky Sedgewick, . . . allow a new way for queer identities to slip and slide around technological interfaces wherein transgressive sexuality only exists in cyberspace when it is targeted for . . . policing."[5]

In chapter 7, there is mention of how in the 1990s there were very few women from the geographic region of India in gay and queer chatrooms because women hesitated to go to public internet cafes where they could go online. However, with the proliferation of mobile phones, there is more internet connectivity possible that allows women access more easily. Still, as Preeti Mudliar notes, this mobile phone connectivity allows for the emergence of yet another dichotomy, where the interplay of technology and physical space is different even when comparing access to these spaces by cisgender male bodies and cisgender female bodies. In her article entitled "Public WiFi Is for Men and Mobile Internet Is for Women: Interrogating Politics of Space and Gender around WiFi Hotspots," she describes "experiences of women who are active smartphone and mobile Internet users, but still find themselves unable to access and use the different WiFi opportunities in the village, owing to gendered politics of space and mobility."[6]

In the interlude with Damini Kulkarni and Debipreeta Rahut in chapter 6, we push against this binary by describing and unpacking specific examples of what might be considered "front stage" versus "back stage" behaviors by some people who discursively perform activist voices and seemingly contribute to the overall movement through sharing protest messages online.

GHAR AND BAHIR

Here, I both lay out the faux binary of ghar and bahir and also insert critiques of the binary. The contradictions entailed in extrapolating from earlier (and implicitly caste and class blind post-nationalist) [7] theorizing of "the women's question" when attempting to take into account the diverse voices of women from India are noted. [8] The project of problematizing the binary while also using it as a framework may seem riddled with contradictions—but the messiness of this book project as a whole in itself is meant to open up questions (later also explored in dialogue interludes) and issues for further exploration across a wide range of contexts, conjunctures, and disjunctures. When the fabric of history is ripped open—there is a tangled mess—it takes many forms of collaborations and repeated reflection to try to unravel the tangles. Thus, for instance, the reader will observe that the dialogue interlude that follows this chapter is centrally focused on middle- to upper-class Indian women in relation to their moving to the United States and how this movement reinstates them in a particular relationship to the domestic (ghar) space. Yet, the dialogue interlude that follows in chapter 3 is with Shilpa Phadke, who is concerned with (re)claiming the streets (the bahir) for women through the #whyloiter movement. This in turn is followed by a chapter that contains dialogue interludes that openly and implicitly put the binary in question by bringing in issues of caste and class. Further, this binary is also problematic in relation to trans folks and queer women as well[9].

The binary of ghar and bahir is an extension drawn from the work of the Bengali novelist Rabindranath Tagore (later developed into a movie by Satyajit Ray). [10] The novel *Ghare Baire* (*The Home and the World*) as read through a feminist lens could be said to center around the dominant-caste female protagonist's struggle toward autonomy as she moves out of her husband's home (ghar) to the outside world to take part in the Indian freedom movement, gets involved in an extramarital affair, and ends up betrayed and destitute. The irony that Tagore points to is the fact that it is the progressive husband who encourages his wife to become modern and to engage in the world outside the home. Her stepping out into the outside world (bahir), however, opens her up to the evils of the outside. Even as she becomes an activist herself, she loses the protection of the home and the patriarchal system that protected her upper-caste purity. [11]

Indian nationalism also adopted this binary to draw a distinction between the material and spiritual during struggles against British colonial rule. This binary of ghar and bahir was a patriarchal binary and reasserted the private as a space for upper-caste and middle- to upper-class women while the public was posited as unsafe for these same women. It is certainly not a framework that was articulated through the writing of women's histories by women, even though the framework was later taken up by South Asian feminists as a point of entry and departure from which to debate and extend discussions around issues of the "'private' and 'public' domain as defined by upper caste and middle to upper class ideologies."[12]

Combine this with the tendency of the Indian women's movement to privilege taking their activism outside the domestic—and with the implicit authentication of feminism as possible through putting the body on the line in physical streets (thus also implying that the body on the line—at risk—in domestic space is either complicit or a mute victim), this leaves the domestic dominant caste space and the nuances of domestic space–based caste oppression untouched by intervention and questioning (in what Ray and Qayum refer to as "cultures of servitude").[13] Patriarchy in the home space is characterized as a homogenous culture, and the nuances of gender hierarchies as well as caste/class oppressions in such spaces are not unpacked adequately. Interventions into domestic violence, rape, and other private sphere–based women's struggles are often treated by the mainstream feminist movement by "[b]ringing a matter into the public sphere" so that the public is still privileged as the route through which is accomplished the "dismantling [of a particular monolithic idea of patriarchy and] its power to subordinate women."[14]

In the case of the digital context, the body tweeting or blogging is in physical domestic space and in some instances the body is in physical streets. But the corporeal body and the affective/subjective body seem out of sync and split (even "disembodied") because of the ways in which our preconceived ideas of dualities and binaries are spacio-temporally static. Implicitly, we view the body in place as corporeal, tactile, and physically tangible; on the other hand, we view the subjective as moving through aspirational, thinking, and imagined space. In actuality, these move together as bodily actions work with instinctual subjective responses. It is our afterthoughts, our conceptualizations, that are often forced into existing sociopolitical frames and place and position us retroactively and strategically as we try to re-sync the corporeal and the subjective/affective encounters in our acts of making sense. Thus, everyday seemingly minor and imperceptible relational shifts contribute to how our body moves through time and space. We transform relationally, along with other people, objects, technologies, the environment, food, sounds, smells, tastes, and so much more through our everyday, but the evidence of these transformations is concretely located. The digital is a moment of affective impact—when it is not a raging flame war—and seems ephemeral. Only some of these momentary impacts on our corporeal subjective selves are locatable; usually they are viewed through preconceived social frames that don't allow us to recognize ephemeral influences triggering transformation. For instance, in several interviews the question of authenticity of protest kept emerging. Some of those interviewed implied that a visible Twitter user in either feminist or anti-caste space wasn't "really" an activist, feminist, or anti-caste in their offline reality. Some of these tensions are visible in the dialogue interludes in chapters 4 and 8.

In other instances, several interviewees pointed to how sharing and clicking on the like feature on Facebook or retweeting and even posting on Twitter did not guarantee that the person offline behaved in sync with what they were performing online. While in the case of some of the self-proclaimed activists on Twitter the question of self-reflexivity was raised, in the case of others there was a clear accusation of hypocrisy. I was told, for instance that some "aunties" and "uncles"—women and men—who shared posts protesting the 2012 Nirbhaya rape continued to victim blame in offline settings. Yet, as others interviewed pointed out, the transformation of subjectivity or the understanding of a social situation from a different perspective does not happen overnight. Perhaps in pointing to particular instances of discrepant behaviors we are being hasty in accusing people of having dichotomous online and offline behaviors. This is further discussed through specific examples in the dialogue performed with Debapreeti Rahut and Damini Kulkarni.

Preconceived social frames in the context of contemporary gendered Indian digital social media spaces, coming to us through mainstream, middle- and upper-class/caste Indian social histories, are the idea of the ghar as women's space and the bahir as men's space. Yet, as Jasmeen Patheja's narration of her more than fifteen years of activist work through Blank Noise reveals, it is possible to see that digital activism is secondary to yet a natural everyday tool that is interwoven with the offline campaigns she has worked on.[15] Thus, in the case of movements that engage the digital, we see that activists are strategic in how these tools are used—they do not consider only digital interaction as sufficient for their activist organizing, neither do they see the digital as unnecessary. Digital tools are used as relevant and necessary. Having said that, not all digitally visible amplifiers of activist movements consider themselves to be activists. For instance, Christina Thomas Dhanaraj has been named by some as a Dalit feminist activist, but she is clear in noting that she doesn't see herself as such—she is an "influencer." For a clear discussion of this, see chapter 8 with Christina Thomas Dhanaraj. Shilpa Phadke, on the other hand, expresses her doubts over being referred to as a "digital activist" even though her team and she use digital tools to spread word of the #whyloiter campaign. So my use of phrases such as "digital activism" and my naming of participants in this book as activists are continually reexamined, contested, and debated.

In this book, I have split the discussion of gendered Indian digital publics into a faux (and conceptual) binary of digital domesticity and digital streets.[16] The overlap and interweaving nature of this faux binary however, means that the analysis here and in chapter 5 often blur into each other; the separation I construct is primarily for organizational purposes. The binaries and boundaries are strategic but are also more affective and political than they are physical or based purely in digital platform/mobile app affordances. Further, the digital publics that emerge as digital domesticity or as digital activism emerge in various ways and are not limited to the examples used in the chapters of this book. The concern with domestic and digital publics dates back to the early years of the World Wide Web—in fact back to the days of Usenet and of text-only MUDs and MOOs.[17]

Conceptual issues around the intersecting of domestic space and digital public space through Indian digital diasporic contexts are discussed through existing literature and by drawing on interviews conducted. Overall, in articulating the private/public binary as home and the world, rather than as "private" space and "public" space as mutually exclusive, I draw on the framework of ghar and bahir, which is an Indian feminist rearticulation of private and public, which was developed through writings in postcolonial theory.[18] This framework, while it is similar to how feminists have nuanced the idea of private and public, has a different history than the Western feminist conceptualization of private and public.

Second-wave western feminists articulated a clear connection between the personal and the political through the now much quoted

phrase "the personal is political" as they exposed the sexual inequalities prevalent in the private sphere. What was happening as consciousness raising among housewives coincided with other movements socially in the 1960s and 1970s. Civil rights activists, students protesting
the Vietnam War, lesbians, and many others were on the streets fighting for their rights. In such a setting, as Joan Landes notes, feminism
"offered women a public language for their private despair."[19]

In second-wave feminism, the private and public binary is revealed
as a social construction that hides women's personal experience and
labor in favor of a patriarchal system that is based in mostly male-
centered publics. Revealing the abuses in private space—viewing the
personal as political—has permitted second-wave feminists to realize
the oppressive nature of private space even while they fight for ownership of their own bodies, decision-making power in deeply personal
issues, and privacy in relationships with the right to say no in the most
intimate and private of situations.

Discourses of women's empowerment emerge and proliferate even
as gendered oppression and exploitation of underpaid female labor continues and the definitions of private and public or of home and the
world outside (ghar and bahir) shift according to what the users affectively define (feel) as home space or outside world space, and based on
the specific affordances of each digital platform and mobile application
used. The binary of ghar and bahir, in fact, maps onto a nuanced notion
of private and public where the idea of ghar includes, for instance, a
culturally or religiously bound community—as in the case of immigrant communities—and bahir refers to anyone or group of people
considered not part of that community (such as members of the host
country). In a move similar to the centering of the "gendered organization of public and private life,"[20] postcolonial theorists and Indian feminists noted the ghar/bahir binary. There is some debate over whether
the concepts of ghar and bahir coincide exactly with private and public
as used in Western feminisms historically. However, since even Western feminists have noted that the binary of public/private does not map
consistently across all gendered spaces in exactly the same way, we can
argue that even in Western feminist history the use of private and
public is more of a continuum than a reference to strict bounded binaries. In modern times (and particularly in the context of digital publics)
what we see is how the private and public work in a continuum that
functions around the production of individualized economic citizens
and social activity formed around economic activity. Both private and

public orient the individual toward becoming an economic citizen. Such an emphasis gives rise to various possibilities for the woman's autonomy as both wage earner and as a consumer citizen leading to a public focus on the economic. Thus, as Hannah Arendt observed even prior to the movements in the 1960s and 1970s,

> The emergence of society—the rise of housekeeping, its activities, problems, and organizational devices—from the shadowy interior of the household into the light of the public sphere, has not only blurred the old borderline between private and political, it has also changed almost beyond recognition the meaning of the two terms and their significance for the life of the individual and the citizen. [21]

Bringing these concepts into discussions of digital space of relational communication, we see that digital publics are a further extension of this blurring of the private and public where the personal is not only political, but also economic. We acquire consumer identities and social value through consumption.

Yet in the case of the ghar/bahir binary, the economic and the social work together through an interplay of caste, class, and cultures of servitude. [22] Ghar denotes caste, class, and gendered enclosures in the name of protection for the woman and the maintenance of culture in opposition to an outside world sociopolitically defined as *culturally* outside—simultaneously in relation to the Western outside and caste/class/racial "outsiders." Ghar is also a place of work for the paid domestic worker and where cultures of servitude contribute to the production of the ideal modern Indian woman.

What happens in the ghar is considered pure. This purity and protection in the home at one extreme even works to sustain and normalize domestic abuse and marital rape as "culture" as they ostensibly occur in "*within-gender* hierarchies," which refer to systems of control among women, where particular subgroups (e.g., older female family members) leverage power against others (e.g., young women) through patriarchal systems of abuse. [23] Thus, rather than characterize private space and public space as clearly demarcated, we must note how publics—whether digital publics or physical publics—of community formation serve as ghars where abuse is normalized in public. The idea of private and public as articulated through Western feminism assumes male-to-female abuse in nuclear family space and misses the protection that the male abuser gets through public discourse and community authorization. Yet the dynamic of public support for the abuse or denigration of women in within-gender hierarchies that mute women's voices and autonomy in certain circumstances is visible to us even in Western and global public media spaces—not just in Indian/South Asian digital spaces. Take for instance how the "public" was characterized through media as implicitly disbelieving of both Anita Hill and Monica Lewinsky. In pre–social media times, the media reports did not problematize this disbelief as openly or as loudly as the social media publics do in contemporary times. Yet, as this manuscript goes to press, sadly, it has also become evident, in the Christine Blasey Ford case, that there is still a struggle over who constitutes the public: those who disclaim Ford's testimony or those who believe her. Yet, because the internet does not produce the illusion or allow media conglomerates to represent a homogenous public and it contains many niche publics and privatized publics, we see the ruptures and debates more openly than we did in the case of Hill and Lewinsky. The disbelief was not characterized by a male/female binary; rather, it was normalized through within-gender hierarchies of race, age, and class. Contrast that with the ways in which the contemporary #metoo movement necessitates and compels us as "a public" to *believe* the women—even while individuals in private space may express doubts. Within-gender hierarchies are being contested as much as male/female hierarchies—even in feminist spaces, as illustrated by the Twitter and blogosphere-based debates around Raya Sarkar's crowdsourced list of sexual harassers in the Indian academy (#LoSHA), for instance.[24] Yet Srila Roy notes that

> the Indian case is evocative of a more general and global predicament that contemporary feminism seems to find itself in. Across the north and the south, there is a new visibility, potency, and legitimacy to feminist knowledges, affects, and struggles, but there is also an intensification of internal contestation, charge, and conflict. If feminists are unable to respond in a unified voice to sexual violence, then they are also faced with an increased backlash from patriarchal forces, not to mention the threat of "co-option" from external agents, such as the state, the market, neo-liberal capitalism, and right-wing nationalisms (Farris and Rottenberg 2017). In short, whether in India or elsewhere, this is a conjuncture in which feminism and ideals of gender equality enjoy more widespread legitimacy than ever before, but paradoxically, at the same time, the fundamental contradictions of feminism as a political project have also never been more visible and obvious.[25]

Online sociality and activism in Indian digital diasporas reproduce the ghar and bahir in different variations. Strategically and simplistically binarizing the ghar and the bahir again, we might say that digital domesticity leads to the construction of digital "homes" for and by digitally diasporic Indian women and that the digital streets are implicitly posited as the bahir. Yet both interweave as they co-occupy space through similar digital and social media tools. Twitter and Instagram hashtags as well as Facebook and blog comment sections occasionally meet and collide, providing interesting ways to problematize issues of caste, class, binary gender assumptions, and heteronormativity.

The framework of ghar and bahir as a way to analyze Indian women's identity and relationship to modernity and public space is based on an exclusion of lower-caste women and women who worked as paid domestic workers in the upper-class/upper-caste households. Thus, the framework itself makes invisible the modern middle- to upper-class woman's reliance on paid domestic labor, with the Savarna woman, the "bhadramahila," as manager of the household. Such an elision of caste/class nuance allows an easy connection with liberal feminist articulations of middle-class women's autonomy and choice without adequate attention to middle-class gendered caste/class complicities. This sense of autonomy, in turn, is what we see in Indian digital domesticity. The discursive formations of networks and the types of content shared, as well as gate-keeping practices engaged in by these women, produce the distinctions between digital ghars and digital bahirs—not because there is a direct patriarchy constraining their agency. Rather, the distinctions come from self-selected behaviors of privilege and upward mobility where individual autonomy and agency can be exercised without having to partake in any kind of accountability based in feminist politics.

The distinction between digital ghars and bahirs, therefore, is more implicitly ideological and not defined by the digital platform being used. These are socio-technical and techno-cultural divides—boundaries propped up through the maintaining of privilege. Further, it is not clearly a Twitter versus Facebook or Facebook versus WhatsApp distinction, even though broadly speaking, affordances within particular apps lend themselves to particular kinds of exchanges. For example, WhatsApp's specific features lend themselves more to the ghar, and Twitter's interface lends itself more to the bahir. But the technical differences also inform which bodies actually access these tools based on what social and linguistic literacies the apps require and on what gadgets people can use them.

Thus, as Donald Norman notes, affordances, or more precisely "'perceived affordance[s].'" by design rely upon "what actions the use perceives to be possible [rather] than what is true."[26] Infrastructural issues have already oriented structures of domination in the production of discursive and affective spaces online, but users still engage in diverse ways within limits and assert a certain amount of agency. Even given a sort of seeming infrastructural agency and access, the cultural ethos of the differing spaces are also defined through offline social hierarchies.

For instance, WhatsApp lends itself to forming more digital ghars, partly because it promises encrypted messaging and ease of access across generations; it consequently sustains intergenerational communities and family networks that serve to contain and hide abuse from digital publics. Intergenerational communities may inhabit networked spaces such as Facebook, but they do so differently. WhatsApp is a tool that seems to allow private enclosures. And, as Maitrayee Chaudhuri notes, "WhatsApp visuals reach a non-literate section in ways that the old media could not."[27] This then nuances the idea of public and private in a different way and disrupts common assumptions about how digital public space is accessed or engaged.[28]

Thus, these conceptualizations do not always correspond to strict binaries of public and private, and there are different ways in which each space and each interaction weaves in and out of ghar and bahir. Interestingly, this continual shifting is both the result of the everydayness of the use of digital tools for the creation of personal and more public relational spaces and also the result of the way in which families negotiate modernity through the ghar/bahir framework. For instance, as Mallapragada notes, "The use of the virtual, interactive, digital environment for religious activities within the domestic household by NRI women destabilizes some of the fixed meanings of the private associated with the individual home and those of the public associated with transnational online spaces."[29] Yet even as there is a destabilizing of the private, the reassertion of domesticity even in its new and neoliberal form often centers a certain kind of middle- to upper-class (and upper-caste) Indian woman's autonomy. This is an appropriation of the digital public as a "ghar" space. A "digital domestic" space of nostalgia formed around cultural practices is also threaded through with religio-nationalist references that are mimetically transferred through image and caption or coded into short videos and tweetable texts.

These digital publics—even as they seem to destabilize physical private space—serve to reinforce the cultural Indianness of ghar space. They potentially invoke connections that are often embedded in the politics of "born again" religious identities through discovery and appropriation of traditions, which are in turn revamped to work with an ethos of consumerism. The multiplicity of interpretations of various mythologies and cultural rituals that have existed across geography, class, and caste—often narrated orally from generation to generation across local regions, contexts, and languages—are flattened into mediascapes of homogeneity. These mediascapes also draw heavily on the many television programs around religious discourse, cultural traditions, and cooking that have emerged since the 1990s and cut across offline NRI community reinterpretations even when these digital spaces are linguistically diverse. This flattening is also an effect of the affordances of various digital formats and how they work across time zones leading to shifts in spatio-temporality of everyday life. Maitrayee Chaudhuri writes:

> One of the profound ways in which the Internet and the new media change the public sphere is through a change in temporality—our relationship and experience with time. Information and images travel the world instantly. The Internet is a highly mediated and highly capitalised form of circulation organized in the 24x7 instant access. The consumer has instant access, but the processes and structures within which messages are constituted and are multiply mediated remain invisible to the consumer.[30]

The hegemony of such content in Indian digital domesticity potentially asserts the role of the digitally diasporic woman as someone who uses modern tools to reinstate tradition and culture in the home space. Thus the privacy of individual homes is indeed destabilized in connecting transnationally but is woven through the safety of digital ghars reaching for content to reinscribe Indianness through digital connectivity. The broader concept of digital domesticity connects with what I am noting as formations of digital ghars through digital publics in the context of Indian digital diasporas. These groups, therefore, can function as a discursive and affective form of "digital ghar."

As implied in some of Sarada Nori's contributions to the conversation in chapter 2 as well as implied in several other interviews I conducted with other women, these enclosures could also serve as consciousness-raising groups that lead to digital street- and physical street-based activisms. Harriet Riches supports these understandings of digital domesticity as a formation that builds intersectional and transnational feminist consciousness-raising practices in her examination of photography and online magazines. This research suggests that digital domesticity could in fact be a pathway to digital and offline streets. Women-centered sociality on the internet does often tend to be more conducive to community building and offline continuities than some other forms of online so-called participatory communities. As Riches notes:

> There is value in that touch. The confessional blogs, sisterly tone, advice and discussion of women's experience online revokes the format of the woman's magazine, offering the hand of digital friendship, and creating online communities, in so doing fulfilling the utopian potential of the web to create vital, truly social networks.[31]

Thus, while Chen has a point about how the domesticity part of digital domesticity potentially serves to perpetuate aspects of women's identity and labor that reinscribe her situatedness within a domestic space that privileges patriarchal structures, there has also been a push back regarding the naming of this form of digital domesticity negatively as a form of "new domesticity."[32]

This push back was quite forceful from several of my research interviewees on another related project examining do-it-yourself (DIY) fiber crafters, for instance. These interviewees were DIY fiber crafters using digital networks such as Ravelry, Etsy, and Instagram as they devoted large amounts of time to their fiber-crafting pursuits. In these interviews, I called attention to Emily Matchar's conceptualization of "new domesticity," which she defines as a "current collective nostalgia and domesticity-mania" that "speak[s] to deep cultural longings" and signals "a profound shift in the way Americans view life."[33] I asked their opinion of her framework by sharing her *New York Times* article.[34] While they acknowledged that their fiber crafting did tend to keep them in the home space—the domestic environment—and that their blogging and image sharing was centered on the home space, their focus was craft, and they asserted their agency through their craft sometimes to the exclusion of any domestic chores. They did not see themselves as part of a "new domesticity." Even though the DIY fiber-crafting communities from which I got these reactions to Matchar's conceptualization of "new domesticity" are different than the mommy and food bloggers that Chen writes about, it is necessary to consider the complexity and ideological implication of the term "domesticity" for the contemporary modern woman who views herself as an autonomous choice-making individual and distinguishes herself from previous generations of women who did not have the choices she has. Thus, the points that Matchar, Lisa Belkin, Linda Hirshman, and others make that these women are making a choice to "opt out" of the feminist fight for equality and are taking either lower-paying jobs or are moving in to domesticity were strongly contested by my interviewees.[35] These women felt that Matchar and other such commentators who talked of new domesticity and opting out in this manner did not have an adequate understanding of the economic everyday constraints faced by the average middle-class American woman, nor did they see the resistance embedded in their choices. Still, based on my observation of interactions online, critical engagement and discussion offline, and qualitative thematic analysis of the interviews, I would agree that in terms of cultural ethos and ideological implications of "deep cultural longings," there seems to be some validity to the points made by Matchar and others. Nevertheless—even if these groups of women in these digital spaces are connected through the commonality of DIY fiber crafting and appear homogenous because of the digital texts they share around fiber and craft—they are a heterogeneous group.

In the case of Indian digital domesticity as well, these nuances, contradictions, and heterogeneities do exist. Drawing from that body of research and using it to understand the interviews I did in the context of South Asians and digital domesticity, I see a similar pushback to the suggestion that Indian diasporic women are opting out of the feminist fight. A return to a focus on domesticity on the part of these women, therefore, is admittedly complex. It is true that these are all practices that connect the digital and domestic; there are moments and instances in which the digital and domestic do work in concert with ideologies of the domestic as women's space. However, it is unfair to oversimplify their turn to domesticity and their use of digital space for domesticity as an ideological return to a 1950s mode of middle-class female heteronormative homemaking.

In general, because of the individualistic nature of how we engage online networks, a rhetoric of choice becomes central to my understanding of these digital domestic practices. We supposedly enter and leave the digital domestic by choice—we are not actually bound by larger community hierarchies and social pressures to the network; we enter and leave with no long-lasting material consequences. Certainly if the digital domestic space is an extension of an offline community that one is inextricably a part of or is being used by one's place of work or has other material or financial connections, it is hard to leave the network, but the choice is still not as difficult as leaving a family or a small local neighborhood community that may have direct impact on everyday life negotiations.

Emotional involvement in terms of individual self-empowerment in such online networks does, however, have influence on the participant. It results in shifts in the actual lives of the women engaged in these spaces. The ideological shifts, communal pressures, and/or empowerment that happen are more affective and manifest in the corporeal day-to-day of the women as choices in their actual everyday lives, as the networks serve more as consciousness-raising through the sharing of information, skill, and experience.

For instance, Radha Hegde's research suggests that some South Asian diasporic women access and write food blogs to reproduce a sense of home and connection with the familiar; interaction with these blogs disrupts feelings of alienation and insularity that emerge in physically domestic spaces.[36] Similarly, Amy Bhatt's ethnographic research on spouses of H1B holders and their dilemmas as they suddenly find themselves stuck in domesticity, so to speak, also shows how building networks through the digital domestic mobilizes affective connections for some South Asian diasporic women.[37] Thus, the way these diasporic women are engaging in digital domesticity differs from the way that the mommy bloggers and others that Chen refers to engage in digital domesticity. Bhatt notes:

> Many turn to the domestic sphere to create new channels for personal development and self-expression, while also grappling with deep challenges to their identities as educated, modern women with potential for launching careers of their own. While some women embrace their reproductive roles, others resist their classification as wives and mothers, and continue to pursue avenues for professional fulfillment.[38]

Thus, through this embracing of stereotypical women's roles through digital connectivity, the private and public are simultaneously inhabited. The corporeal self may appear to be in physical home and private space, yet the body and mind engage the public sphere through the digital gadget, reorienting both the corporeal and subjective through shifts enabled through exposure to and negotiation of global connectivity and online sociality. This positioning is oriented physically toward a subjective immersion in social spaces outside of the brick and mortar home. Yes, we might expect that the home that is being reproduced and built through the digital (as a digital *ghar*) is happening through explicit reinforcements of ideologies of domesticity; heteronormativity; and, in the case of Indians, ideologies of Hindu nationalism. And, indeed, the digital ghar does serve to produce "a place to affirm one's Indianness" where "the Indian woman is [yet again] expected to be responsible for maintaining this Indian home in [digital] diaspora by remaining true to her Indian womanhood."[39] Similarly, Hegde has noted how affective and sensory digital enclaves are formed around various Indian regional food blogs and around Carnatic music blogs that serve to create "portable traditions in the diasporic contexts."[40] Such digital encapsulations of "tradition" and circulation through the digital are certainly susceptible to the creation of oppressive within-gender hierarchies where true Indian womanhood is potentially reasserted.[41] In fact, this is clearly visible in digital domestic circulations through intergenerational exchanges via WhatsApp communities.

Yet these connections to nationalist ideologies are not always straightforward or clearly visible. Indian digital diasporic spaces—especially food blogs—are based in South Asian hybridities, so when recipes go digital, the hybrid identities can be mobilized in the marketing and branding of these blogs. For the most part, the women engaged in such digital domesticities are subtle in their endorsements of nationalist and religious ideologies in an effort to maintain their cosmopolitan and neoliberal entrepreneurial image. While the Hindu religion-based digital domestic sites that focus on rituals and the circulation of religious doctrines and related cultural practices do tend to be based more clearly in nationalist identities that connect Hindu ways of living with Indian national loyalty, the food blogs and celebrity blogs tend to be less overt. Thus the larger ethos of Indian digital domesticity is complex; it cannot be flattened in description as either global/cosmopolitan or a reproduction of Hindu nationalism. The contemporary and digital diasporas from India bring together gendered laboring subjects through digital interfaces from various geographical locations including India itself. However, even as contemporary digital diasporas include engagement from people of various social locations in India (across the diversity that is India—religion, language, and caste), the discursive space that forms as "India" online tends to marginalize and invisibilize non-Hindu and non-dominant-caste participation. Therefore, the reader will note that while this book as a whole references "Indian digital diasporas" it sometimes slips into a characterization of "Hindu" digital diasporas. Dating back to the 1990s, as noted in the introduction to this book, it is possible to see how Indian internet spaces have produced, intensified, and now normalized "Indian" as "Hindu."

A salient ethos characterizing the activity of gendered subjects engaged in labor and leisure in Indian digital diasporas reveals self-expressions of autonomy where "performances are constructed with predominantly entrepreneurial [digital] enclosures . . . where various media forms converge."[42] In addition, even as these performances "speak to their transnationally mobile forms of belonging," they do so in varying "registers that are at once nostalgic, traditional, cosmopolitan and at times postfeminist."[43] These forms of belonging are reinvigorated through the circulation of affect that potentially connects with exclusionary nationalist ideologies through religious and cultural practices as they are disseminated transnationally.

Therefore, the affective and discursive production of Indian digital domesticity is also nuanced by the fact that this policing occurs through sexual harassment and violence in digital streets through what Sahana Udupa names "Gaali cultures," based on a conceptualization of "Gaali" (a word that means "curse word") which, as she describes,

> implies a continuum between democratizing participation and regressive silencing. It gestures towards complicating the prognosis of the online discourse in terms of the polar opposites of a normative order, and to those practices where the experience of participation through maverick tactics slides into abuse of more intimidating nature as they interface larger structures of hegemonic power as well as the online ambience to "noise it out" on the web.[44]

However, in digital domesticity, the intimidation could occur in social within-gender hierarchies, too. Women's spaces in the home or in digital domesticity are not necessarily safe spaces when they are implicitly or explicitly based in the reproduction, revival, or update/modernization of tradition and culture within nationalist/communal loyalty structures.

SOUTH ASIAN WOMEN ONLINE

South Asian/Indian women's presence online dates back to the late 1980s and early 1990s. The binarizing of gender in much work about Indian women and the internet excludes transwomen and queer women. With the recent protests in response to the criminalization of transgendered populations in India, there has been much transgender community–based activism through social media. However, as is visible in campaigns such as #touchofcare, this attention also comes in the form of corporate appropriation of (trans)gender autonomy to garner more consumer attention.

Such Othered, non-cis, and non-Savarna gender identities do get included in digital domesticity through tropes of motherhood and other acceptable forms of domestication, but often it is also through certain commercialized hashtags that these issues come into digital domestic spaces. For instance, using the hashtag "touchofcare," the Vicks company produced several videos about motherhood, one of which was a video about a transwoman and her demonstration of care for her child through the use of Vicks Vaporub.[45] This sort of visible inclusion of transwomen as mothers in digital domesticity coincides with a so-called "Protection of Rights" bill proposed in Indian Parliament in 2016, which reasserted problematic essentialized cisgender binaries through implicit assumptions of "transgender."[46] It led to a proposal for the "verification" of transgender identity through body inspection. This was because, as Sharanya Gopinath notes in her post on the feminist blog *The Ladies Finger!*, the experts who helped define this policy, such as Dr. Piyush Saxena, have very debatable ideas on what "transgender" means and thus the very definition of transgender used in the bill is problematic in that it notes that a transgender person is "neither wholly female nor wholly male":

> This "definition" also flies in the face of the Supreme Court's own ruling that people have the right to gender self-determination. Not to mention that transgender and intersex are not interchangeable terms at all and it's problematic for this Bill to say they are.[47]

The introduction and circulation of the #touchofcare advertisement seems to suggest then that corporations' representations of trans folks in digital domesticity are more progressive than the government's continued stance on transgender rights.

The inclusion of these issues in corporate settings and advertisements leads to a double-bind. While the inclusion functions to make visible these identities through the corporate and NGO campaigns, the way in which the inclusion is done also functions to tame the issues and place the activist protests within the realm of bahir, or even ghar, where the protests might also be placed in digital domesticity. For instance, it was in a moment when the rights to self-determination of gender identity were being attacked in an attempt to define the trans body through particular detectable biological characteristics that legal trans-motherhood became woven into digital domesticity as well. Queer and transgender activist spaces as well as Dalit, Bahujan and Adivasi (DBA) women activist spaces tend to be "outside" the domesticity of Indian digital diasporas. This is not to suggest that queer, transgender, or Dalit and Bahujan women do not participate in the blur of activity that appears discursively to be heteronormative or that they do not engage in discussions around domestic life or are not consumer subjects themselves. However, the preservation of "ghar"—domesticity—is a classed activity. It is a particular classed activity that requires an implicitly "housewife" location. Whether or not participants claim that location, the performance of domesticity in modern nuclear family formations draws on that model. In the United States, such a housewife/homemaker location is socially also racialized—it's a location shaped through aspirational whiteness. In an Indian context, a "ghar"-based domesticity likewise is based in a mix of dominant caste and white-aspiring modernity. Digital ghar spaces that rely on subject formations around such modes of domesticity tend to exclude, for instance, African American and Dalit identity performances of self.

In my conversations with Divya Kandukuri (who is a Bahujan activist and co-founder of "EverydayCasteism" on Twitter, Instagram and Facebook), as we worked on a dialogue interlude (included in chapter 4) and developed plans for future collaborations, she critiqued the class-ist and caste-ist focus of movements like "Pinjra Todd," noting that that the ghar/bahir binary plays out differently outside of caste and class privilege. For instance, in her interview with me—leading to her dialogue interlude in chapter 4—she says:

> I worked with Pinjra Todd for two years continuously very actively when I was in college but I had to quit—because I felt I was not there—I was there but not really there. This whole thing about reclaiming the streets—for me it was—our women are on the streets since *when*—we never talk about . . . [*who's* reclaiming streets and how it is relevant to only women of caste privilege]. I need to be inside—I don't want to come on the streets again. Besides, this whole idea of reclaiming streets, loitering also demonises the men on streets - who are these men that they talk about? Bahujan men of course. Harassment doesn't happen inside the households of savarna feminist's houses or what?[48]

I realized I was putting all my energy into making posters and rallying on streets and making slogans for a cause that excludes me .Why don't they have any Bahujan woman in decision making roles? or running their online pages. They didn't take stand during #LoSHA when all of us were demanding for it, so on whose interest do these collectives run? Sisterhood in the Indian women's movement is a farce for me.[49]

Shailaja Paik similarly implies the problematic nature of the ghar/ bahir frames adopted by Indian feminism in her work on Dalit women's education and in the context of describing how Dalit populations were uprooted from their lands in nineteenth-century Maharashtra and had to move to urban locations. In urban locations, city construction and planning in modern India led to the poor people and Dalits living in rapidly growing slums. In such a context, there was no privacy "and there was no dichotomy between the home and the world. The ghar, home, was indeed bahar, in the outside, open world."[50] Sharmila Rege also points to the problems of this binary as she examines the problematics around the framework of "difference" in relation to the Dalit feminist standpoint.[51]

Thus, a key problem with even the mainstream of Indian feminist thinking, where they still implicitly draw from frameworks of postnational framings of the "woman problem," is its class/caste location. She notes that the "reinscriptions of [Dalit women's] struggles in our historical mappings—poses a challenge to Chatterjee's (1989) analysis of the 'Nationalist resolution of the Women's Question,' an analysis that has come to inform much theorization on gender and nation."[52] This problematic of caste is marginalized even in the subaltern studies project.[53]

Thus, in digital spaces of domesticity, the embodied experiences of queerness or Dalit-ness are not singularly emphasized. Both Divya Kandukuri and Christina Thomas Dhanaraj have very clearly noted this issue in conversations with me and in their own public writings on social media and elsewhere.[54] As Rege observes, "issues of caste become the sole responsibility of dalit women's organizations."[55] When they are emphasized, it is to note the *difference* and risks of exposure to caste, class, and heteronormative prejudice. Thus, the practices of domesticity that may be associated with queer, trans, or Dalit locations are not always identified as such, since these are groups of people who have had reasons to be fearful of revealing their identities in mainstream Indian social spaces. It becomes a form of self-exclusion within a digital domestic space that claims an Indian identity. It is in the self-naming of the speaking position as queer, trans, or Dalit that these subjects become Othered. Thus, as Hegde notes, these digital domestic spaces do not exactly replicate what might be considered traditional Indian domesticity, but rather they resist and reorient them transnationally. She argues that this signals a "new moment in the transnationalization of regional Indian food," which is in turn "rendered possible through the home labor of diasporic women building culinary linkages to the nation."[56]

This nation that they link to is implicitly a bourgeois heteronormative, upper-caste/class and middle-class India and in turn, I would argue, reinstates an Indianness that excludes Dalit, queer, Muslim, and trans Indian identities among others that might be marginal to this notion of a modern, cosmopolitan, transnational, tech-savvy Indian woman. Thus, even while ideologically these spaces may offer possibilities for transformation, agency, and liberation for heteronormative Indian women—and while several of these spaces might get past religious and linguistic divisions and seem progressive in their attempts to include queer, trans, and caste issues in their discussions—they are still limited socially and privilege heteronormative middle- to upper-class women.

INDIAN DIGITAL DOMESTICITY

Digital domesticity as it emerges in Indian digital diasporas through post-information-technology (IT) generations and their migration outward from India, whether to Dubai, Norway, or the United States, relies on the re-domestication of the diasporic Indian woman. Field research combined with interviews that I conducted within South Asian migrant communities and with Indian IT professionals and their wives in Norway suggest a similar dynamic. More recently, my conversations with interviewees in The Netherlands also reinforce this social and gendered phenomenon of re-domestication of professional women.

On the one hand, individual woman's autonomy is strongly asserted through the carving out of women's spaces, and on the other, the physical domestic space of home is recovered as a cultural site for reinforcement of communal identity. Yet the digital streets are not that far away from digital domestic spaces. Disruptions in physical domestic space—which performatively and visually serves as a physical space of cultural patriarchy—have occurred and continue to occur as my interviewees attest. Movements and shifts occur relationally in domestic space even as in the larger Indian diasporic society transnationally the figure of the woman within South Asian diasporic spaces continues to perpetuate what Anannya Bhattacharjee characterized as the "habit of ex-nomination."[57] Yet Elaine Salo has noted that

> in the contemporary moment we have to take into account the complex, multiple terrains of women's gendered struggles in the context of the local neoliberal economic climate, dominant new forms of nationalist masculinity, and globalization and determine how these struggles are expressed in relation to women's hitherto muted identities and differences.[58]

The joint forces of neoliberalization and globalization impact specific national contexts differently and also impact how women reach outward into South Asian digital diasporas with digital tools and through specific local geographical and sociopolitical contexts. Digital ghars in South Asian digital diasporic spaces thus are mostly centered around cisgendered, middle- to upper-class, heteronormative discourses. Othered identities mostly become visible as activist formations.

The writing in this chapter and much of this book does not include an examination of distinct visible/discursive self-expressions by a portion of women who are digitally connected and who work in domestic spaces for wages; thus there is definitely an absence of a certain classed location in the spaces of which I write. The staging of such working-class-based subaltern identities from places like India is evident through "digital subalternity" produced through philanthropy sites, microfinance sites, and through employment-oriented platforms such as "bookmybai.com" and "urbanclap.com."[59] In addition, a portion of women from rural India as well as from urban slums such as those researched by Payal Arora and Laura Scheiber are also not represented.[60] It is possible that these women also engage in digital domesticity in different vernacular languages and through the very same social media tools that their employers use.

CONCLUSION

In order to think through expectations, manifestations, and materializations of what appear to be activist and autonomous subjects and their aspirations for global/local coalitions, we need to raise questions about whether these emerging digital publics are indeed in binary opposition to digital domesticity. If so or even if not, I ask, then what makes these two forms of digital practice appear in binary opposition as ghar and bahir? Is there a difference in content, politics, and form of engagement? Does it emerge from what the tools/platform/code enable or it is a feature of the affective formations around certain technomediations and offline events? And yet again, is there really a binary at all? True, the binary is derived from discursive analysis of online spaces and from interviews. The binary I posit, therefore, has evidence supporting my broad-sweep observation, which, when examined in more specific contextual engagements is troubled (as we see in the dialogue interludes that reveal pauses and stutters as well as outright contestations of the binary).

For instance, interviewee comments do indeed suggest there is a perceived binary between comparatively "safe" social spaces online and more exposed spaces online. Some of this comes out in discussions around Facebook versus WhatsApp, Twitter versus Instagram, Tumblr versus Twitter, Tinder versus Shaadi.com, and so on. However, depending on who is being interviewed, the perception of a feeling of safety or of communal inclusion/exclusion shifts. Thus, on average, women interviewed who primarily connect to online community formations for the sake of getting information around family caregiving, food, and culture considered online social spaces (on blogs, in WhatsAppified communities and social media platforms such as Facebook mostly) safe to engage in (until they encountered harsh disagreements or attitudes they felt as oppressive to them personally). Women who were heavily engaged in activist, social change, and human rights work noted that Twitter allowed them an outlet and opportunity to reach for communities of global activists. Yet we know from existing research that trolling is heavily prevalent in the Twittersphere—the deactivating of accounts by Twitter, the harassment and hate messages that Dalit activists receive who are calling out Brahmin patriarchy, for instance.[61] While some clearly noted that Twitter, for instance, by no means felt "safe," they still felt that it was a platform that allowed them to find people fighting for the same cause by building bonds of security and support—"in knowing that such people exist."[62] Such mixed feelings toward being on Twitter—where the activist user felt unsafe, but still valued being able to reach out and connect with other activists engaged in similar struggles—were evidenced in my Skype conversations with both Christina Dhanaraj and Divya Kandukuri (see also chapters 4 and 8), and also in the Twitter direct messages and email communication with Varsha Ayyar and an anonymous Dalit-identified Twitter user. It is clear that "Twitter" or "Facebook" as platforms and as corporate entities are not in themselves supportive of this digital activism, but that they try to capitalize on such use to their advantage. An event worth noting—that is going viral in the Dalit and Indian Twittersphere as of November 2018—is the image of Twitter CEO Jack Dorsey[63], amid a group picture with several Dalit feminists, holding a "Smash Brahmanical Patriarchy" poster.[64] Apparently a representative of Twitter India, Vijaya Gadde, sent out an apology that the poster is *"not reflective of our views."*[65] Gadde tweeted:

> I'm very sorry for this. It's not relective [*sic*] of our views. We took a private photo with a gift just given to us—we should have been more thoughtful. Twitter strives to be an impartial platform for all. We failed to do that here & we must do better to serve our customers in India.[66]

In her message it is again clear who is considered "Indian" by even transnational corporations. This image continues streaming to the hashtag of #SmashBrahminicalPatriarchy on Twitter, Facebook, and Instagram and is continuing to collect hate responses.[67]

In continuing research, therefore, it might also be worth examining what features of the tool/platform/code might be sustaining or disrupting the faux binaries posited. Who are they even relevant to? How do affects get generated and to what effect are they mobilized? Digital tools for digital domesticity and for digital activism/advocacy do not differ per se. Rather, the nuances and differences are more in the content and the forms of sociality that are performed in these public spaces. The same actors may participate in the creation of both, so that these spaces are not separate or mutually exclusive; instead they weave in and out of each other.

NOTES

1. Radhika Gajjala, et al. (2017). Prosumption. In Van Zoonen, L. (Ed.), International Encyclopedia of Media Effects. Hoboken, NJ: Wiley-Blackwell.
2. Maitrayee Chaudhuri, *Refashioning India: Gender, Media and a Transformed Public Discourse* (Hyderabad, India: Orient Blackswan, 2017), 22.
3. Radhika Gajjala, "The Sawnet Refusal: An Uninterrupted Cyberethnography" (PhD diss, University of Pittsburgh, 1998), 78–79, ProQuest (304446170).
4. Rahul K. Gairola, "Digital Closets: Post-millenial Representations of Queerness in *Kapoor & Sons* and *Aligarh*," in *Queering Digital Activism: Activisms, Identities,*

Subjectivies, ed. Rohit K. Dasgupta and Debanuj DasGupta (Edinburgh: Edinburgh University Press, 2018).

5. Ibid., 59.

6. Preeti Mudliar, "Public WiFi Is for Men and Mobile Internet Is for Women: Interrogating Politics of Space and Gender around WiFi Hotspots," *Proceedings of the ACM on Human-Computer Interaction* 2 (November 2018): 4, doi: 10.1145/3274395.

7. Amongst the critiques of this binary are critiques of its situatedness in caste hierarchy – see Hugh Gorringe and Uma Chakravarti for more on this.

8. Partha Chatterjee, "The Nationalist Resolution of the Women's Question," in *Empire and Nation: Selected Essays* (New York: Columbia University Press, 2010), 116–35.

9. See also Sudipta Kaviraj, Hugh Gorringe and Ursula Sharma for discussions of the home and the world in relation to caste.

10. Rabindranath Tagore, *The Home and the World*, ed. William Radice, trans. Surendranath Tagore (London: Penguin Books, 1985).

11. This is my reading of a translation of Tagore's original, from watching the derivative film *Ghare Baire* (Ray, 1984), and from reading Anita Desai's introduction to the English translation of Tagore's original work, which was in Bengali. The novel itself is far more complex and layered than my simple outline would suggest.

12. Kumkum Sangari and Sudesh Vaid, "Recasting Women: An Introduction," in *Recasting Women: Essays in Colonial History*, ed. Kumkum Sangari and Sudesh Vaid (Brunswick, NJ: Rutgers, 1990), 9.

13. Raka Ray and Seemin Qayum, *Cultures of Servitude: Modernity, Domesticity, and Class in India* (Stanford, CA: Stanford University Press, 2009).

14. Nandini Deo, *Mobilizing Religion and Gender in India: The Role of Activism* (New York: Routledge, 2015), 25.

15. While I interviewed Jasmeen several times in relation to this research project, I was unable to pull together a performative dialogue interlude with her because of time constraints.

16. Gina Masullo Chen, "Don't Call Me That: A Techno-Feminist Critique of the Term *Mommy Blogger*," *Mass Communication and Society* 16, no. 4 (2013): 510–32, https://doi.org/10.1080/15205436.2012.737888.

17. These systems refer to synchronous or real-time interaction that takes place on multiuser domains: MUD is an acronym for multi-user dungeon or domain; MOO is an acronym for MUD object-oriented servers.

18. For example, see Kumkum Sangari and Sudesh Vaid, *Recasting Women: Essays in Colonial History* (New Brunswick, NJ: Rutgers University Press, 1990).

19. Joan B. Landes, ed., introduction to *Feminism, the Public and the Private* (Oxford: Oxford University Press, 1998), 1.

20. Ibid.

21. Hannah Arendt, *The Human Condition*, second edition (Chicago: University of Chicago Press, 1998), 38.

22. Ray and Qayum, *Cultures of Servitude*.

23. Bipasha Ahmed, Paula Reavey, and Anamika Majumdar, "Cultural Transformations and Gender Violence: South Asian Women's Experiences of Sexual Violence and Familial Dynamics," in *Gender and Interpersonal Violence: Language, Action and Representation*, ed. Karen Throsby and Flora Alexander (London: Palgrave Macmillan, 2008), 45. Emphasis in original.

24. Though the list is no longer public, see Elizabeth Cassin and Ritu Prasad, "Student's 'Sexual Predator' List Names Professors," BBC News online, November 6, 2017, http://www.bbc.com/news/blogs-trending-41862615, for more information.

25. Srila Roy, "#MeToo is a Crucial Moment to Revisit the History of Indian Feminism," *Economic and Political Weekly* 53, no. 42 (Oct 20, 2018), https://www.epw.in/

engage/article/metoo-crucial-moment-revisit-history-indian-feminism?fbclid=
IwAR3RHHfal_dRESLmsDSUaYaA4dNl9V8zCs2dT3IhBr5M65ZGZ0g59RR_VMU.
  26. Donald Norman, "Affordances, Conventions, and Design," *Interactions* 6, no. 3
(May/June 1999): 39, doi: 10.1145/301153.301168.
  27. Chaudhuri, *Refashioning India*.
  28. Radhika Gajjala and Tarishi Verma, "Whatsappified Diasporas and Transnational
Circuits of Affect and Relationality," in *Appified: Culture in the Age of Apps*, ed.
Jeremy Wade Morris and Sarah Murray (Ann Arbor: University of Michigan Press,
2018), 205–18.
  29. Madhavi Mallapragada, *Virtual Homelands: Indian Immigrants and Online Cultures in the United States* (Champaign: University of Illinois Press, 2014), 60.
  30. Chaudhuri, *Refashioning India*, 21–22.
  31. Harriet Riches, "*Pix* and *Clicks*: Photography and the New 'Digital' Domesticity," *Oxford Art Journal* 40, no. 1 (2017): 196, https://doi.org/10.1093/oxartj/kcx010.
  32. Emily Matchar, *Homeward Bound: Why Women Are Embracing the New Domesticity* (New York: Simon & Schuster, 2013).
  33. Ibid., 4.
  34. Emily Matchar, "Sorry, Etsy. That Handmade Scarf Won't Save the World," *New
York Times*, Sunday Review, May 1, 2015, https://www.nytimes.com/2015/05/03/
opinion/sunday/that-handmade-scarf-wont-save-the-world.html.
  35. Linda Belkin, "The Opt-Out Revolution," *New York Times Magazine*, August 7,
2013, http://www.nytimes.com/2013/08/11/magazine/the-opt-out-revolution.html?rref=
collection%2Fbyline%2Flisa-belkin&action=click&contentCollection=undefined&
region=stream&module=stream_unit&version=latest&contentPlacement=2&pgtype=
collection; Linda Hirshman, "Unleashing the Wrath of Stay-at-Home Moms," *Washington Post*, June 18, 2006, http://www.washingtonpost.com/wp-dyn/content/article/2006/
06/16/AR2006061601766.html.
  36. Radha Sarma Hegde, *Mediating Migration*, Global Media and Communication
(Cambridge: Polity), 2016.
  37. Amy Bhatt, *High-Tech Housewives: Indian IT Workers, Gendered Labor and
Transmigration* (Seattle: University of Washington Press, 2018).
  38. Ibid., 17
  39. Anannya Bhattacharjee, "The Habit of Ex-Nomination: Nation, Woman and the
Indian Immigrant Bourgeoisie." *Public Culture* 5, no. 1 (1992): 32. doi: 10.1215/
08992363-5-1-19. Here I repurpose Bhattacharjee's original quote.
  40. Hegde, *Mediating Migration*, 19.
  41. Bipasha Ahmed, Paula Reavey, and Anamika Majumdar, "Cultural Transformations and Gender Violence: South Asian Women's Experiences of Sexual Violence and
Familial Dynamics," in *Gender and Interpersonal Violence: Language, Action and
Representation*, ed. Karen Throsby and Flora Alexander (London: Palgrave Macmillan,
2008), 44–65.
  42. Hegde, *Mediating Migration*, 82.
  43. Ibid., 73.
  44. Sahana Udupa, "*Gaali* Cultures: The Politics of Abusive Exchange on Social
Media," *New Media & Society* 8, no. 2 (2017): 190, https://doi.org/10.1177/
1461444817698776.
  45. Vicks India, "Vicks—Generations of Care #TouchOfCare," YouTube video,
3:37, March 29, 2017, https://www.youtube.com/watch?v=7zeeVEKaDLM&t=64s.
  46. Rohan Abraham, "All You Need to Know about the Transgender Persons Bill,
2016," *The Hindu*, last modified November 30, 2017, http://www.thehindu.com/news/
national/all-you-need-to-know-about-the-transgender-persons-bill-2016/
article21226710.ece; Arvind Narrain, "How the Centre's Bill to Protect the Rights of
Transgender People Will Actually Hurt Them," *Scroll.in*, December 1, 2017, https://

scroll.in/article/859620/how-the-centres-bill-to-protect-the-rights-of-transgender-people-will-actually-hurt-them.

47. Sharanya Gopinathan, "Why People Are Freaking Out about the New Trans Bill," *The Ladies Finger!* (blog), December 7, 2017, http://theladiesfinger.com/trans-bill-2016/.

48. This point is also engaged with in research by Hugh Gorringe, Ursula Sharma, Uma Chakrovarti and others who note how the ghar/bahir binary noted by nationalists and postnationalists ignores caste and class dimensions of society.

49. Divya Kandukuri, in discussion with the author, 2018.

50. Shailaja Paik, *Dalit Women's Education in Modern India: Double Discrimination* (New York: Routledge, 2014), 192.

51. Sharmila Rege, "Dalit Women Talk Differently: A Critique of 'Difference' and Towards a Dalit Feminist Standpoint Position," in *Feminism in India*, ed. Maitrayee Chaudhuri (London: Zed Books, 2004).

52. Ibid., 212.

53. While Kancha Iliah has been a contributor to the collected essays, volumes from the subaltern studies collective, and even while several of the collective founding members do note the significance of caste, what is missing is "a systematic engagement with questions of caste inequality, even though caste continues to be the primary form through which hierarchical discrimination is practiced even today." Ramnarayan S. Rawat and K. Satyanarayana, eds., *Dalit Studies* (Durham, NC: Duke University Press, 2016), 13–14.

54. See dialogue interlude with Divya in chapter 4, my dialogue with Christina Thomas Dhanaraj in chapter 8, and various other writings by Christina Thomas Dhanaraj for more information.

55. Rege, "Dalit Women Talk Differently," 211.

56. Hegde, *Mediating Migration*, 71.

57. Bhattacharjee, "The Habit of Ex-Nomination."

58. Elaine Salo, "South African Feminisms—Coming of Age?" in *Women's Movements in the Global Era: The Power of Local Feminisms*, ed. Amrita Basu (Boulder, CO: Westview Press, 2010), 32.

59. For more, see Radhika Gajjala, ed., *Cyberculture and the Subaltern: Weavings of the Virtual and Real* (Lanham, MD: Lexington Books, 2012); and, Radhika Gajjala, *Online Philanthropy in the North and South: Connecting, Microfinancing, and Gaming for Change* (Lanham, MD: Lexington Books, 2017).

60. Payal Arora and Laura Scheiber, "Slumdog Romance: Facebook Love and Digital Privacy at the Margins," *Media, Culture & Society* 39, no. 3 (2017): 408–22, doi: 10.1177/0163443717691225.

61. Udupa, "*Gaali* Cultures."

62. Divya Kandukuri, WhatsApp exchange with author, following the writing of our dialogue interlude, 2018.

63. Seehttps://www.theguardian.com/technology/2018/nov/20/twitter-ceo-jack-dorsey-criticised-for-upsetting-hindu-nationals-india-visit

64. Divya Kandukuri, "Outrage Over Jack Dorsey Holding Smash Brahmanical Patriarchy Poster Shows Casteist Souls Can't Face Reality," *News 18*, last updated November 20, 2018, https://www.news18.com/news/opinion/outrage-over-jack-dorsey-holding-smash-brahmanical-patriarchy-poster-shows-casteist-souls-cant-face-reality-1945061.html?fbclid=IwAR3feMH4X_pX_ytOUtE5hbjy_H-d68WTrn2sTLwBACnBCKbiwLe-kmtvi10.

65. ThePrint Team, "Twitter's Apology a Cop Out or Was CEO Jack Dorsey Wrong to Hold Brahmin-Patriarchy Poster?" *ThePrint*, November 20, 2018, https://theprint.in/talk-point/twitters-apology-a-cop-out-or-was-ceo-jack-dorsey-wrong-to-hold-brahmin-patriarchy-poster/152114/.

66. Vijaya Gadde, Twitter post, November 19, 2018, 2:28 p.m., https://twitter.com/vijaya?lang=en.

67. Thenmozhi Soundararajan, "Twitter's Caste Problem," *New York Times*, December 3, 2018, https://www.nytimes.com/2018/12/03/opinion/twitter-india-caste-trolls.html.

Chapter Two

Dialogue Interlude

Ghar and Bahir

Radhika Gajjala in conversation with
Sriya Chattopadhyay, Sarada Nori,
Shobha S.V., and Puthiya Purayil Sneha

This dialogue draws on interviews that provide some of the evidence for what is theorized in later chapters as well.[1] Salient themes that surfaced in the interludes center on literacy, access, capital, and negotiation of public space as gendered bodies. Several of these concerns are, as Divya Kandukuri, a Dalit feminist activist notes, dominant-caste/class problems. This chapter is based on evidence from upwardly mobile dominant-caste women.

The framework of ghar/bahir, which has been rightly critiqued as based in dominant-caste Indian women's experience by scholars such as Sharmila Rege, is retooled here similarly to how Anannya Bhattacharjee has adopted this framework in nuancing "private" and "public" to demonstrate how the negotiation of ghar/bahir and its impact on gendered bodies functions through an immigrant community's attempts to recover its "power of ex-nomination" whereby its aspiration to remain un-named relies on the reinstating of woman as the cultural center of the home.[2] In later chapters of this book, as the Savarna centeredness of both Indian women and Indian diasporic feminisms is made evident through interactions, it is possible to see how the Indian immigrant community's aspirations toward a recovery of its bourgeois unnamed status also relies on the exclusion and naming of Dalit and Muslim Indians, for instance, as Other. In fact, the Dalit feminists I later interviewed for this book would suggest that even postcolonial and transnational feminists articulated in the context of Indian diasporas are blind in the way they adopt some basic assumptions through liberal feminist frameworks. Even as each of the individuals cowriting here is interpellated by complex *intersections*, the dialogue interlude stays—performatively—in a caste- and class-exclusionary space. These women have a different history also from second- and third-generation diasporic Indians in the United States, let alone in other parts of the world.

Coauthors in this chapter have conducted interviews with women working for pay through domestic space in a variety of ways—common to all, however, is the use of digital tools in their work. Most of the women we have interviewed either aspire to or are actually doing entrepreneurial work through the home space with the aid of various tools for connectivity. The collective pool of unstructured interviews that we draw on comprises more than one hundred South Asian women in diverse locations. Radhika conducted over three-fourths of the interviews over a period spanning 2014 to 2017 with a diverse pool of women in digital spaces, not restricted to South Asians. This chapter only draws from a section of those interviews.

Sorting through these interviews over this fairly long timeline in terms of technology use and adoption was a challenge. The interviews were uneven in terms of early adopters, frequent users, and so on, but what was consistently evident was the reliance on digital tools in everyday life for a variety of everyday activities and across a range of socioeconomic contexts. Rather than mobilize the interviews as inert data that implicitly positions researchers as outside viewers looking in on their lives, we locate ourselves within the "data." We do this by acknowledging the subjective and relational processes of engaging each other and our various interviewees as part of the knowledge-building process. We highlight the social, technical, and affective contexts of our database of interviews by narrating through and in relation to ourselves. That which is superfluous and excessive—while it activates slippery openings for escape routes from pinned subject positions—cannot be contained in writing about findings in static formality. Readers must work with us here.

Two themes foreground this conversation. One is the idea and/or the actuality of moving to the United States; the other is a personal and professional engagement with the digital. Each of the coauthors thus uses her personal experience and maps how she inhabits a particular social and professional trajectory. The main commonality we share is that each of us identifies the nation-state of India as our point of origin and inhabits digital space through a spectrum of mobile and internet-based tools. Sadly, there is no diversity in terms of class or religious location among the authors in dialogue in this chapter.

Our dialogue surfaces themes that include women's work in domestic and professional spaces, the dilemmas of middle-class women in their negotiation of home and profession, as well as aspirations from India toward the United States and aspirations and struggles within the United States. Some of the interviews that we refer to are with women in the United States who have work permits for legal US employment but find it hard to find full-time work. These women, however, use their inability to get employment as an opportunity to be flexible in negotiating home and work by seeking out work from home (telecommuting) opportunities. The flexibility to work either from their office or home seems appealing to them for a variety of reasons. As Sarada noted in our conversations, this flexibility in IT work is quite rare in India. SN's observation was found to be a "plausible account" by RG based on conversations she had with women looking for telecommuting opportunities in India. Caste or religion do not emerge as categories in this performative dialogue; however, in the introduction to this book Radhika has speculated on this issue.

Three coauthors, Sriya, Sarada, and Radhika, start with talking about their move from India to the United States and the juggling of home and profession. Shoba and Sneha, on the other hand, reside in India as professionals. While one (Shoba) negotiates society as a single woman, the other (Sneha) juggles her roles as mother, wife, and career woman. Sneha and Radhika jointly interviewed several women (and some men) in India who worked from home and in some sort of computer-related work.

One of us (Radhika) is of an older generation of women who moved to the United States as the wife of an aspiring academic and who herself eventually became an academic. She belongs to a generation and category of dominant-caste married women for whom leaving Indian society opened up opportunities for professional growth. Based on the selection of interviews conducted, her experience is not unique. The struggle between individual and community, career, and home that Indian women face when they leave the home nation allowed Radhika's generation a degree of outside-ness and choices that are not available when a woman is immersed fully in the context of either the home or host nation. Thus, the betweenness became an opportunity, even as the loss of community and associated caste/class privilege within mainstream society created other kinds of issues of struggle and social isolation (which in most cases is remedied through strong affiliation with the immigrant Indian community and its biases). In the case of Sriya and Sarada, however, each of them faced her encounters with the United States differently. While they were going through undergraduate education, it was assumed that they would have professional lives. In fact, their income became a valued addition for them in the marriage market, as many young men today prefer to marry women with professional training who have their own income. A two-income family was the norm for SC and SN's generation (as also noted by several interviewees of their generation and younger).

MOVING TO THE UNITED STATES

In this section the conversation revolves around all of our personal life trajectories in relation to "moving to the United States." While Sarada, Sriya, and Radhika did move, the other two live in India.

SN: I move to the USA as a spouse—a wife and mother—I experienced loss of identity as an information technology (IT) professional because of this move to the USA.

Indian women who work in IT play many roles in the US. A main aspect of their lives involves the juggling of multiple roles. For instance, they supervise their children's extracurricular classes and homework, but they also take early-morning conference calls, perform late-night production checks, do the laundry, and so on.

In my circle of friends there are women who do a variety of technical recruitment jobs that could be done from home because they lack official permits to work in the US. This work does not need a permit and helps employers recruit a multitude of IT workers who are waiting to get placements in the US. Apart from this, I have interacted with small business owners selling jewelry, food, and beauty parlor services, which were run out of homes using closed Facebook groups. The women who actually had permits to work had a slightly different lifestyle compared to the IT workers in India. They had flexibility to work from home and could step out of the office before 5 p.m., which is unthinkable in India. The IT culture in India is very different. The longer we stay at the office, the more "productive" we are assumed to be. The offshore on-site IT work used to force people to spend late hours at night. Women in the US do have to take night calls but have options to physically not be at the office. In one way, I feel this is due to childcare facilities closing at 5 p.m., unlike in India where grandparents and domestic helpers manage the show.

Currently, as an entrepreneur running a dance school, I am engaged in different journey as compared to the IT jobs that have a structured pay scale. Small business (running a school) must be made legitimate to receive consistent recognition in a foreign country. For instance, registering the dance school, venturing out into multicultural spaces like libraries, art councils, etcetera, have to be visible in American society. The most challenging aspect however is to retain students, as they need to be taught how to connect with an ancient Indian art form and appreciate the underlying magic it can create.

SC: I was a journalist in India. I finished college and immediately entered the profession. I moved to the US as a spouse of a graduate student, with child, but I was somewhat naive in assuming I would get a job sooner than later. I did get three job offers within the first year of coming here—but legal issues around work visa procurement created problems. As a spouse of an international student in the US, a legal alien, I had no right to work on my F2 visa status.

Negotiating domestic work also became an issue—I did not identify as a homemaker, yet there I was, bound to the home space. I did not get a driving license and hence was dependent on my husband for transportation to places that were not within walking distance. Domestic chores, when they are the only thing one is *allowed* to do (in my case, due to visa issues), become tedious and set certain boundaries to one's life.

RG: I did not come to the US expecting to be a professional. I did, however, expect more social freedom to be an intellectual outside the home than I had felt I had while in India after my marriage when I had to present a socially acceptable image as the daughter-in-law of a high-level bureaucrat in North Indian, upper-class, and English-educated society. I did come expecting to speak my mind more often, as I had done before I was married. As it turned out, both my husband and I were not well equipped to do any sort of women's labor at home, apart from childcare. This turned out to be an advantage in a sense, because we had to learn together. There are still many household things we are not comfortable doing, but we manage fine. I entered academia quite by accident, even informally, one might say. In fall 1989, I started to attend classes because some professors at the university were kind enough to let me "sit in."

Socially and age-wise, I am two generations ahead of the other four coauthors. I am a product of a 1970s Indian feminist climate, where my feminism moved into the ghar space and remained hidden in creative writing, since I was married and had a child in my early twenties. I engaged the public mostly through my occasional publications in regional and national newspapers and in women's magazines.

SN: I acquired a "master's in computers" degree in 2002. The call-center boom was at its peak. Youngsters had suddenly found themselves in fancy offices working night shifts with amazing salaries. I started working in this sector even after marriage. A year later my husband was asked to travel to America. We waited for work opportunities for me to become available in the same geographical location before moving. I worked in the US for two years. I took a break when I had my son. This resulted in the loss of a work permit. Stuck at home, I focused on turning my passion for dance into an alternative career. This got me teaching music and dance. I had prior experience in the art world, as my mother is a puppeteer who runs her own nonprofit organization.

RG : *[Thinking to herself, wonders if . . . as she considers making connections with scholarly writing and theorizes]*

Machinic subjectivities unhinged from that tight system—upon migration with spouse
Women's tech labor becomes invisibilized again.

Machinic processes mobilized in home time management

Quotes: Thus as Sangeeta Kamat, Ali Mir, and Biju Mathew point out, in the case of India, "the growth of the IT labour sector was based on changes in the immigration policies of the US. . . . These policy changes reflect how nation-states alter their national policies to meet the demands of the global economy. . . . [and] are indicative of the unique political context and culture of each country. In the case of India, the education policy changes relate to caste politics while immigration policy of the USA shares the legacy of US race politics."[3]

EDUCATION

SC: Though I am a '99 graduate (BA), I am actually the only female in my family to start working at a job outside the home immediately after college. My mother never worked in the professional world, nor did my elder sister, though she had enough and more options to do so. My father always said, "She is like my son." I took great umbrage to that. I did not aspire to be "like a son"; I wanted to be referred to as a hard-working, career-minded person—why the gender distinction in the first place? In many ways, I felt dissociated from female family members. Their world, to my mind, is narrow and closed. They have never experienced the challenges of the office, coworker issues, the pride of a promotion, salary increments, an extra bonus, issues of managing a big team—the many joys and vagaries of a workplace. This is what had nurtured me and kept me going in India. Sitting at home, planning dinner menus, checking my son's homework—these are all very good for some women maybe, but not for me. In India, I have not needed to negotiate much to ensure continuity of my professional life, barring the visa hurdles mentioned earlier, but balancing schoolwork with the demands of family life in the US, where daily domestic help is rare and super-expensive, is a new kind of challenge.

SSV: I am a single child of my parents; I belong to a Tamil Brahmin family. My mother was a professional. She was a teacher. According to her father, teaching was a profession that helped a woman run a family despite going to work every day. However, she has a very interesting story as far as her studies are concerned. Her family was struggling economically when she was around seventeen years old. So much so that her further studies could have been stopped. But my mom really wanted to be a graduate. So she started teaching during the day (thanks to a teachers training diploma she had!) and went to college in the evening. She completed her BA and her B-Ed this way. But she tells me how my grandmother extracted a promise from her to be a "good" girl and not go astray before she granted her the permission to study in an evening college. Anyway, I digress here a bit.

Since both my parents were working professionals, I was forced to be an independent child. As a child, I was expected to do well in academics. Even though my mom was a professional, she always looked at a career as a "necessity." If my father was super rich, she would have happily stayed at home. Or that's what she used to say. For her, her primary role was that of a mother and my caregiver. The career was secondary. That's not the same with me. I have been working for over a decade as a journalist, researcher, and as a digital media professional in a women's rights organization. I cannot imagine myself "unemployed" ever.

SOCIAL ADJUSTMENTS

PPS: As with some of the others in conversation here, the choice to begin working immediately after college was never a difficult one for me, as for other women of my generation in my family. All of them, including my younger sister, are well educated with successful careers, which has also shaped so many of their choices in life—whether in moving away from home or finding a life partner. Yet it is with each passing year that I realize how much it means to be able to work without having to deal with a lot of the struggles that were persistent even with a generation just before mine. My mother is a homemaker, so I have grown up being accustomed to her presence in the house; I always wondered about the overwhelming dependence that my family has on her for everything, and the burden that such a responsibility often entails. This is not to say that household work is not shared; we have never had any domestic help, so it was always expected that everybody at home would do their own chores. I am used to seeing my father do things around the house, but daily, mundane responsibilities still fall on my mother simply because she is always around. Suggestions that we hire help, like when we had my bedridden grandmother at home or when both my parents were unwell for an extended period of time, have always been brushed aside hastily, almost like it is an affront to her capabilities as a homemaker—a tendency I have noticed in most women in my family. There is a certain pride in being able to do domestic work, doing all of it and doing it well, which has led to some exacting standards and expectations for the younger women in the family, but not so much the men.

As with most traditional families, a big concern at home until a few years ago was that I will not be able to "adjust" to another household after marriage, something I always vehemently questioned and dismissed as unimportant. Conflicts come up time and again, especially in the context of what is often seen as my "unrealistic expectations" of sharing domestic responsibilities with a partner. In conversations that I have with the women in my family about marriage, work, and child-care, I understand where some of those concerns are coming from.

SC: Depression is a serious consequence of alienation, social isolation, or other perceived/actual distances associated with migration. This is also true in university towns, such as the one where I now live. I know a couple who live a few houses down the lane from my current apartment. The woman comes from a South Asian country where not too many women are encouraged to work even today, but she stepped out of her home and worked in a company after completing her graduation program. But since coming to the US with her husband, she has been unable to find work and she doesn't want to go back to school like me. She is suffering from depression, but due to the seemingly prohibitive cost of student health care costs (even after paying the monthly premium), she does not seek a cure for her depression. She cannot go back home because that will seem like a betrayal of her marriage vows—more to his and her family than in her own mind. This is like a trap, and looking at a possible four-to-five-year stay under such conditions seems quite tough. Internet use seems to help her connect with friends and family.

SN: Although in my first few years at home I did notice myself and some others in a state somewhat similar to what SC mentioned, I have seen a drastic change over the last five years (out of the eight years I have been here). Facebook has been very useful in helping me look around and contemplate why this happened. With more and more Indians migrating here, several immigrant women have started Facebook closed groups to sell services like baking, small party cooking, rotis, daily tiffins/meals, tailoring, beauty parlor services (out of two-bedroom apartments), and childcare services. Another set of women has started selling jewelry (handmade terracotta, silk thread), kurtas (Indian clothing), mangoes (yes, mangoes shipped from India), and so on. Such services are a boon to busy doctors and IT professionals stuck working extra hours with outsourcing companies (night calls with offshore teams). Those meals and rotis help reduce the time spent on mundane activities for these professional mothers. Also, who would provide a home-cooked meal for $8 or a one-hour facial for $20 in a country like the US? The low cost for such service/labor is unthinkable in the US.

Having come from a family where livelihood comes only from an office job or teaching an art form, I started to wonder why these women were engaged in these domestic service activities. It struck me that we grow up interacting with the same class of people as we go to colleges and school (I grew up in a metropolitan city). But we must remember the immigrant workers who come here are not just from metropolitan cities. They work hard and get to the US. The wives may not have a college degree, but they do look for business opportunities. Every penny matters, as they have people to send money home to family. In my interviews I have come across women who have parents living in small towns and villages who look forward to the money sent to them. Also, some of these services would have not been offered by these women (of dominant caste and class) back in India. For instance, we can't be a "maid" or a "tailor" or a "cook." But they can offer those services here in the United States and the husbands will not object. Is this liberation for women who migrate?

DOMESTIC WORK

RG: Reading for my research on women's work historically, I am mapping them by picking up whatever existing writings and research I can find about women who used to spin yarn. I know that women always did productive labor even while being less paid for it under the social assumption that their natural role was to perform reproductive labor, which was always unpaid/unremunerated. While we still negotiate some of these basic issues of social expectations and lesser pay in comparison to men doing the exact same job, we live now in a moment in history when these conditions are not for the most part "taken as given" as they used to, for instance in the times of women doing productive work through domestic space as spinners in New England mill towns back in the 1700s. [4] *What is interesting, of course, is how middle-class centered this tug of war is.*

Reading historically, I drift away from thinking of this present situated discussion, for as I read more about women's work historically I realize how clearly class—being in professional classes—shapes our perception of domesticity. A domestic space we take for granted, as we write against it, is how this domesticity traps or holds us in place. The domestic is also layered in hierarchies of work—it is not a homogenous "women's" space. The domestic was where the white slave owner's wife managed female slave workers in the home space and the domestic is where upper-caste housewives had lower-caste servants doing menial tasks. The domestic has always been in motion—never stable: it serves us as women of a certain class, as much as the patriarchal systems we talk back against, this domestic as a place for family and home. When women of upper classes and castes migrate, they migrate to upward mobility—when women migrate as domestic workers, they are socially immobile. As Tanu Priya Uteng notes: "The positive mobility of skilled

*women is taking place at the cost of the immobility of the gendered
service class in the form of domestic workers, who are forced to adopt
mobile livelihoods and shift to urban areas due to changes made in
their original habitat by interventions such as those made by mining
industries."*[5]
*This "migration" is happening internationally—as work such as Eileen
Boris and Jennifer Klein's* Caring for America *reveals—with domestic
workers and nannies being imported from the Global South to Global
North countries.*[6] *Interviewing care workers in India, for instance, I
found that some interviewees—nurses and other at-home care workers—would try to find out if I would be able to find them employment
with a family of non-resident Indians in the US. Even websites such as
BookMyBai.com—which translates to "book my servant"—that are set
up locally for Indians, have an option for "Overseas Maid."*

SC: Having lived in India for the first fourteen years of my professional life, I have had domestic help who would take care of all the
household chores for us. And since moving to the US, my husband and
I do share most of the load. But here, I noted something interesting
when talking to a cousin who also came to the United States earlier this
year, and is the earning member of the family. Her husband has yet to
find a job, so he does the household work for the time being. But her
response to this was to say: "Poor fellow, he is washing dishes and
doing the laundry every day. It is so tough for a man." For any professional to just sit at home if they have to quit their job for any reason is
difficult. What has "for a man" got to do with it!

PPS: While I spoke earlier about the satisfaction and pride that
many women have in doing housework, and unreasonable demands this
often makes on them or others, it makes me also think more about the
respect and support for different kinds of work. I studied English Literature and have been working in the nonprofit sector doing research in
humanities, education, and technology; there are few other people in
this or a related field in my family, so it becomes a little difficult at
times to explain what exactly I do. I understand my privilege in being
able to explore and make some of these choices and in resisting others.
Here I find some resonance with my aunt, who is today an eminent
artist but had her own share of struggles in the early years, because
apart from it being a difficult field, I don't think everyone understood
her decisions then, or that in some cases, withdrawal or absence can
also be a form of support. Also I often wonder if some professions
allow for a greater degree of self-reflexivity and choices in life that are
away from the beaten track so to speak—but I believe all kinds of work

and a measure of independence should offer that. I know that a lot of my understanding about life and identity comes from my work. I cannot imagine a life where I am not working.

I see some of this reflected through some of the interviews we did for this book—especially women who are trying to juggle careers with family, particularly with the needs of young children, trying to strike that all important balance between both. Even if some of them have the opportunity to work flexible hours/work from home, there is a constant renegotiation of schedules, often making instantaneous decisions, and dealing with unexpected situations—trying to balance both professional and domestic needs and aspirations. Recognition and respect for work they do as something that is meaningful to them becomes important here.

LOITERING

SN: Loitering always felt unsafe for me when I was growing up. I used to walk to college from other classes and felt that cheap bikers were waiting around the corners just to quickly drive by and touch in inappropriate ways. This was something I noticed in middle school. I always used to walk away toward the corners of the road to avoid such experiences. Once I grew up and had a vehicle of my own, I was more protected. But I always felt India was a country where people stare even if you wait outside a class for a friend.

Girls at Dhabas reminded me of an interview that was given by one of the rapists before his death sentence (the 2012 Delhi gang-rape and murder).[7] He said that the group of men who did it wanted to teach a lesson to the girl/or send a message to the society that women should not be in that place at that time of the night with that person. I was terrified to even listen to a statement like that from someone who was facing a death sentence. The defense lawyer stated women should not put themselves into these spaces. If they do, it is obvious that they will face such consequences. This says a lot about what Indian society thinks of women in public spaces, especially during the night; deeply these thoughts are rooted.

SC: There are so many personal stories I want to share upon reading the Why Loiter? blog.[8] I studied in an all-girls convent school in Kolkata, India, where the Sisters told us—even when we reached grade ten—that "there are boys out there. You have to be very careful." The gender distinction was made always clear when we were warned not to loiter around the school or our own neighborhoods in school uniform. The reason: the school refused to be held accountable for what happened to students if they loitered around. The uniform would brand us as schoolgirls, and therefore, easy targets when we loitered. It continued in family admonitions about loitering, too. Only the "loafers" loitered—meaning, the unemployed young men who sat at street corners smoking cheap cigarettes or bidis (cigarette-like, but with pot or some kind of nefarious substance inside). A young woman, unless of low moral character, should not therefore be branded in the same way. It also brought about—and still does, I suppose—the binary of "good girl" versus "bad girl."

Taking off from what SN says about loitering, I want to add that, yes, I felt the same way too. But the difference I felt when I moved to Ahmedabad was notable. Gujarat is a dry state (prohibition, so no alcohol), and it was always reiterated by the locals that because there is no alcohol freely available to be purchased and consumed (no bars or liquor shops), the men are not inebriated, and therefore, do not trouble the girls. It was almost as if it was only under the influence of alcohol that men misbehave, and it almost sounded like an excuse to me. But it was true that there were few rare instances of women being attacked/molested in that city. Girls rode their bikes to work and back; I went for night shows of movies that ended at 1 a.m., and hailed taxis and returned home alone at that hour. No untoward incident ever.

PPS: This discussion makes me reflect on so many efforts that are still being discussed to make public spaces safer and more accessible to women, and it often comes down to brass tacks—streetlights, patrolling, public transport, restrooms, helplines, childcare facilities, even surveillance of women (which is problematic). Thinking of spaces where we have the freedom to loiter, to sleep, or feed a baby in public still seems a bit far away. I also think of my own experiences of commuting and travelling, for work or leisure—and the extra effort that goes into planning these, thinking about my safety, and allaying concerns of people back at home.

A friend of mine, a woman, once remarked that women do not walk in Delhi—they are visible in cars, or the metro, in malls and restaurants, but not so much on the streets. I speak from no experience of living there, but having enjoyed visiting and exploring the city. Walking around even late in the evenings, I found that observation rather bleak. Needless to say, it seems to be indeed true as there are relatively fewer women in public spaces in the city after dark. I once took a cab from the airport at 1 a.m. in the rain; nothing untoward happened, but it still was nerve-wracking. But then again, surely it is something I would think twice before doing in Bangalore, where I live, as well; regardless of the city, we are always careful. These experiences make me realize how limiting such fear and caution can be, and encourage me to find ways to overcome it where possible. I also understand I can still make those choices, but for many women working late hours, working outdoors, or for those who cannot afford private transport, these are additional, difficult conditions of work that are to be constantly negotiated.

NEGOTIATING GHAR

When gender ideology is challenged through feminist politics, the dichotomy between the binary of public and private space comes to the fore.[9] We draw on our lived experiences and conversations/interviews with other women to understand the context of family life and how gendered roles are brokered to fit the diktats of an immigrant family. In this, too, there are links that hold the private and public parts of our lives together, but at times the roles are reversed—the man stays at home, and the woman goes out to work. Mayuri Samant traces the start of women's studies/gender studies to the 1970s when women's studies centers were established, and the United Nations declared the Decade for Women in 1975. However, "the women's movement, with its emphasis on violence against women, tried to politicize the personal."[10] To extend a feminist critique of the contradictions and challenges noted here, we turn again to our lived experiences and narrations to look at role reversals and how this affects a woman's handling of both the public and private space.

SN: In my circle of friends, I have noticed at least four friends in the role reversal. But unfortunately in two of those cases the men have given up the responsibility of earning while taking care of household chores. Sadly this is more noticeable in situations where we are immigrant workers. In some families, I notice men taking up less stressful jobs as the wife has night duties or long hours so they can be with their child.

SC: I cannot relate to my aunt (sixty-four) when she serves my uncle his meal, when she says she is unaware of their joint bank balance, or when she seeks a male relative's help during medical emergencies. To me, each of these issues are gender-neutral. If there is a medical emergency, I would need help, too, but from a person, male or female. My family seems unable to understand me. But my peers seem different. There is not a single friend of mine who doesn't work in a professional capacity. In a reversal of traditional ways, my cousin—a woman—came to the United States earlier this year on an L1 visa (internal company transfer). She is a director of an MNC [multinational corporation], and came over with her young child. Her husband came many months later, and is even now on the lookout for a job. Her salary is the only one for the household, and her husband is homebound, as he is yet to learn driving. It is a complete role reversal for many married couples of, say, twenty to thirty years ago when the wife usually followed the husband who came on an H1B or L1 visa. And my cousin is not the only one, I am sure.

PPS: One of the interviews we did for this book involved a role reversal of sorts, as the man was working from home; he spoke about how it has been a learning experience, as it also meant he had to take care of most domestic responsibilities. They had managed to figure out a comfortable division of labor, but we also discussed how this in some ways still replicates an existing structure. I see this also with married friends who constantly have to work out how to share household chores, sometime due to external factors; my friend's refusal to wake up early in the morning and cook simply because she does not like to do it is still met with alarming disapproval by her in-laws, although that has never been a problem for the couple. Even where men contribute equal or more time to domestic work, it is still considered by families as "lending a hand" or taking up responsibilities that should primarily be handled by women. Among friends and cousins, I definitely see now a greater flexibility of roles in relationships—women who are working late, traveling or putting in more hours than their partners, and men who often rearrange schedules to devote more time to housework and children. They however have to deal with a lot of expectations from families, as gendering of some kinds of work as "women's work" continues to complicate these relationships.

FINAL THOUGHTS

In interviews with women who share certain similarities with our movements, as well as with those that branch off tangentially, we are faced with the awareness that what constitutes the home space and labor therein is a construct that is dependent on the social site and/or channels that are fluid and flexible according to the time, space, and location of the person(s) experiencing it. Each of the varied experiences noted by the coauthors, be it their own or that of their friends/relatives, suggests that there are many layers to the issue of ghar-bahir, how women's work is negotiated, and how labor takes on different hues when performed at home (ghar) and outside the home space (bahir).

NOTES

1. Dialogue interludes are transcribed by Radhika Gajjala with light editing by Kaitlyn Wauthier.
2. Sharmila Rege, "Dalit Women Talk Differently: A Critique of 'Difference' and Towards a Dalit Feminist Standpoint Position," in *Feminism in India*, ed. Maitrayee Chaudhuri (London: Zed Books, 2004), 211–35; Anannya Bhattacharjee, "The Habit of Ex-Nomination: Nation, Woman and the Indian Immigrant Bourgeoisie," *Public Culture* 5, no. 1 (1992): 32. doi: 10.1215/08992363-5-1-19.
3. Sangeeta Kamat, Ali Mir, and Biju Mathew, "Producing Hi-Tech: Globalization, the State and Migrant Subjects," *Globalisation, Societies and Education* 2, no. 1 (2004): 5, https://doi.org/10.1080/1476772042000177023.
4. Thomas Dublin, *Women at Work: The Transformation of Work and Community in Lowell, Massachusetts, 1826–1860*, second edition (New York: Columbia University Press, 1979), 2.
5. Tanu Priya Uteng, "Rethinking 'Mobilities': Exploring the Linkages between Development Issues, Marginalized Groups, and Gender," in *Gender, Mobilities, and Livelihood Transformations: Comparing Indigenous People in China, India, and Laos*, ed. Ragnhild Lund, et al. (London: Routledge, 2014), 30. Emphasis in original.
6. Eileen Boris and Jennifer Klein, *Caring for America: Home Health Workers in the Shadow of the Welfare State* (Oxford: Oxford University Press, 2012).
7. Girls at Dhabas Facebook page, accessed March 13, 2018, https://www.facebook.com/girlsatdhabas/; for information about the 2012 case, see "2012 Delhi gang rape"; "2012 Delhi Gang Rape," Wikipedia, last modified March 8, 2018, https://en.wikipedia.org/wiki/2012_Delhi_gang_rape.
8. *Why Loiter?* (blog), http://whyloiter.blogspot.com/.
9. Mayuri Samant, "Re-inventing 'Public' and 'Private' in Social Experience of Movements: A Case of Magowa Group," *Contributions to Indian Sociology* 50, no. 3 (2016): 415–35, https://doi.org/10.1177/0069966716657467.
10. Ibid., 420.

Chapter Three

Dialogue Interlude

#Why Loiter

Radhika Gajjala in conversation
with Shilpa Phadke

This chapter is performed in dialogue form. The theoretical insights—as in all the dialogue interludes in this book—emerge through our encounters and narrations of experience.

RG: Hi Shilpa. Thank you for agreeing to do this written dialogue interlude. You and the "Girls at Dhabas" were some of the first few South Asian digital feminists that I interviewed extensively. Our first interview was in fall 2015.

This conversation does not have to be led by me throughout; you should feel free to take it any direction you feel is relevant in the context of Indian feminist activisms. You have read the drafts of the chapters in this book, so you should feel free to contest any of the points I make as well. *To start us off, could you describe #WhyLoiter and your motivation for starting this movement, responses to it, and so on?*

SP: I am really delighted to be having this conversation with you even as I have begun thinking via our conversation in 2015 much more about the internet as a public space or what you call "digital streets." I am both gratified and puzzled to find that you would think of me as a "digital activist"; although we started the #WhyLoiter, we never have thought of ourselves as "digital activists." Rather we are people who use the internet to invite people to think about the joys of loitering. When I say "we" here, I refer to my colleagues Sameera Khan and Shilpa Ranade along with myself. In the first phase of the campaign, 2014–2015, we also included Neha Singh and Devina Kapoor in a supportive role, who had started the Why Loiter Movement in the city, about which I shall talk later.

We saw the internet merely as a way of "performing" loitering that was already taking place on city streets online. Our first invitation as part of #WhyLoiter in December 2014–January 2015 invited women to post pictures of themselves having a good time in the city to make the point that women have the right to fun in the city. It is only more recently that I have begun to think about loitering online and I talked about loitering online for a workshop titled "Feminist Internet" organized by Point of View in Mumbai. Even more recently, I was really excited to discover that Wendy Chun and Sarah Friedland have already used our work on loitering to think about loitering online.[1]

RG: So how did "whyloiter" come about?

SP: #Whyloiter comes out of our research and scholarship on women's access to public space. Our research focused on women in Mumbai. In our book *Why Loiter? Women and Risk on Mumbai Streets*, we argued that what women needed in order to access public space was not the conditional protection offered by "safety," but the right to take risks.[2] Our right to be in public space should not be questioned. We argued that the only way in which women could have unconditional access to public space was if everyone else, especially other marginal citizens, including those who were perceived to be unfriendly to women also had unconditional access. We argued that if everyone could loiter in public space we would also simultaneously subvert the neoliberal ethos by claiming public space while challenging the demand for the constant appearance of productivity.

#WhyLoiter began in December 2014 after a woman was raped in an Uber. Victim blaming followed. The focus was on the fact that the woman had fallen asleep in the taxi. In response, we wanted to focus on women's right to fun in the city.[3] Also, the two-year anniversary of the December 2012 gang rape and murder was close, so we decided to begin on December 26, 2014, and run it until January 1, 2015. The response was overwhelming. The internet was suddenly full of women having a good time in public space and sharing it online. The campaign has limitations—women need to have access to the technology to post pictures; there was also no necessary commitment to feminist politics.

This is a political limitation but also a way to demonstrate that whether articulated as feminist or not, being able to have fun in the city was important to women.

Our Twitter account became a space for the broadcasting of our activism around loitering. Earlier we had focused more on our Facebook page, which still continues to be the more active of the two.

I want to pause here to separate #WhyLoiter from the Why Loiter Mumbai movement started by Neha Singh, a theater professional and children's author who read our book and began loitering in the city. Singh and Devina Kapoor started a blog to talk about their adventures. Digital activism around loitering therefore includes their blog as well. This blog is separate from the #WhyLoiter movement, which is led by the three of us, authors of the book. The blog is maintained by Neha Singh and can be found at WhyLoiter.Blogspot.com.

In 2015–2016 we collaborated with several other groups, such as the Girls at Dhabas of Pakistan and actually organized park loitering days. We also had several conversations online focusing on different cities and the efforts to loiter in these cities.

RG: Your collaboration with Girls at Dhabas is transnational. Can you say more?

SP: In 2016–2017 the campaign ran in collaboration with the Girls at Dhabas. We had Twitter chats and ran them in tandem. This, I think, was an important moment in our "digital activism" and a space created by digital spaces—the possibility of collaboration across fraught borders. This space requires no visas for us to meet and connect. The digital space in this sense allows for subversions that take on larger politics as well to make the clear point that our governments do not represent us in this instance and in many others too. We spoke about the many similarities in the ways in which patriarchy frames norms and codes for women in the two countries. The collaboration allowed for the conversation to become transnational in many ways.

It's also interesting to me that the Girls at Dhabas in Pakistan ran into some of the same concerns that we faced when we began talking about loitering. Feminist scholars and activists suggested that this form of claiming of the public was at best addressing a minimally important facet of the problems women faced. However, since December 2012, in India, loitering has become a way of responding to the narratives of danger in relation to the city that emanate from the media. Loitering as a form of protest and claiming public space has entered the feminist lexicon. The word loiter is now likely to appear in the mainstream media when speaking of women and safety as well. This is a huge transformation from when we were struggling to legitimize our arguments around the right to loiter for everyone.

RG: Were there any issues around operationalizing the framework?

SP: Once we'd made our arguments, everyone kept asking us how we planned to "operationalize" the idea of loitering. We'd often leave the conversation not sure how to respond. Neha Singh's intervention—the act of reading the book and then acting on its politics—provided us with a response that was exciting.[4] Neha Singh was doing such an amazing job of operationalizing our framework. The Why Loiter Movement in Mumbai was followed by similar though less prolific ones in Jaipur and Pune—Neha Singh was in conversation with both of these.

When Neha Singh began loitering, she was responding to the book. She did not contact us as authors. We contacted her when we accidently discovered her photographs of loitering on social media. Neha Singh has also argued that while she appreciates the performative space of the protest or the Take Back the Night March, on a personal level there are few substitutes for actually loitering on the street, to claiming it with your body. When we wrote our book, the idea of loitering was somewhat abstract and utopian. Neha Singh's work has taught me that micro-transformations matter.

Later, in 2016, another theater professional, Satchit Puranik in conversation with Neha Singh directed a play titled *Loitering* based on the ideas from the book. The play explained the ideas from the book to speak of loitering in myriad forms. Sameera Khan, Shilpa Ranade, and I were delighted at the ways in which people had read our ideas and run with them in exciting directions. The Girls at Dhabas have also been really generous in articulating how much our work has meant to their own endeavors.

RG: How would you respond to the critiques that these are neoliberal forms?

SP: The ideas of loitering, of action heroes (Blank Noise), the early Pink Chaddi Campaign, the claim-staking of the Girls at Dhabas have at various points been accused of being neo-liberal—targeted at a group of middle-class women—and even more so when we visibilize our project online. Our research demonstrated unequivocally to us that it is not only middle-class women; women across class, especially lower-income women, desire to access the city for fun. Not only do they desire to do this but they do so when they can. More recently I have encountered narratives from young women from lower-income families in regard to the kind of access to the outside world their mobile phones provide them. In the absence of physical mobility, the internet becomes their conduit to the outside world. They also use the mobile phone to actually access public space while being able to stay in touch with their families.

There is of course the issue of using online corporate platforms like Twitter, Facebook, and Instagram for hashtag campaigns like #WhyLoiter. This is a much more complex question: How does one speak to this space? The fact is that these spaces have been useful to connect globally; for instance, many campaigns such as #YesAllWomen and #MeToo have gone viral. However, these campaigns also constitute "data" that are mined by these companies to sell us products, to more malevolently influence elections, to build personality profiles that are sold for profit. I do not have a response to this really: How do we build a space that is more democratic and does not lend itself to misuse in this form?

RG: This is not just a question for feminist movements, though. This is a question for a lot of the world: What sort of public sphere do we have in today's world? Populist? Elitist? Empowered? Datafied? Constantly surveilled? Paranoid? Why assume that these sorts of public spaces will lead to democratic interactions? What's hidden and what's visible? How is this refiguring our social spaces for posterity? When will someone reach for a switch and turn it all off? As Trebor Scholz notes:

> The Internet has become a simple-to-join, anyone-can-play system where the sites and practices of work and play increasingly wield people as a resource for economic amelioration by a handful of oligarchic owners. Social life on the Internet has become the "standing reserve," the site for the creation of value through ever more inscrutable channels of commercial surveillance.[5]

What are the implications and repercussions of the forms of digital labor and affective networks we produce in public, leaving behind incomplete spontaneous archives in data space through these forms of social movements and through the particular hashtags you refer to? Hard to say.

But even if we had an evaluation or an answer, it's part of our everyday life now. We cheer when young people suddenly find themselves at the center of activist movements (as in the recent case of the young folks in the US fighting for gun control and safety in schools), from having tweeted in anger and outrage from their living rooms or back seats of their parents' car. And then the close community members, family members, and friends suddenly find themselves having to cope and become strong support communities for these young activists. When one or two names emerge as the celebrity names of the movements and become public figures, the labor of the victims and their families and of the inadvertent and accidental activists from the close community isn't even acknowledged.

We live in a time of visibility politics where the corporate ethos of the platforms with their embedded marketing and extreme binarizing structures and their exploitative underpinnings become our tools for transmitting and communicating in times of crisis and outrage. Once a simple micro movement emerges organically, there are groups of actors that surround the visible space of the movement fighting against it, questioning its authenticity as a movement or trying to connect with it as a brand to get their names and organizations attached to it by association for fame and profit. Note for instance how your movement was picked up as a brandable/marketable movement by an advertising professional. As Indian rapper Sofia Ashraf notes in her podcast interview with Ian Cook, activists as much as any other actors in social media are competing for attention—they have to find effective ways to catch the attention of the users of digital tools.[6] Further, as Pallavi Guha's work reveals, this attention is garnered only in particular instances: class, caste, and region play a role (implicitly and explicitly) in how any event is picked up and brought into visibility.[7]

The contradictions are many. Who is accountable and what is honesty of representation?

SP: Taking the discussion back to feminism, I want to ask you a question now. I have been reading about hashtag feminism and what it achieves and what is lost. I'd really like to know, what do you think this space has done for feminism?

RG: For me, hashtag feminism is not a thing by itself. Historically, what different tools for mobility and for communication do in our everyday life and the fact that we have them available at any point in time has shaped the ways in which different groups of people have been able to conceptualize their autonomy in relation to power structures and fight for their rights in different ways. Hashtagging is just one mode of activism in a long history that we haven't even yet documented in full. Take for instance the printing press and Christianity, or the newspapers Benedict Anderson discusses in *Imagined Communities*.[8] Also in the case of women's movements, we know of how Susan B. Anthony used her bicycle and made activist history. So I don't see the use of hashtags in feminist or other kinds of movements as a deliberate choice in opposition to other forms of activisms as much as a move toward using what is available in the everyday for certain groups of people. It is both a choice and not a choice in that the global publics that a lot of us interact in are being defined through these social media spheres. To participate in certain global settings, therefore, we have to be "here." Yet we know that while these "heres" are visible globally, there are many "theres" that are not; there are many micro-struggles happening in unconnected space—they have always happened and they continue to do so. We live in an ethos that privileges only particular movements as authentic and real, however, and if it's a movement we have not heard about through particular hierarchies of information, we tend not to consider it an authentic act of activism. The micro-movements that shift hierarchies happen both online and offline and locally and globally, though—and not all make a big splash in the news.

This actually reminds me to ask, to push on: What might have been some foundational thoughts and assumptions for your group as you ventured into the use of hashtags for your movement? Also, picking up from an earlier point, can you elaborate on the question of who is a digital activist, who authenticates you as such, and how does the authentication happen?

SP: Like you say in your response, we didn't think of hashtags as separate from other forms of feminist organizing. At that moment it seemed one way in which we could reach out to a larger audience and talk about the right to fun in public. When we spoke of loitering in the beginning, it was often the young women in our workshops who seemed to be excited by the idea of loitering. In some ways it was these women we wanted to speak to via social media to invite them to participate in what we hoped would be able to demonstrate that women access the city streets for fun, for purposeless pleasure. Our invitation specifically invited women to share updates and pictures of themselves having a good time in public space.

The hashtag was an extension of our politics around loitering. It was the idea of loitering that was important. The idea of the hashtag was actually Nishant John's, so we can't take credit for it. But it seemed like a good way to be able to archive the posts that appeared as part of this campaign. Even now people will occasionally post using #Why-Loiter. In the last few years of intensified activism around public space we have seen the feminist discourse turn from one that focused on safety to one that focuses more on citizenship and the claiming of rights, which I think is an important move and has been possible only because multiple voices are speaking in multiple contexts on city streets; on digital streets, to use your term; in workshops; conferences; schools; colleges; and other organizations.

I think your question of who is a digital activist is a very important one. We see ourselves more as researchers who chanced into digital activism. Who, then, is the digital activist? I see my role as a facilitator of conversations.

RG: I myself am neither an activist in the physical streets nor the digital streets. I am a feminist researcher of internet-mediated space. I am primarily a feminist teacher and mentor.

For my research I enter through the internet first. And yes, I do extensive interviews and offline ethnographic work in rural locations, in urban locations—anywhere I can and need to go to get further insight into what I see online and also to get an understanding of the absences, of what I am NOT seeing online. But the internet is my point of entry. So . . . for me, you and your collaborators are on the digital streets—I see you on the internet.

Also in the short history of Indian digital feminisms, those that have written about this phenomenon in academic work such as Trishima Mitra-Kahn, Padmini Ray Murray, Sonora Jha, and others have noted your pioneering role in hashtag feminisms.[9] Just as we wonder about why the Delhi rape of 2012 gained such global visibility as opposed to other equally horrific violent rapes in India (I ask this question in an earlier chapter, but Pallavi Guha and I also unpack some of these issues in our dialogue interlude), we might ask how and why some hashtag movements and not others get picked up by academics or reporters to showcase as activist projects. My wondering this of course does not take away from the important work you and your team are doing—it's something to wonder about just the same, and I know you too wonder.

SP: I love how you characterize the act of being on the "digital streets" of the internet as digital activism. If we think about loitering online as an act that is as subversive as loitering in city streets, then perhaps we might see all of us who are online articulating feminist positions, debating, engaging as digital activists? If it expands our vision of digital activism to include all those who subvert and transform the misogynist and often exclusionary space of the internet, then clearly many more of us are digital activists than recognize ourselves as being such.

I guess our foray into "hashtag feminism" via #WhyLoiter also firmly locates us as people who have used the online space to popularize a feminist idea.

NOTES

1. Wendy Chun and Sarah Friedland, "Habits of Leaking: Of Sluts and Network Cards," *Differences: A Journal of Feminist Cultural Studies* 26, no. 2 (2015): 1–28, doi 10.1215/10407391-3145937.
2. Shilpa Phadke, Sameera Khan, and Shilpa Ranade, *Why Loiter? Women and Risk on Mumbai Streets* (New Delhi: Penguin Books, 2011).
3. The advertisements are available at: Why Loiter? Facebook page, accessed March 23, 2018, https://www.facebook.com/Why-Loiter-193556873988115/.
4. Neha Singh, *Why Loiter?* (blog), http://whyloiter.blogspot.com/.
5. Trebor Scholz, "Why Does Digital Labor Matter Now?" introduction to *Digital Labor: The Internet as Playground and Factory*, ed. Scholz (New York: Routledge, 2013), 1.
6. Radhika Gajjala and Sofia Ashraf, "Cyberfeminism and Content Creation," by Ian M. Cook, *Online Gods*, no. 6, podcast audio, March 2, 2018, https://www.stitcher.com/podcast/online-gods/e/53542877.
7. Pallavi Guha, "Mind the Gap: Connecting News and Information to Build an Agenda Against Rape and Sexual Assault in India" (PhD diss., University of Maryland, 2017).
8. Benedict Anderson, *Imagined Communities* (London: Verso, 1983).
9. Trishima Mitra-Kahn, "Offline Issues, Online Lives? The Emerging Cyberlife of Feminist Politics in Urban India," in *New South Asian Feminisms: Paradoxes and Possibilities*, ed. Srila Roy (London: Zed Books, 2012), 108–30; Padmini Ray Murray, "Bringing up the Bodies: The Visceral, the Virtual, and the Visible," Keynote Presentation at Diginaka, Tata Institute of Social Sciences, Mumbai, January 6–8, 2016; Sonora Jha, "Gathering Online, Loitering Offline: Hashtag Activism and the Claim for Public Space by Women in India through the #whyloiter Campaign," in *New Feminisms in South Asian Social Media, Film, and Literature: Disrupting the Discourse*, ed. Sonora Jha and Alka Kurian (New York: Routledge, 2018), 63–84.

Chapter Four

Dialogue Interlude

Centering Marginalized Feminists

Radhika Gajjala in conversation with Sukhnidh Kaur, Varsha Ayyar, Nithila Kanagasabai, and Divya Kandukuri

The interludes in this chapter were started in March 2018. These interludes serve to rupture the mostly Savarna narrative of digital access and of postnational and postcolonial Indian feminist frameworks that still tend to draw on the ghar/bahir framework. The interludes center feminist voices and issues that are usually on the margins of a postnational, postcolonial "Indian women's movement."

DIALOGUE INTERLUDE WITH SUKHNIDH KAUR: QITAABZINE

RG: Hi Sukhnidh, thank you for agreeing to dialogue with me. Our Skype session covered a range of topics—expectations of LGBTQ identity performance in media space; emotional labor; feminist start-ups; the invisibility of subaltern feminist activism (even when they are on Twitter); and, your own role in digital space as founder and editor of the Qitaabzine (https://www.instagram.com/qitaabzine/). Can you elaborate on some of the points, please?

SK: Feminist startups and organizations are responsible for creating inclusive spaces that reflect the ideologies they propagate. However, incorporating such ethics is complex. There are multiple issues that plague digital feminisms, and I believe they can be traced to two root causes: the profit incentive, and blindness toward the struggles of other marginalized communities.

Feminist publications in the digital space are starting to be widely recognized, having created a niche for themselves. We are currently living in the age of cyber-activism, and these portals are marketed to young women and men who are willing and eager to consume feminist content. Two questions on this matter that require in-depth thought are: Where does this content come from? What drives these portals in terms of traction and sustenance?

These portals often ask for long hours of unpaid labor in terms of writing, graphic design, and social media management, and pass it off as prestigious internship experience that provides exposure and affiliation with the organization. In doing this, they create an exclusionary space that leaves out those women who cannot afford to sustain themselves on mere exposure and one free lunch a day. Feminism entails access to fair means of work and wage, and many web portals tend to overlook that. Moreover, they do not publicly credit women—a problem faced by women historically, which one would hope would be tackled by the feminist-activist organizations in question. For example, a graphic designer's work on an organization's page will be credited to the organization itself, but the young artist's name would probably appear in fine print somewhere else on the website. Young people looking to actively contribute to a cause they believe in are easily lured by the prospect of working in digital feminist space, and these organizations benefit from that by exploiting them in the name of contribution to activism.

Further, these publications, articles and op-eds that surface are often reflective of a largely privileged perspective. This content is palatable and relatable for the similarly privileged, upper-middle-class, upper-caste individuals who consume it. While #MenAreTrash is discussed at length, caste, class, and sexuality are only tagged as keywords for when the next tragedy happens—like the murder of a Dalit woman or an infuriating comment made by a figure of political authority. Pop-feminist articles gain more traction, and hence their mainstreamism is unsurprising. This comes at the cost of burying and neglecting issues that plague the underprivileged majority of the country. Consumers buy into it because this is a mutually beneficial equation born out of convenience—they don't want to read "boring" longforms. Publications can hence gain traction by introducing lighthearted pieces that do not accurately reflect the reality of how India lives today. This content is far easier to produce and it is eagerly consumed. Feminism has never been easy. It has been a struggle, but this process seems to be slowly, but steadily, watering it down and leading to the commodification of feminism.

Feminism is now used as a tagline for commercial purposes, and consumers are buying into it like never before. It will generate more sales, and corporations will profit from publicly affiliating. A company selling feminism-related merchandise at INR 300 per T-shirt and INR 250 per mug, each with a quirky catchphrase, probably does not care about the cause—it cares about how easily it can be exploited.

If a well-known brand "comes out" as feminist and paints its profile picture rainbow in solidarity with the LGBTQ+ population, is it championing the causes, or is it using them as tools of public satisfaction, enragement, and discourse? It may well be a strategic PR move—and it seems to be working incredibly well. A question of ethics surfaces. Is benefiting off of these causes justified if doing so spreads the message of awareness simultaneously?

RG: Srila Roy has written about the first lesbian advertisement—for the apparel line Anouk—in Indian media in her Oxford University Press (OUP) blog post, "Lesbian existence and marginalization in India."[1] What do you think?

SK: I do agree with what the author of the article has said. If I had to tell you about one LGBTQ+ Indian issue that I think desperately needs attention, it is the Indian idea of "elitism" of LGBTQ+ folks (with Hijras being an exception). Anouk's ad is, simply put, not a black and white matter!

RG: I've been mulling over this. On the one hand the visibility cannot be fully discounted; and on the other, there is a global move to using philanthropy and activism as content to move technology and other corporate startups forward (my collaborators and I have commented on some of this in my last book). Do you think, though, that sometimes in our contemporary modes of existence we might be acquiring "voice" and visibility through consumer citizenship?

SK: Consumer interaction and response is a key factor in directing the growth of a brand's image. Growth-oriented corporations and startups have their fingers on the pulse of trend trajectories, and they utilize these trends to their fullest advantage. A fine example of this is Women's Day activities conducted by brands. Products such as makeup and lingerie are some of the most marked-up commodities in the world in terms of price, so when brands offer 15 percent discounts on Women's Day, they are not making a real adjustment or compromise for the benefit and recognition of women. They are brand-building. It is a growth strategy.

How does one decide whether visibility through consumer citizenship is ethical? Impact evaluation is an effective approach. Has the corporation/startup brought about tangible change in the areas covered by the causes it champions? Have genuine efforts been made towards the same? If not, chances are, it is a farce and a PR strategy. This is a harsh evaluation, but it also explores the most telling approach. Accountability is essential. We must hold brands accountable for contribution and investment into the causes they support.

RG: And finally, tell us about your wonderful work with Qitaab! What have been your motivations, processes, goals, etcetera?

SK: I started Qitaab with a small team of people in 2018. It is a web-based zine and news dissemination portal that allows young Indian citizens to submit their art, photography, and writing centered around the queer Indian experience.

We are currently witnessing a surge in LGBTQ+ visibility in the media, in particular social media, but there is not much content that is India-specific. Young Indians do not have access to desi, feminist, intersectional, inclusive LGBTQ+ content. Cultural differences in the approach to queerness exist, and it is unfair to expect Indian members of the community to adapt to Western ideas of activism. We have our own unique struggles, and visibilizing them is incredibly important.

We pay whomever we can pay, and explain to contributors that we are brand-new and just starting out, and hence cannot give monetary compensation yet. Everybody is credited and recognized for their work. Inclusivity and intersectionality are emphasized—I force myself to explore the intersections of LGBTQ+ in caste and class. I reflect on my own experiences with privilege and acknowledge them. I am trying to keep Qitaab's approach as ethical as possible, and all of us still have much to learn.

The response to Qitaab was expected—queer Indians are brimming with ideas, intellect, and talent, and they are grateful for being given access to a platform that welcomes them. I am humbled by the experience of going through their works, interacting with them, and listening to their perspectives.

DIALOGUE INTERLUDE WITH DR. VARSHA AYYAR

RG: Dalit feminist engagement through Twitter, Facebook, and other transnational/global social media platforms is indeed very vocally present on Twitter. It exists both as a protest space, community space, and as a space that turns its back (loudly) against Savarna Indian and global academic theorizing and appropriation of the Dalit spaces. To start us off, can you tell the readers about your work and how you use the digital space to engage in anti-caste feminist work?

VA: Thank you Radhika. I will begin with a brief background. My name is Varsha Ayyar; I am a sociologist and faculty at Tata Institute of Social Sciences. My engagement with the digital space has been primarily in a range of roles as a user, as an academic, researcher, as a Dalit, and as a Dalit Feminist and a concerned "netizen." I must underline I am serious, mindful, and very conscious regarding the enormous possibilities of using the internet, but also of its limitations and violence that is embedded. I also pay attention to how digital technologies—smartphones, the internet, and social media—are transforming the nature of social interactions in a highly stratified society like India, where caste and gender lines often restrict social interactions broadly. What social differences emerge now in India as we interact through messaging apps like WhatsApp and platforms such as Facebook—now that they're available in local languages? What is also alarming is the new kind of caste abuses visible online—new forms of digital violences, Savarnaization of digital spaces, and how the dominant modes of sharing information, stories, and greetings are Brahmanical. For instance, the WhatsApp Group culture can be extremely misogynist, sexist, casteist, and very terrifying—you do not know who is reading your messages, how sensitive they are to your opinions, especially if you are liberal, feminist, and anti-caste!

To many women, the WhatsApp patriarchy will be familiar. Often we hear how people want to know your whereabouts, why you are/were online at a particular point in time, whom you were chatting with—all these interrogations are largely reserved for women. So on one hand, we are a country that shares the memes, fake news, and good morning/ good night WhatsApp forwarded messages, but underneath this, most of the people are sharing content that is mostly misogynist, sexist, racist, and casteist. The only way to counter this culture is by participating in and challenging as much as one can. And this incredible work begins at home. What kinds of groups do we have? Are they inclusive?

Are they mindful of the content that is shared? How many women administrators run these groups? For example, how do we respond to groups that seem politically neutral—like those formed around school/ batchmate groups—but that are also composed of a bunch of digitally active adults who may very well be very political and not necessarily progressive?

Unlike my senior Dalit generation that keeps forwarding messages—particularly women groups where Brahmanical Marathi writers and their posts are forwarded with implied casteist, Brahmanical superiority and bigotry toward Muslims, Dalits, working classes—I have not only intervened but also pointed out to how the upper caste/upper class dominate social media discussions. I think I am not a meek, submissive "harijan" that Gandhi and Savarna India loves—offline and online; neither am I a "domesticated woman." If I am engaged in any discussion or part of any forum, I ensure my voice (i.e., of a Dalit and a feminist) is heard.

My first initiative dates back to creation of a group on Orkut in 2005–2006 when I created a group for Dalits to contribute and commemorate Dalit food. Orkut was the networking site—Facebook—of that era. The inspiration for the group was primarily my interest in "everything Dalit"—the food, the social life, Dalit politics, the social movement, Dalit leadership, and so on.

I began my doctoral studies at Bombay School of Sociology and was researching Dalit lives in the slums of Mumbai. In the course of my work, I had applied for a research-based fellowship (via a Yahoo group started by a social work graduate of Tata Institute of Social Sciences, who later did an MPhil at the Indian Institute of Technology and PhD at Indiana University) and I was selected out of a pool of hundreds of applicants. I was a fellow and had visited New York City for a research project. This is where I met one of our fellows from the United States, Tiffany Gardner, a law graduate from Columbia University and an African American. Tiffany gave us a tour of Harlem— showing us around the neighborhood and its historic places, giving its historical background, the rich African American culture, and the literary and social activism of Harlem. We were very fortunate to attend a Sunday mass at the Abyssinian Baptist Church, walk around the beautiful neighborhood on a November morning, see Italian brownstone homes and the fall colors, and we ended our little tour with a lovely brunch at Amy Ruth's. I learned of the interrelated sides of Harlem during this visit: on one hand, I learned of histories like that of the

Mosque of Islam founded by Malcolm X; and on the other hand, I discovered the world of "soul food." Both these histories and the Harlem neighborhood are very close to my heart as a Dalit.

Dalits (ex-untouchables) and African Americans have a lot in common—especially their lived experiences in social hierarchies, their resistance practices, and their long struggle for the civil rights are eerily similar. And these two social groups historically have extended their solidarities with each other and continue to build bridges to carry forward these conversations of the two most remarkable and greatest struggles in human history.

Brunch at Amy Ruth's actually led me to develop the Orkut group, and I started posting Dalit recipes, foods, and cultures specific to Dalits in Maharashtra. Very quickly, I had two hundred-plus followers; many were curious and interested and wanted to learn, contribute, and know about the "Soul Food of India"—the Dalit food. That was my initiation into the digital medium. I did not continue running the group nor did I migrate to Facebook as Orkut died; however, I did inspire many and got academics interested in researching and talking about Dalit foods. Since then there has been a steady rise and interest in Dalit foods. Since then I have used the digital medium, social media, to bring awareness to Dalit issues, the Dalit–African American solidarity, and to "educate" about the history of reservations. I also hosted the first Facebook page on Dr. B. R. Ambedkar and W. E. B. Du Bois. I was introduced to Du Bois as a sociologist, not through the Indian curriculum but through a Macmillan sociology textbook that I had received as a sample copy.

I was struck by the relevance of Du Bois's sociology for Dalits and yet found no mention of Du Bois in Indian sociology, which was filled with Eurocentric and upper-caste male sociology. I was curious to find out more about Du Bois and started reading him. I was also reading Ambedkar for my doctoral work. I came across the letters exchanged by Du Bois and Ambedkar. I was thrilled to see these two giant intellectuals writing in solidarity and addressing each other as "My dear." I asked my family friend Mangesh Dahiwale to find out more from American academics, as I was interested in mapping the exchange and finding out if Ambedkar and Du Bois ever met or continued their exchange beyond these letters. A detailed response was posted by an American professor in the form of an e-memorandum in 2008, and since then, many have created Facebook posts, Twitter handles, and so on.

Since my visit to Harlem, NYC, in 2006; my meeting with Tiffany
Gardner; and more than a decade in academia, I have continued my
interest in the Dalit–African American research and solidarity and currently I am doing some interesting digital projects with Indiana University and Columbia University that are historic in nature and profoundly
significant for Dalit Studies/South Asian Studies and African American
Studies. Most of these projects deal with social justice, Dr. B. R. Ambedkar, and Dalits in western India, where I come from and work. It has
been an exciting journey to brainstorm and be the co-PI with some of
the scholars associated with Ambedkar and Dalit movements.

RG: These are important moments that you describe! Can you say
something about your experience, exposure, and engagement through
social media?

VA: Although I started using Twitter when it was very new, as with
almost all social media platforms I have tried, tested, and even abandoned—Orkut, Myspace, Yahoo Groups, Facebook, WhatsApp, and
now Twitter—I have used it mostly to advocate and educate my friends
and followers. Being in academia, we have access to several insights,
debates, and current and advanced knowledge that many people outside
academia are not exposed to. For instance, many online discussions
centered around discussions of how reservations represent incorrect
information. Especially on social media when you are connected
through different kinds of networks, all kinds of people participate in
such discussions. Often I intervene, post, debate, and argue, but I also
ensure that the layperson who is not exposed to the latest studies or
research gets information. For example, I would quote Professor Sukh-
deo Thorat's study; share newspaper articles, lectures, and videos; and
summarize findings of research and post it for the community to read
and engage. These are the small ways of using one's knowledge for
public good—particularly to advance social justice and Dalit rights. I
am also critical of masculinity and the absence of Dalit Feminist points
of view and try to incorporate as much as I can in my social media
engagement. Most of the time, I have been able to reach out to activists
and Ambedkarites, who have been extremely receptive.

RG: Varsha, your valuable interventions reinforce the point that
Twitter and Facebook are not the first entry points for Dalit digital
feminisms—neither is Dalit feminism something "new." Thank you for
giving so much of your time to this dialogue interlude. [2]

DIALOGUE INTERLUDE WITH NITHILA KANAGASABAI

RG: Nithila, thank you for agreeing to do this dialogue interlude with me. One of the issues highlighted by recent debates and clashes in feminist space is the need for more "intersectionality" within the Indian women's movement. In talking to several young women participants during a seminar I was teaching in Pune, India, in 2018, I found that some were making a distinction between the Indian Women's Movement and Indian Feminisms. Also, in another dialogue interlude for this book with Pallavi Guha, we discussed some issues around lack of representation of rural feminist struggles and also caste and class issues. I know your work engages these issues through your research in Tamil Nadu: can you talk about how you see the digital being taken up by different groups of feminists? Do you see this as interlinked (or not) with making visible ruptures in how the Indian women's movement has functioned thus far as a mostly dominant-caste and upper-caste movement?

NK: I am delighted to be having this conversation with you. First off, I must confess that I do not consider myself to be a "digital activist" or even an activist in the traditional sense of the term. I would like to position myself as a feminist researcher in this context. This is not to posit either an easy binary or a hierarchy between the two terms but simply to claim an identity I am more comfortable with.

In my research on women's studies (as a politics and a discipline) in Tiruchirapalli and Coimbatore in Tamil Nadu I was looking at students pursuing higher education in state-funded Women's Studies Centers (WSC) in two universities. My curiosity was piqued when I first met some students from these universities at the National Conference organized by the Indian Association of Women's Studies in Guwahati in 2014. Many of them were first-generation graduates who had stumbled upon Women's Studies (WS) at the master's level after having faced rejection or complete alienation from their previous disciplinary backgrounds—which varied from zoology to economics to computer science. They hailed from working-class families and from Dalit, Bahujan, Adivasi communities in villages around Trichy and Coimbatore. Most of them had initially signed up for the MA in women's studies not because they were motivated by feminist politics, but largely because this was the only course that was willing to accept them, because their parents thought of it as a "safe" course for women (most of the students enrolled in WS in these locations were women), or because they were told that they would be able to find a job after completion of the course. But they also went on to speak about their journeys within the discipline and articulated their arrival at a "women's studies perspective," distinct from feminism, which they perceived to be both more "Western" and more "academic."[3] They spoke of their active involvement in campus politics, their participation in Gender Study Circles and Ambedkar-Periyar Study Circles, their activism via extension activities, and their contribution to women's studies academia.

These narratives were in stark contrast to the available academic literature on WSCs in non-metropolitan locations in India, which more often than not, rued the "NGOization" and "professionalization" of WS courses and the consequent deradicalization of the discipline itself. In some ways, it is this "professionalization" that has, I have argued in my MPhil dissertation, enabled a democratization of the discipline—with more students from various marginalized locations now accessing the discipline, who are not just being transformed by this experience, but also actively transform the academic feminist discourse in India, which has long been dominated by the metropolitan feminist speaking either about herself or the Other (the underprivileged, rural woman). While voices from non-metropolitan locations have been recognized within the Indian women's movement, it is often as the grassroots-level activist, not as a feminist/women's studies scholar. The WS scholars I worked with saw themselves as contributing to the creation of a women's studies that drew as much from the works of Iyothee Thass, Periyar, and Ambedkar as from contemporary Tamil feminist authors and poets such as Kutti Revathi, Salma, Bama, and Sukirtharani and from academic feminist scholars in India and elsewhere. Following from Gopal Guru's argument, they criticized metropolitan feminists' impulse to hastily classify work of Dalit Bahujans—poems, novellas, and songs—as merely "empirical," as "data," that need to be processed within institutionalized academia to produce legitimate "sociological knowledge."[4] Keenly aware of the hierarchies of knowledge production and the politics of citationary practices, they spoke of their struggles *within* and *against* patriarchal Brahminical academia.

Even as I engaged with the "experiences" of WS students in these locations, I was cautious of the stereotypes that I might be playing into. This was heightened by the recognition of "the double bind of distance and closeness" I shared with the participants.[5] I spent my formative years in a small city in Tamil Nadu and have myself come to women's studies after engagement with various other disciplines. But in terms of my class (middle) and caste location (Savarna), I am undeniably much more privileged than most of the research participants. More often than not, a person belonging to a marginalized community is seen unproblematically as "the one who speaks from the gut, who righteously praises the concrete over the abstract, the material over the theoretical."[6] In order to avoid this, I frame the experiences of my research participants as critical texts that both speak *of* and *from* the field. While this does not erase hierarchies, it allows me to work with them.

The participants of this research saw themselves as very much a part of the Indian women's movement, but articulated a strong sense of alienation with regard to feminism, especially academic feminism, Indian or otherwise. This, however, was not due to a postfeminist ethic, as is the case in most metropolitan locations, where young people often feel that the project of feminism is redundant in the current scenario. The ambivalence and sometimes outright rejection of the term stemmed from the idea of the locatedness of theory as academic white philosophy that can sometimes be irrelevant to their lived realities and from their perceived lack of competence—to be a "feminist," one had to meet an ever-receding horizon of expertise, of authority.

Most scholars in this location accessed online spaces through desktop computers in the library on campus. Though most students owned a cell phone, almost no one had a smartphone with internet connection. Things have changed quite a bit since my first visit to the universities in April 2015. Now, in 2018, more and more students have mobile phones with 4G connections. WS scholars here engaged with Tamil little magazines—literary journals that have a small, hyperlocal circulation—in the online space. Before these magazines were available in the online space, it was particularly difficult for women to access them because they were usually sold in crowded public places young girls were discouraged from frequenting. These journals also featured feminist poets and authors whose work was central to the enterprise of formulating a feminist language that spoke to their location. A number of research participants spoke about entering online social networks after being introduced to it by peers in the university and how following feminists online has led a deeper everyday engagement with feminist literature. While many of them admitted to not posting much online, they said that they would discuss with their peers posts with a feminist take on current affairs or those with feminist poetry they came across. Social networks were also widely used in organizing meetings and study circles and distributing reading material for the same. They also frequently shared information on academic research/training workshops that were being offered specifically for Dalit Bahujan students. These were workshops organized locally to train students from marginalized locations for competitive exams like those for the civil services or the National/State Level Eligibility Tests for qualifying to be appointed as assistant professors. Some of the research participants were also involved in creating and editing local-language Wikipedia entries of "Western" feminist philosophers. They curated lists of these links and passed them on to their juniors and peers so they could access these pages for a preliminary understanding of Western feminist thought. They also worked on developing Wikipedia pages for feminist authors and poets writing in Tamil. In all these cases, it was interesting for me to note that the digital circuits that they were a part of rarely tried to explicitly transcend the local or the present. The digital was often used to address the immediate and communicate locally rather than to communicate with an elsewhere.

RG: So the assumption that using the digital to communicate means you are targeting an "elsewhere" audience is proven incorrect. What you describe is a local contextual use of the digital. Would you consider these to be digital publics? Can you elaborate a bit more on your points?

NK: Many of their engagements on digital platforms do not explicitly attempt to be legible to a larger audience. For instance, a lot of participation on Facebook happens on closed groups with members largely from the university or the same geographical space. They saw their attempts at creating local-language Wikipedia pages also as addressing their immediate needs. While most of their interactions in the online space did not aim to transcend the spatial or the temporal, they did employ these platforms strategically to facilitate engagement in ways that are meaningful. When students protested the wrongful termination of one of the faculty members by staging a *dharna*, they mobilized support for the professor through what may be called traditional media—by writing letters to the governor and to various teachers' associations in the state. [7] But they extensively documented their protests on Facebook as evidence. Social media in this particular case was employed toward a subversive memory-making rather than a means of communication. This was because they felt that they could not mobilize more student support through social media because students from other departments were sternly cautioned against participating in the strike with threats of suspension, and students from other universities might not have locus standi regarding this issue.

In their own narratives, their initial months on social media networks were more observational than conversational. This was attributed to both non-expertise and fear of being policed by brothers or other family members who were participants in the online media space. However, with time, their interactions with feminist and Ambedkarite activists and authors increased. They used the space to highlight mainstream media's silence on caste-based atrocities while furthering engagement with alternative media like Round Table India, Countercurrents.org, TwoCircles.net, and Savari to debate sexist or casteist depictions in popular Tamil cinema, comment on opportunism and appropriation in electoral politics, and also engage in participatory scholarship like in the case of Dalit History Month. In doing this, they marked themselves as being an important part of the growing Ambedkarite counterpublics in digital spaces.[8] "Counterpublics" becomes the appropriate iteration of their practice because they recognized their exclusion from not just feminist digital publics, but also from metropolitan feminist academia, and consequently they articulate through alternate discursive practices. They enable the widening of fields of discursive contestation because they do not perceive this as a matter of inclusion, or even intersectionality, but as a means of calling out caste privilege. In a certain sense, the purpose of their presence and performance in digital spaces is not so much persuasion as it is agitation. This was viewed as an attempt to cultivate their own vocabulary, to articulate their identities, and adopt what Rege calls a "dual strategy" of seeking both alternate means of organization and communication, while simultaneously staking claims of entry into unmarked publics.[9] They can also be considered counterpublics because they continue to be seen, at least by some sections, as fracturing the feminist movement and are often called upon to maintain status quo and affirm either metropolitan or Savarna feminism, or identify themselves as a counterpublic.

Then there is also the question of self-presentation. Computer skills were linked to ascendancy in the workforce, and employment was a huge concern. They saw their engagements in digital media as familiarizing themselves with the "system" (as the computer was often referred to). In fact, some of them, based on their newly acquired skills, had already secured part-time employment as data entry operators. This was helping them fund their own education and sometimes even that of their younger siblings. But engaging with digital media or computers needs to be read in the specific context of the linking of technological capability, development, and aspiration in the postcolonial situation. In Tamil Nadu, in particular, where engineering is seen as more prestigious than pursuing a degree in pure sciences, and much more so than higher education in social sciences or humanities, research participants indicated that being able to "work with computers" can fashion respectability, especially in semi-urban and rural areas. While most families from land-owning dominant castes routinely sell land to be able to fund their children's higher education in engineering at one of the over five hundred self-financed engineering colleges in the state (Tamil Nadu has the most number of engineering colleges in the country), participants of this research belonged to marginalized castes and consequently their families were unable to afford the fees in private engineering colleges. In such a situation, being able to use computers or digital media was not just seen as an attempt to cross class/caste boundaries, but also generate respectability for both the discipline of WS and its scholars. The argument that I am trying to make is that digital media is always experienced from within one's social world.

Because my research was on pedagogical practices in non-metropolitan women's studies, my focus was not on addressing how digital media was employed in these contexts, but rather exploring different media that the students were choosing to engage with for purposes of communication, self-presentation, and memory-making. Consequently, the circuits enabled and the identities activated. It was not simply activism in corporeal spaces spilling over into digital spaces, or the other way around. Rather than a simplified cause-and-effect relationship between activism and media platforms, the focus was on teasing out the modes of being and becoming political.

RG: Nithila, thank you for this dialogue exchange—I know it's fairly short, but your points serve to nuance and even provide evidence for some of the larger conceptual analyses and questions in other parts of this book and I appreciate that. Do you want to say anything to wrap up our conversation?

NK: Thank you for this conversation. It allowed me to think through shifts in the nature and form of feminist academia and the women's movement, and emergent practices reshaping the contours of feminist engagement in digital spaces. The idea is not to offer up the local in opposition to the global, as something more real or true, but simply to articulate differential modes of political participation; it was to think through how global digital platforms could be mobilised to enable processes of localisation of feminism, activate latent ties critical to the making and remaking of counterpublics, and open up dialogues around possibilities of the present.

DIALOGUE INTERLUDE WITH DIVYA KANDUKURI: "EVERYDAY CASTEISM"

RG: Divya, thank you for agreeing to do this dialogue. It has been a pleasure knowing you even if only through WhatsApp and Skype. I've been following the Twitter handle @DivyaKandukuri and your instagram account @anitcastecat where you share messages on the topic of "everydaycasteism. I'm also following your latest project "blue dawn" around mental illness, gender and caste. You and I have talked several times even before deciding to do this dialogue interlude. In our conversations we talked of many things related to the Indian higher education system's social context and also your own personal history and aspirations. You spoke of your use of Facebook as well as Twitter. You also talked of your work with Buzzfeed. In our conversations, I suggested that you take the lead in framing this dialogue by making the decision on what you wanted to talk about in the context of digital streets. Some of what you said serves to socially situate the ghar/bahir framework of how both Indian nationalist discourse and mainstream Indian feminist movements have implicitly framed women's lives as contained in the "ghar." For instance, you note how movements such as Pinjra Todd are not intersectional and that the issues are more upper caste/class in relevance.

In this dialogue, let's focus on how you became a digital activist. Why and how did you get into digital activism, particularly in relation to your work with EverydayCasteism, Smashboard, and Buzzfeed.

DK: I'll start by talking a little about myself. I'm from Coastal Andhra Pradesh. I did all my schooling there. I come from a varied social background—from a family of three religions: my mother is a Dalit Muslim and my father was a Hindu OBC[10] who is now converted into a Christian. I identify as a "Bahujan." Through childhood I had to hide my caste identity because of social bullying and mistreatment. I wanted to prove that I was not a "reservation" student, so I worked very hard to excel in everything I did so as to escape the bullying that proceeds after people get to know when someone is a reserved quota student. For college I moved to Delhi and entered one of the top colleges and was admitted through merit. I got 97% and still people looked down on me as my admission is under reserved quota. I was looked down upon both because of how I dressed (coming from a non-metropolitan South Indian location, I was not yet in sync with the Delhi fashions) and because my leisure reading and viewing had been focused on the regional—Telugu-language novels and media and so on. I was, in short, not "cool" enough for the social classes in that space. [11]

RG: What you also said was that they also made fun of you for not having read bell hooks and Audre Lorde, yet they themselves obviously had not thought through their own social location while being exposed to those African American feminist works. I find that very ironic indeed. So tell us about how you started forming social awareness groups.

DK: I feel that intersectionality should not be considered a subtheme of feminism—if you are not intersectional, I don't consider you a feminist. Anyway, the result of this negative climate in the elite college I was at led to me falling behind academically. There were other structural issues as well—where even some of the authorities also spoke badly about Scheduled Caste/Scheduled Tribe ("SC/ST") employees and implicitly supported caste-ist culture in the college.

RG: When and how did you begin activist organizing?

DK: I started exploring activism on the ground; I started attending talks. When you are in a situation of crisis, you look for people who are in crisis too—you relate to them. A few of us connected; it turns out that all of us were from a "reserve" category. One fine day we decided we should have an Ambedkar reading circle—although we didn't quite call it that. We started meeting regularly and started reading anything on anti-caste literature. We started meeting in a small shed. One day we put up posters around campus to invite people to our talk on reservations, but the college officials removed our posters. They thought our posters were disruptive. Anyway, we still managed to hold our event on campus. But we realized that we are now under surveillance for doing this. So we moved our events and meetings to the small shed. We had talks on Dalit Feminists—we also had a talk on manual scavenging. This was around the time when the Rohit Vemula thing was also happening. [12] So we called activists from Hyderabad Central University (HCU) and asked them to speak to the group. All this activity started to give me confidence actually. It's like you are asserting your identity with strength somewhere.

RG: So when did you begin to see utility in using digital tools for the work you started doing offline? Based on the Rohit Vemula comment, I'm assuming you were organizing locally around 2015–2016.

DK: I graduated in 2014. After that, I came to Tata Institute. A PhD student there used to post under the hashtag of "EverydayCasteism," and I really liked it. Many people started using it. I thought we should make this into a page—a larger campaign. So with her permission, both of us started a facebook page with that handle, and started to post daily messages—normal everyday casteist slurs that we hear every day. Things like "Oh, you don't look like a Dalit"; "You can't even speak English. How did you get admitted to this college"?; "You have an iPhone, but you have admission through reservation"; and many other things. On the Facebook page, people used to post submissions, so we started posting those as well. We got messages from some upper-caste readers saying, "Thanks for doing this"; they said they were now aware of what not to do and so on. But when I posted things around reservations, the same upper-caste people started to argue that reservation should be along economic lines and not based on caste and so on.

RG: So it sounds like a lot of what you do is also triggering to you and still you continue to use the social media space to engage Savarna people and challenge their assumptions and biases.

DK: I feel as if I need to do this. My major idea and why I exhaust myself doing this is I somehow feel as if I should engage with Savarnas. Maybe there is a chance that they might change their views. But I get push back from them and see some hypocritical behavior and it hurts.

RG: How did you start making videos with Buzzfeed India?

DK: They approached me. After starting EverydayCasteism on Twitter, I realized it was a very small community. It's very recent for us. There are very few people on Twitter who talk about caste and there is much pushback from Savarna people on Twitter. But when I started work on Twitter, media organizations like Buzzfeed India approached me. So I started making videos for them. This media form can have a larger reach. So I started making videos for Buzzfeed India. One is on mental health, one is on caste in film, one is on casteist slurs, and one is on Savarna feminism. There have been more than eighty thousand views. In India, through mainstream media, I cannot reach such a large audience. Not from my caste and gender location.

RG: Divya, this was an excellent conversation—most informative. I know we have spent several hours talking and there is so much more you've told me. However, we will use some of that for our further cowriting. I look forward to that. I also just noticed that Christina Thomas Dhanaraj tweeted along similar lines—describing her experience being teased and treated badly by other students in school and college. It seems right to end our conversation with a quoting of one of her tweets:

> Dalit women are human beings, period—in that sense, we are not all that different. This means that love, respect, freedom, and everything else that life has to offer is our right. We are beautiful. We are equal. And we deserve to be celebrated every single day. [13]

NOTES

1. Srila Roy, "Lesbian Existence and Marginalization in India, *OUPblog* (blog), Oxford University Press, June 25, 2015, https://blog.oup.com/2015/06/lesbian-marginalization-india/.

2. Note: For further reading on some of the points raised by Dr. Ayyar see Varsha Ayyar, "Caste and Gender in a Mumbai Resettlement Site," *Economic & Political Weekly* 48, no. 18 (May 4, 2013), https://www.epw.in/engage/discussion/caste-and-gender. For Dr. Ayyar's response during the aftermath of #LoSHA in December 2017, see Varsha Ayyar, "Caste-Gender Matrix and the Promise and Practice of Academia," *Economic & Political Weekly* 52, no. 50 (December 16, 2017), https://www.epw.in/node/150602/pdf; Also for a discussion of #LoSHA and #metooIndia in relation to Dalit women, listen to Christina Thomas Dhanaraj, "#MeToo, violence against migrants in Gujarat & more," *Reporters without Orders*, ep. 40, podcast audio, October 11, 2018, https://www.newslaundry.com/2018/10/11/reporters-without-orders-ep-40-metoo-migrants-gujarat-haryana-rohtak?fbclid=IwAR12lv6EmGy4Qrva4PEMWuCI9AVhunLNwMDvk-GuG53iuV5KtqP4wh0h870.

3. Nithila Kanagasabai, "Possibilities of Transformation: Women's Studies in Tier II Cities in Tamil Nadu, India," *Discourse: Studies in the Cultural Politics of Education* 39, no. 5 (2018): 1–15, https://doi.org/10.1080/01596306.2018.1448702.

4. Gopal Guru, "Dalit Women Talk Differently," *Economic & Political Weekly* 30, nos. 41–42 (October 1995): 2548–50, https://www.jstor.org/stable/4403327.

5. Kanagasabai, "Possibilities of Transformation."

6. bell hooks, *Teaching to Transgress: Education as the Practice of Freedom* (New York: Routledge, 1994), 68.

7. *Dharna* refers to a peaceful sit-in protest.

8. Sharmila Rege, *Writing Caste, Writing Gender: Narrating Dalit Women's Testimonials* (Delhi: Zubaan, 2006).

9. Ibid.

10. "Other Backward Caste"

11. see Divya Kandukuri's video on the topic of "How Casteism Leads To Severe Mental Health Problems" for more detail athttps://www.facebook.com/1494596163934604/posts/2021449771249238/

12. "Suicide of Rohith Vemula," Wikipedia, last modified November 30, 2018, https://en.wikipedia.org/wiki/Suicide_of_Rohith_Vemula.

13. Malarăsculat (Christina Thomas Dhanaraj), Twitter post, November 18, 2018, 9:55am, https://twitter.com/caselchris1.

Section II

Chapter Five

Gendered Indian Digital Publics

Digital Streets

Radhika Gajjala

In the 1990s, access to the internet was comparatively limited, and access for women from the Global South was even more limited than it is now. At that time, I was critical of the idea of cyberfeminism being possible through Global South locations.[1] While some of my critiques from that time are still relevant, it is also true that now in 2018, access to the digital—through computers, mobile phones, gaming consoles, tablets, iPads, and several other gadgets—is part of everyday sociality in much of the world through varying degrees of access.[2] In the contemporary digital moment therefore, the phenomenon of women in digital publics has spread globally. This has led to a generation of young women who have become feminist to varying degrees through their digital connectivity. Sujatha Subramanian recounts this process in her contemplation of a comment made by one of her feminist professors about the apathetic and apolitical nature of the younger generations of women. She writes:

> To me, who had always held my peers in high regard for their feminist politics, this came as a surprise. While I would not admit this out loud, I had learnt more about feminist theory through interactions with my friends than I had inside the classroom. Where was this disjunction in opinion coming from? I realised then that while I sought feminist interaction and politically charged conversations with fellow feminists on Facebook, my professor saw the empty streets as evidence of our lack of

113

interest in feminist politics. In the span of a generation, the political actors had not changed, but the space of politics had been transformed.[3]

In addition, even women who may not see themselves as feminist draw inspiration and direction from these digital spaces in their struggle for individual autonomy in their ghar/bahir settings. Thus, these young women live in a pervasive, overall contemporary ethos of entrepreneurial agency and neoliberal empowerment that centers women's autonomy.[4] The interesting result of this move of feminist dialogue and engagement through the digital reveals a generation of young women who are very vocal in their feminisms.

Yet the social and economic divides along class and access lines may be recontoured differently. Can we say these access lines are purely along economic and/or along lines of access to higher education? Are the boundaries along lines of metropolitan versus rural? Are they along boundary lines formed around vernacular languages or English? Where is subalternity shifting to? Who is accessing these spaces? Who are these feminist advocates for Self and subaltern Other along a spectrum of gender and human rights? Who is naming whom as "subaltern"? What hierarchies are implicit even in an apparent quest for the margins from each particular center? These questions emerge in the book as a whole, but the questions are reasserted in this chapter in relation to social media–based activisms from India. These are also questions that are never fully answered and that need to be taken up in further detail and further nuanced in continuing investigations.

This chapter continues the conceptual engagement with digital ghars/bahirs that I began in chapter 1 and focuses the discussion of gendered Indian digital publics on the visible activisms in the digital streets. It considers and thinks through issues and contradictions that emerge in the context of Indian digital activism focused on gender, caste, sexuality, and human rights issues that emerged from 2004 to 2017.[5]

The dialogue interludes in the previous and the following chapters are conversations with feminists and researchers in these digital streets and their attempts to include their voices. Whatever the emerging and/or transformative potential of politics that gendered bodies come into contact with in these spatial and discursive formations, a crucial point to return to is the fact that the body is a focal point for gender and human rights activism in these digital streets. Despite the split placement of corporeal and affective bodies—a seeming out-of-body spontaneity—the body itself also becomes the medium for protest. There are two ways in which the body becomes a medium for protest: one is based in representations of offline communities through discursive and legal frameworks and identity politics. The other way this happens is through organized activities offline based in corporeal meeting spaces. Thus, in looking at digital streets and the centering of the body in online social media activisms, we must keep in mind the online/offline interplay in how the digital space of protest comes into being.[6] As Marwan Kraidy alerts us, we tend to restrict our examination of contemporary activisms in social media to the digital, while forgetting that "social media" is in fact far older and stretches beyond the digital. In his commentary on the body as medium in the context of the Arab spring, for instance, he writes,

> Focusing on platforms instead of processes essentially reduces "communication" to "media" in fundamentally uncritical fashion. Focusing on "new" digital media ignores "old" media—the human body, puppetry, poetry, singing, graffiti—that animated Arab uprisings in Egypt and Syria a century ago, and continue to thrive in recent Arab rebellions and activism worldwide. . . . [E]pisodes of acutely contentious public debate are best understood as *hypermedia* events sustained by permutations of words, sounds and images circulating between a variety of interlocked media platforms—old and new, material and virtual, local and global— that create . . . hypermedia space.[7]

Therefore, the discussions here contribute to investigations along broader questions regarding what sorts of recontourings and disruptions of gender, caste, and class are being fostered and what coalitional practices, if any, are produced and in turn produce these differently mediated activist subjects in such digital publics.[8]

DIGITAL ACTIVISM IN THE SOCIAL MEDIA ERA

Digital activism manifests as a citizen's media paradigm on one hand and a call-out culture on the other. The citizen's media paradigm of access to publics is based in aspirations and hopes that individual citizens and groups of citizens can address structural bias in news reports as well as government and corporate reports. The call out culture that has emerged in social media shapes the tone and performance of much activism in online discursive space. Yet the success of digital activism relies on two factors: the ability to tap into existing virtual communities and the formation of affective publics through networked affects. Further, as Sofia Ashraf suggests in a podcast interview, activists and NGO workers aggressively compete for public attention in social media spaces, not only with each other, but also with multiple other online pursuits and messages.[9] Merely posting something online or tweeting it does not ensure that the message is read and circulated widely. It needs to be amplified and marketed. This resonates with what scholars such as Clifford Bob have already noted about the competitive nature of advocacy work in an era of NGO professionalization and the increased use of social causes as marketing tools for established corporations.[10] What may have begun as a move toward citizen media reporting to counter the hegemony of news organizations has shifted in the case of the NGOs and several feminist digital startups. Digital street activity is increasingly an activity of dissemination of news from various outlets through a series of retweets and expressions of outrage. While these activities have a role in activism, the role is different from that envisioned as a citizen media, alternative format. Further, even feminist startups have begun to compete over visibility and around the creation and dissemination of content. The success of feminist activists and of feminist startups therefore relies on metrics of access, retweeting, and dissemination, just as the success of commercial enterprises and political organizations using social media does. Branding and visibility politics shape digital streets activism and require an intensely competitive framework.

Labor issues emerge in these contexts: contestations occur around the labor of creating hashtags and questions of hashtag ownership, as well as the labor and ownership of developing unique feminist content. The comparatively higher resourced feminist startups (which are backed by international funders, for instance) have the benefit of better-planned campaigns, since they are able to get paid help and organize better.

Thus, just as digital domesticity relies on feminized consumer labor, the digital streets rely on the labor of activist and NGO worker labor that includes careful curation of the content that gets distributed. Elizabeth Losh points out how important the labor around hashtagging, retweeting, and overall content curation is to activist movements. In "Hashtag Feminism and Twitter Activism in India," she examines how organizations such as Blank Noise and Breakthrough used hashtags to curate content during the 2012 activism in response to the Delhi rape case of Jyoti Singh Pandey. Losh observes that such work is "important hashtag activist labor," and important circulation and curation work occurs even through tasks such as the

> retweeting [of] content from feminist power users with large bases of followers such as @Kavita_Krishnan and @UN_Women. The new media ecologies of online social movements are often characterized by a mix of original content generated by specific grassroots activist groups—such as Breakthrough and Blank Noise—and reposted content from like-minded political celebrities or well-established organizations. Similarly, primary and secondary content-creation is often intertwined.[11]

This labor is very much like that of the digital housewife Kylie Jarrett describes, in that it is both affective and behind the scenes. While we might be able to digitally trace and map some of the labor of hashtagging and retweeting and even document the planning of campaigns offline, the labor of victims, their social groups, and associated subaltern groups remains invisible. How might such a reformist, welfarist feminist politics be implicated in what Devaleena Das notes as the "erasure of embodied existence of the Other" and a "purposeful denial of their bodies"?[12] In fact, there is not even an awareness of such support structures and contributors on the part of corporate social responsibility groups and some NGO workers. Because this activism is implicitly and explicitly framed as "giving voice" or as "empowerment" of the subaltern, the subaltern community and the victims' labor in mobilizing the social movement and potential social change is rarely acknowledged. As Brittney Cooper has indicated in her work *Eloquent Rage*, this is a major issue in contemporary neoliberal activisms. She writes, while noting the difference between 1930s radical left organizers and contemporary neoliberal activist organizing, that in the 1930s, the radical left organizers in the United States at least "seemed to understand that if they were going to use Black women's labor to build movements for social change, they had a responsibility to care about the quality of Black women's personal lives."[13]

In contemporary mediascapes—even as Dalit-Bahujan[14] activists on Twitter repeatedly protest the tendency of dominant-caste (Savarna) and upper-class academics, activists, bloggers, and writers to appropriate anti-Brahminical language in order to be viewed as progressive— there is very little acknowledgment of the invisible labor of Dalit-Bahujan communities and activists, or of the transgendered communities whose labor amplifies some of the feminist activism,—from Sa-varna women.

High-profile activists and support organizations still function in a framework of shepherding that privileges a Savarna hierarchy—by default—since infrastructure of access still functions on ideas of "inclusion" that place the onus of change on the underprivileged victim. There is a process of selection (that is sometimes spontaneous and undocumented, but important to consider) of victim stories and causes. For instance, the question has been raised in discussions about how and why the 2012 metropolitan-based rape gave rise to a global explosion of activism and why such massive mobilizations have not occurred around, for instance, one of the many equally violent Dalit women's rapes in rural India.

A major and most obvious reason for the social media–based visibility of the 2012 rape (apart from the brutality of the event and the fact that it happened in the capital city of India) that is often given seems to be that young people in the metropolitan center of India were (and are) more digitally networked through their everyday use of smartphones than those in rural areas. On the other hand, the reason most often given for the lack of visibility of Dalit women's rapes is that rural women are less networked through digital tools in their everyday lives and rely on mainstream media outlets and local activist networks to create protest networks. There is some truth to that, but work by Ayesha Vemuri and Pallavi Guha reveals some nuances related to issues around class, caste, and location, and how both activists and mainstream media responded differently to these two cases. [15]

Guha examines three cases of sexual assault and rape coverage in India with a focus on how these were reported in major Indian newspapers and how access to digital technologies impacted the overall media landscape. [16] Two of the cases she looked at were in metropolitan centers of India—Bangalore and Delhi (this was the Jyoti Singh case); the third case was in Perumbavoor, Kerala, and occurred in 2016. The victim in this third case was a Dalit woman and the rape was as brutal as the Jyoti Singh case. All three cases, Guha writes, were of women brutally raped and killed. Yet this third case failed to get the attention of the media or policy makers in the way that the Delhi rape case did. Guha notes that there were many similarities in terms of the brutality of the incidents. Yet there were differences in how the two cases were reported both in traditional media and through digital activist venues. [17] In mainstream media, the usual suspects of geographical location and caste/class location certainly contributed to more exposure for the 2012 case than for the 2016 case. But, what factors might have shaped the relatively lower level of uptake in the digital streets for the Kerala case? What contributed to the comparatively fewer number of activists willing to perform the techno-mediated labor required to publicize this event? Why didn't this event carry the kind of social value for activists seeking to create visible social movements around social issues that the Jyoti Singh case did? The Dalit identity of Jisha was repeatedly focused on by mainstream media and digital activists, said Pallavi Guha during our Skype conversations as we continued to discuss her work.[18] Jisha was being stalked in the lead-up to her rape, but her complaint was ignored by police, who claimed that a Dalit woman would find it difficult to get support to fight against sexual violence. The media too did not engage in the kind of activism that they did in the case of the Delhi Rape case (that of Nirbhaya) of 2012. There were no quotes from celebrities and hardly any visibility in social media.

Thus, as I proceed to discuss some of the digital platforms for activism and acknowledge the good work they are doing, the contradiction to keep in mind is that the victims' families and communities of support contribute to the labor of making events visible.

There is also considerable subaltern labor and visualization of subaltern images mobilized as a strategy to foster affective connectivity needed for the building of momentum toward digital activism as much as the technical labor building the campaign through digital know-how and access. The process of building a digital social movement, therefore, is based in multiple layers of offline engagement.[19] Further, each movement that uses digital tools in its advocacy and activism should be viewed in context. Thus, while it is true that, as in the case of the Egyptian or Tunisian activists interviewed by Ramesh Srinivasan, activists in the physical streets function under different conditions of physical vulnerability than the activists that use social media, the one does not necessarily need to discount the other as "slacktivism" or as ineffective. Each has its role. "Slacktivism" is not what digital activists who use social media tools strategically do, so it is unfair to conflate the two—the slactivist followers of activism and the digital activists implement a well-thought-out campaign that works with offline strategies. As noted by David Wolman in his article about Egyptian activists using social media:

The ease of participation cuts both ways. At first glance, this form of online activism might seem ineffectual, even frivolous—a brand of sacrifice-free protest sometimes derided as "slactivism."[20]

However social media's combined potential of reaching large external audiences through global leisure spaces as well as reaching unexpected local audiences through small screens can lead to the mobilizing of large groups. This contributed to shifts in public opinion and awareness. Differing and unexpected forms of physical street activisms are enacted. Such impact was observed in a movement during the mid 2000s—prior to even the now famous Delhi rape protests of 2012. The power of the small screen messaging was evident in local contexts of activism in the Jessica Lal case. News reports combined with effective mobilization of text messaging unleashed large crowds of protests leading to the reopening of a case against Jessica Lal's murderer, who had been acquitted.[21]

Further, in some instances, the digirati mobilize social media with a primary goal of reaching global audiences while local activisms occur in the streets and through other forms of media. There is also extensive local use of digital tools by activists to stay networked as well. As noted by Bahujan feminist activist Divya Kandukuri in my interview with her, the use of digital tools has to be considered alongside the physical space–based organizing that happens—whether in trying to understand digital activisms or in trying to "overcome the conceptual gaps in feminist theorizations of empowerment and violence." Richa Nagar's point that it is only "serious engagement with social spaces in grass-roots activism [that] . . . enable[s] us to . . . apprehend more adequately the nature, content, and meanings of women's political actions" must be recognized.[22]

DIGITAL STREETS

In celebrating its ten-year anniversary in March 2017, Twitter listed the ten most influential hashtags centered on social justice movements. These were ranked by frequency of usage. The contradiction inherent to digital activism: the corporation benefits from activism, regardless of the message of the activity. The more conflict around a particular hashtag there is on the platform itself, the more the usage statistics improve. Regardless of whether the activist use of the platform benefits or oppresses the subaltern sphere, Twitter benefits. There is no morality to this success. Yet, as several activists have noted in their conversations with me and in their posts on Twitter, this is a contradiction they are willing to work with because the platform affords them a way to reach a global audience for their advocacy efforts. Thus the logic underpinning the use of social media is the same whether an activist group is using it or a corporation is using it for its marketing campaign.

Digital streets, therefore, are where corporate marketing/branding, NGO advocacy, human rights activists, right-wing and left-wing radical groups, Dalit-Bahujan activists, feminist activists, transgender activists, queer activists, and others come together, interwoven with the personal and leisure use of social media. Yet whether we see these social media spaces as political or not varies with how we as the users selectively engage the tools; therefore, as noted earlier, these same tools can be used in digital domesticity and in other kinds of leisurely social activity. The tone is what defines the space rather than the platform for engagement. Facebook, blogs, Tumblr, Instagram—these all contribute to digital streets depending on how they are used. WhatsApp, too, lends itself to being a tool of digital street activism. But Twitter tends to reveal more characteristics of digital street interaction than any other platform at this moment in internet history. As noted in chapter 1, digital domesticity is produced through particular kinds of affective exchanges around topics that generate feelings of comfort, companionship, and "home." Digital domesticity also manifests in the sharing of information around homemaking activities including cooking, childcare, and elder-care. Digital street activity, on the other hand, is focused on advocacy and protest.

While internet-based activism has existed since the Internet became accessible to the larger publics with users beyond specialized scientific communities, global modes of digital activisms with their global access points and potential for citizen media reporting emerged visibly after about 2005. Thus we saw moves to build blogging communities around citizen media reporting. For instance, in an effort to bring together a platform for global digital activisms with a view to highlight Global South activisms, Rebecca McKinnon and Ethan Zuckerman began the citizen media platform Global Voices in the year 2005 (https://globalvoices.org/). In India, individuals and groups created blogging communities such as Kafila.online for critical engagement with contemporary events. This blogging, though, has been mostly in English, and so this narrows down the readership. Even so, there has been video blogging, such as that by the "Video Volunteers" (https://www.videovolunteers.org).

The sharing of blog posts through Twitter and Facebook became regular practice for those NGOs, activists, and journalists who were quick to incorporate social media into their daily routines. Even though the concept of blogging—through weblogs and on personal websites—was prevalent since 1995 when the World Wide Web opened up through the hypertext markup language (HTML), blogging became more global after platforms such as LiveJournal became popular among the youth of that time. LiveJournal was an early social networking platform—a precursor of sites such as Friendster, Myspace, Orkut, and Facebook—where bloggers functioned as a community rather than solely as individuals by adding friends, sharing posts, and commenting. Subsequently, easy to use weblog templates offered up by services such as WordPress, TypePad, and Blogspot (later acquired by Google) became easier and available for free to a larger public:

> According to Google Trends, the public interest in the term "blog" peaked in 2009 and has been steadily declining since then (Google Trends 2016). Platforms such as Blogspot and LiveJournal, while still used by networked audiences globally, are superseded by newer social media platforms and mobile apps, such as Snapchat and Instagram, built around instant messaging and microblogging.[23]

Parallel to the growth of the blogosphere and the availability of social media tools such as Myspace, Facebook, and Twitter, YouTube also appeared on the global scene. It was through this blogosphere, linked with social media outlets such as Facebook and Twitter, that what we now see as digital activism emerged with its tone of spontaneity and calls for action. In India these tools became more mainstreamed by activists and journalists after an anti-corruption social movement in 2011.

Yet, as Zizi Papacharissi and Maria de Fatima Oliveira note, the use of social media by journalists is most effective when they engage with "*premediated* situations where the story is changing so quickly that TV or print media do not have the time to develop a fully sourced story" rather than merely forward traditional news articles converted into digital formats.[24] This is where the labor of "digital natives" and populations with technical know-how and an understanding of global marketing began to be mobilized by activists, NGOs, government publicists, and news organizations.

Globally, digital streets activism came powerfully into public notice during the "Arab Spring" protests. There are other highly visible social justice campaigns that are also notable as having been effective, such as the Black Lives Matter movement. These contributed to the development of a process and the standardizing of best practices for the implementation of digital activism through the strategic use of social media platforms. As Zeynep Tufekci and Christopher Wilson note:

> Since the "Arab Spring" burst forth in uprisings in Tunisia and in Egypt in early 2011, scholars have sought to understand how the Internet and social media contribute to political change in authoritarian regimes. Perspectives range across the full spectrum from those who view the Internet as potentially disruptive (Aday et al., 2010; Howard, 2010) to those who argue that it may even support authoritarian regimes (Morozov, 2011).[25]

Overall, both in existing literature and in the interviews I conducted (including the dialogues), it is clear that there is no consensus around whether or not the term "activism" can be used and whether the label "activist" can be applied to those who are using social media tools for advocacy and campaigning if they are not also on the physical streets experiencing tear gas and baton beatings (or "lathi charge" in the Indian street context). I would argue, however, that being immersed in the use of digital media is a form of *living in digital place*. Granted the experience of being in place and being placed in digital streets is different, the embodiment and vulnerability experienced is less immediate and differently tactile. Yet it is a physical and embodied placement of the self in a digital public, visible and potentially within interactive reach.[26] Indeed as Christina Dhanaraj notes in her dialogue with me in chapter 8, the tweeting body can disconnect, but bodies on the physical streets cannot. But, just because a person has been on the physical streets and participated perhaps in a few protest marches, being on the streets alone does not qualify someone as a lifelong activist. This is a much larger discussion looping back to the points I raised in the introduction to the book. Later chapters—particularly the dialogues—explore some aspects.

INDIAN FEMINISTS OUT ON THE DIGITAL STREETS

In October–November 2017 the Indian digital feminist spaces exploded with debate around what came to be known as #LoSHA (a list of sexual harassers in the academy—specifically Indian academics). This list originated on the Facebook wall of law student Raya Sarkar (now "Raya Steier") and then traveled as a Google Doc where others could anonymously add to it. This was a moment of high visibility and debate in the Indian feminist discourse. The "digital streets" became alive with open debate in a larger Indian feminist community in a way that some earlier social media–based feminist campaigns such as Blank Noise campaigns, Pink Chaddi, Why Loiter, and Girls at Dhabas did not.

In 2012, the social media–based global visibility of Delhi rape protests was made possible through the use of Global North–oriented/ situated social media platforms such as Facebook and Twitter. In 2016, the digitally public visibility of the death of a Dalit student Rohit Vemula[27] on social media marks a moment of global visibility of issues around caste discrimination in Indian academic structures. But #LoSHA produced visible debate and made visible ruptures in received narratives of "Indian feminism." Two things happened in discussions and debates around #LoSHA in 2017 (I mark 2017, because in 2018, exactly a year later, #metooindia brings back discussions and questions about #LoSHA as well) on the Indian digital Twittersphere: first, there was a renewed sense of discovery of "empowerment" through digital feminism; and second, discussions emerged around whether or not mainstream Indian feminist movements were truly "intersectional" or not.[28]

Thus for instance, in the #LoSHA discussions, Dalit feminist voices were highlighted. Statements coming from activists such as Thenmouzhi Sounderarajan (aka Dalit Diva) that rejected dominant-caste and upper-class academic frameworks (such as those of the subaltern studies collective) and favored connecting with African American feminist networks were retweeted and circulated. To be clear: Dalit-Bahujan feminist activism online is not new—neither is Dalit-Bahujan presence online recent.[29] However, as Padmini Ray Murray notes, mainstream media reports and characterizations of feminisms in India routinely omit significant Dalit-Bahujan feminist online platforms (such as Savari and Dalit Women Fight) and rural feminist organizations staffed by women from non-dominant-caste communities. These presences are often "only mentioned [in the media] as an afterthought following a talking head snippet advocating the need for intersectionality."[30] Further, as Timothy Loftus notes, Dalit feminism faces "a larger problem in the academy in which Dalit intellectual production is ghettoized."[31]

#LoSHA was an activist moment that centered on problems of gender and caste in Indian educational institutions. Caste issues in the context of higher educational institutions in India are different from caste/class issues that emerge when dealing with concerns that surface in spaces where the victims are illiterate or literate only in regional languages. Caste and gender—more than class—were at play here, even though many opponents of #LoSHA still keep raising questions of class. The Dalit-Bahujan students' experience of the educational institutions in India is conveniently overlooked in such questionings of class location.

The ensuing discussions around #LoSHA invite feminists of South Asian descent to interrogate assumptions about who an activist is; what the object of activism should be; and, how and when activism is legitimized. We also encounter questions regarding the victim's autonomy and the evaluation of evidence. As Arpita Chakraborty notes, discourses of sexual violence have been based on "the presence of a victim, [with] a surviving body as the evidence of survival."[32] In the case of the list, however, the bodies of the victims/survivors remained hidden while the voices and autonomy of the victims were heard loud and clear. They were not asking to be represented by savior activists—even though Raya Sarkar's name is visible in a facilitator role.[33]

Further, the move of post-2010 activisms to social media space has not left the body behind. Online is not "virtual" offline and is not the only "reality." Neither are "online" and "offline" mutually exclusive ways of being and interacting. Rather, we see different kinds of activisms based not only on access to the internet and to gadgets but also on a potential for visible victim autonomy through these spaces. Even as the accessing of digital publics might occur through physical space-based subterfuge these women and non-binary people, as well as other marginalized groups (whether because of caste, disability, race, or some other unnamed category), find ways to express themselves publicly through individual voice. They have discursive presence as agents. To quote Adrija Dey,

> the participation and involvement of "the individual" in gender activism
> has resulted in a wide range of ideas, thoughts and opinions in the
> activist space. . . . [W]ith social media, there is a fundamental shift from

activists leading the discourse or the activism carried out by non-profits to represent others, to individuals carrying out their activism on their own terms. [34]

Upon interviewing several digital feminist activists and social media based influencers around issues of gender, geography, sexuality, caste and class - such as Jasmeen Patheja (Blank Noise collective), Shilpa Phadke (#WhyLoiter), Raya Steier (#LoSHA), Sukhnidh Kaur (Qitaab zine), Noopur Tiwari (genderlogindia, smashboard), Divya Kandukuri (EverydayCasteism), Christina Thomas Dhanraj, Ditilekha Sharma[35] and also the young women behind the Pakistani site Girls at Dhabas, I learned about their process. In actuality this process is fairly generic and standardized and works very much as such a process in mainstream public relations, marketing, or strategic communication campaigns would. The process is shaped by access to financial resources and to people willing to put in the work. Thus, their process is the result of a neoliberalizing logic that is almost ubiquitous. Yet not all of these activists make the same kinds of market-oriented arguments. [36] In the case of the individualizing of Dalit-Bahujan female voices online, it is suggested that perhaps these writings have a "different lineage of foregrounding the individual and individual autonomy than that in neoliberalism."[37]

Time, literacy, capital, and value for exchange of work/labor (even when labor was offered up as voluntary "free labor") were key factors. Capital of course includes access to digital gadgets as well as wireless and internet services. I also interviewed women who were not working from metropolitan areas who were digital natives and working on regional-language Wikipedia editing projects. They saw this editing work as feminist and also as a form of non-Western intervention into the politics of knowledge creation online. Some of those interviewed participated in dialogue interludes featured in chapter 9.

In the context of Indian digital feminist activism, the history of social media use for activism is usually traced back to 2003 when Blank Noise was formed as a response to street harassment. Blank Noise is an artist collective that is currently described on its website, BlankNoise.org, as "a community of '*Action Heroes*,' individuals and citizens united to eradicate gender based and sexual violence." In fact, Trishima Mitra-Kahn even goes so far as to say that later Indian digital activists "are enabled by Blank Noise's pioneering efforts to break the silence on public sexual harassment and prise open various dialogic spaces."[38]

Examining these campaigns in their early stages through "the minutiae of the ethnographic field," Mitra-Kahn describes how contemporary middle/upper-class women emerged as political citizens using social media tools.[39] Noting that an "affirmative, hopeful, playful politics" emerged through such movements,[40] she argues that they also contest "the multiple hegemonies that regulate the corporeality of middle-class women's gendered lives."[41] The Pinjra Tod (break the cage) movement and the Pink Chaddi movement, for instance, attest to this point. In interviews I have conducted with various such digital feminists, I have noted a mix of anger and playfulness in the way that they engage digital tools for protest. These movements mark the beginnings of social media–based Indian digital feminisms and highlight a particular set of online and offline activist processes and logics of labor and affective networking.

While Mitra-Kahn's work is centered on noting activist subjectivity and how that shapes digital activist spaces, Losh notes the reliance of this public activism and feminist discourse on the labor of producing "shared terminology in metadata"; in looking at labor issues, she particularly

> focuses on the informational labor of two specific activist groups in India—Breakthrough and Blank Noise—and how careful hashtag use reflected their policy decisions and deliberative activities about metadata management, which is becoming an increasingly important aspect of transformative social movements that bring citizens out into the streets.[42]

Sonora Jha, on the other hand, compares the #WhyLoiter campaign with earlier campaigns of #SlutWalk and #BlankNoise to "examine the political choice of this campaign to foreground pleasure in public space."[43]

Examining some of these same movements in her master's thesis, Ayesha Vemuri focuses on three particular campaigns around rape and domestic violence. She delves deep into the very construction of the victimhood while critically examining how such campaigns contribute to "transnational discourse(s) about Indian women's safety or lack thereof."[44] She notes how the fact that all three campaigns address middle-class audiences who are English speaking limits them locally in relation to subaltern populations, but it also allows them to be visible

internationally. The labor in putting forth the activist material therefore
is implicitly West oriented. Vemuri observes:

> [T]he creative and symbolic elements that grab attention on social me-
> dia and encourage users to like, share, comment and participate in these
> campaigns [and] [t]he images used in these works simultaneously situ-
> ate [the campaigns] as being specifically Indian and talking about In-
> dian femininity, whilst also being readable by global audiences. [45]

This element of readability by global audiences seems key to all forms
of digital activisms, and therefore, structural elements limit subaltern
access to these spaces of activism.

Pallavi Guha takes the thinking around hashtag activism to examine
why certain hashtags do not "trend" and highlights the uneven resources available to rural and subaltern feminist activists. In her research on feminists working in rural India, she found that while they
work effectively with mainstream media, the potential for these activist
movements to enter global digital streets is more difficult than for
urban, metropolitan-based feminists even though they share common
ground in terms of experience and responses to issues such as sexual
harassment. Guha notes that

> for the feminist activists from the rural areas, networking is less on
> social media networks and more on community networking. Rather
> these rural feminists organize through open spaces—courtyards. They
> network in their villages with one another and look for solutions to their
> problems. Similarly, Sampat said that girls in her organization meet
> regularly to discuss their issues and try to help and give support to each
> other. Their personal experiences moved from personal to political, and
> networked spaces. [46]

Here we are reminded once again of Kraidy's point about how a focus
on new "digital media ignores 'old' media—the human body, puppetry,
poetry, singing, graffiti." [47] Yet, we must be careful about drawing ro-
manticized binaries between these village courtyard gatherings and
gatherings around digital tools.

A point to be noted is that while some of these points ring true in
terms of process even for Dalit-Bahujan activists in social media
space—their use is distinctly different and deeply rooted in community
formation (offline and online). Further, allies are requested to amplify
Dalit-Bahujan voices but are discouraged from speaking for them.
Most often, they use the opportunity to connect to subaltern commu-

nities to develop transnational activist connections.[48] They thus write what Pramod Nayar terms alternative global histories, "where linkages across geography and geopolitical boundaries based on a shared vulnerability and suffering are possible through new media."[49] Dalit-Bahujan feminists, for instance, identify more clearly with African American feminists than with postcolonial and transnational feminists of South Asian origin. Dalit Diva,[50] a transmedia artist, for instance, states a preference for African American and Latina feminists in the following Twitter thread in response to questions about Spivak's "Can the Subaltern Speak."[51] They wrote:

> A11. For me #Bellhooks, #GloriaAnzaldua, #AudreLorde, #Derrick-Bell, #Cornellwest #chinua achebe #kimberlycrenshaw are all so crucial for me. #WriteBackFightBack #WriteBackFightBack
> A11. I also want to flag that for South Asian folks often people lift up post-colonial writers like #GayatriSpivak as other sources. But from the #DalitBahujan perspective many of the #postcolonial thinkers were uncritical about their hegemonies of #caste. #WriteBackFightBack
> A11. That is why when folks ask me about #Canthesubalternspeak, I roll my eyes. Why would I accept my own denigration in trying to imagine tools for my freedom. Sub to whom I would ask, and who would write that positionality? #WriteBackFightBack[52]

Varsha Ayyar, in her dialogue interview with me (included in chapter 4), points out, for instance, that

> Dalits (ex-untouchables) and African Americans have a lot in common—especially their lived experiences under caste/race, their resistance and the long struggle for the civil rights are eerily similar. And these two social groups historically have extended their solidarities with each other and continue to build bridges to carry forward these conversations of the two remarkable and greatest struggles in the human history.[53]

The process of digital activism relies on a lot of intensive offline labor—both paid and unpaid, visible and invisible. The offline processes and engagements may be different in terms of how space is occupied and how digital tools are mobilized, but digital street activism does not occur without offline processes, deliberation, and planning. I point to the rural women feminist scenario not to binarize the offline and online as mutually exclusive—rather to point to degrees of access to digital and other mediated publics. The rural feminists cannot bypass main-stream media as easily as the urban feminists.

MORE ON THE QUESTION OF THE SUBALTERN
IN DIGITAL ACTIVISM

Gayathri Spivak's well-known intervention into the project of Subal-tern Studies attempts to reveal the "domain of the popular."[54] While commendable in the 1980s, this approach does not adequately take up issues of the gendered subaltern or of Dalit-Bahujan subalternity. It does not in itself redress the caste-related silence of Indian feminisms of this generation. Nilsen and Roy therefore ask, "So how can we think about subalternity in an alternative way?"[55] They suggest that instead of assuming there is only one way to look at the issue of subaltern agency in an either/or binary, we must understand that subalternity is

> (a) relational—that is, subalternity is above all a positionality of adverse incorporation in a certain set of socio-historical power relations; (b) intersectional—that is, subalternity is constituted along several axes of power, whose specific empirical form must be deciphered in concrete empirical settings; and (c) dynamic—subalternity does not preclude agency, but agency arises and develops within and in relation to domi-nant discourses and political forms.[56]

This relational, intersectional, and dynamic subalternity, however, is visible more in some digital publics rather than in others. Spivak her-self has also urged intellectuals to unlearn their privilege and has sug-gested that such unlearning may lead to relational understandings of subalternity. Yet we must be careful when we talk of intersectionality and relationality from a location as (possibly) dominant-caste and mid-dle- to upper-class academics whether situated in the Western acade-my, where we become people of color and experience forms of margi-nalization through travel into Western spaces, or situated in India, where we retain our caste/class privilege without being compelled to unlearn this privilege in everyday practice. We need to be mindful of the locations through which we are naming intersections and relation-ships. Thus far, Indian theorizing around subalternity is still occurring through an academic space occupied predominantly by dominant-caste men and women even if their politics are left of center and progressive.

This hierarchy of knowledge production is made more evident as it is countered and contested actively in digital streets by Dalit-Bahujan intellectuals, artists, and activists who do indeed have a lot to say.[57] While it may be argued that the fact that they have access to the internet and have the language with which to protest means that they are no longer "subaltern," the truth, as we know, is that Dalits in India continue to occupy a subaltern position structurally in the Indian national context—but "subaltern" may not be the word we should be using. Structurally and historically oppressed peoples shouldn't have to "prove" their "subalternity" in fighting for rights for their communities. The question "can the subaltern speak" traps historically oppressed community members in an individualistic framework—where they either speak as individuals and then get considered as merged within spaces of privilege or they remain as visible named "subaltern" victims. "Speaking" from oppressed communities is enacted in varied forms— whether as individuals or as a community. The Dalit-Bahujan or Adivasi woman, who has been violently abused, raped, and killed hardly ever gains media visibility, yet, witness how the death of the University of Hyderabad Dalit doctoral student Rohith Vemula opened up a space for the public visibility and speech of his mother Radhika Vemula.[58] In addition, it is important to note, as Nayar reminds us, that central to Dalit presences online is "the construction of a different, or alternative, history of India."[59] Thus, as a historically oppressed community in India, Dalit-Bahujan communities are formed online by speaking in global contexts where they potentially align with other historically oppressed groups, such as African American communities in the United States. As Nayar notes:

> Dalit activism when it goes online enables a transnational subaltern project, seeking and establishing links with sympathizers, activists, NGOs, transnational organizations as well as with other histories of oppression—the blacks, mainly, but also African Americans. Thus the "alternative history" . . . must be redefined as "alternative global history" where linkages across geography and geopolitical boundaries based on a shared vulnerability and suffering are possible through new media.[60]

In the context of digital Dalit activism, and in a manner similar to Tamil Eelam networks of the 1990s and early 2000s, online Dalit presences are moving toward exploiting digital connectivity "in order to constitute a citizenry and nationality without territorial confines."[61]

Does the fact of global access through digital tools make them "digirati" and thus potentially negate the authenticity of Dalit-Bahujans and Adivasis as "subaltern"?[62] The issue of subaltern agency and voice in this instance—as in the instance of Black Twitter—is nuanced.[63] The access to and use of digital tools is not unilaterally elite anymore. Further, we know that in the United States, the case of Black Twitter defies all notions of digital access being restricted to elite populations.

According to a 2013 Pew study, African Americans at that time were one of the three top Twitter user groups.[64] This is sometimes seen as surprising precisely because the African American community is considered to be subaltern. Yet as we know by now, Black Twitter is a reality and is a collective where primarily African American Twitter users engage in community building online. As André Brock notes:

> Twitter's discourse conventions, ubiquity, and social features encouraged increased Black participation; Black Twitter is Twitter's mediation of Black cultural discourse, or "signifyin'" (Gates, 1983). In particular, Black hashtag signifying revealed alternate Twitter discourses to the mainstream and encourages a formulation of Black Twitter as a "social public"; a community constructed through their use of social media by outsiders and insiders alike.[65]

In the Indian context the Dalit-Bahujan Twitter similarly serves as a protest zone.[66]

Contemporary Dalit activism in digital space, however, is different from the kinds of staged subalternity on philanthropy websites and in marketing campaigns about the empowerment of women, people of color, and poor populations from the Global South that my team and I have written about elsewhere. The trope of "subaltern" is mobilized to market products—thus the term itself comes to have market value.[67]

Starting with B. R. Ambedkar's leadership, we know that Dalit resistance has been asserted in forms of the burning of the Manusmriti or later the burning of nationalist-era Hindi writer Premchand's novel *Rangbhumi*. There is already a strong postnationalist movement of Dalits in India and there are contestations around "standards of 'authenticity'" as applied "to Dalit identity and experience as well as contested standards of legitimacy for literary representations of a Dalit perspective."[68] Against such a background of already existing debates and struggles around Dalit-Bahujan identity and activism, the social media–based Dalit-Bahujan presence further subverts the either/or framing of subaltern agency. In this regard, Gyanendra Pandey suggests a conceptualization of the "subaltern as subaltern citizen" as he examines both African American and Dalit subaltern locations while reminding us that there are "different locations of subalternity" and that it is important that the subaltern not be presented as ahistorical and static and as merely acted upon rather than being an actor through diverse nuanced and contradictory modes of action and speech. [69]

This tendency to approach subaltern and gendered agency as static and within an either/or framework is also critiqued by Nishant Shah in his thought-provoking essay that lays out the contradictions emerging from digital gender. He writes of the need to "relocate agency and question the paradigm of the body as actor/the body as acted upon that is invoked in thinking of body-technology relationships." [70]

Shah describes how a video of two underage students from Delhi that went viral in 2004 initiated discussions focused on the young woman out in public, thus marking the digital public as an "outside"—a *bahir*. This, he notes, is a precursor to the attitudes and actions of the right-wing Ram Sena goons who suggested that young women out in public with their male romantic partners on Valentine's Day were "empowered by access to the Internet and cell phones, have become sluts and . . . have been corrupted by technologies." [71] In response to this violence, the Pink Chaddi campaign, one of the early Indian digital feminist campaigns in the social media era, emerged.

EMPOWERMENT AND/OR ACTIVISM THROUGH THE DIGITAL

Over the past three decades of shifts, Global South feminisms have spearheaded the transnationalization of struggles around both subaltern and metropolitan middle-class women's autonomy, integrating the language of feminism into their local, national, religious, ethnic, racial, and caste contexts. The increased use of information communication technologies (ICTs) and digital financialization have had a significant role in this shift—as have the increasing "NGOization" of feminist movements. [72] This has resulted in a different attitude than the postcolonial Indian national attitude to feminism as "Western." As I observed through my engagement with women NGO workers in India in the late 1990s and early 2000s, there was a visible struggle around feminism as a mode of empowerment versus what was viewed as a broader framework of livelihood promotion in rural areas. For instance in 1998, while my coauthor and I were writing an article for the journal *Gender and Development*, we positioned ourselves in a binarized dialogue between activist and academic.[73] This binary, once again, is a problematic and even false binary, but at that time it reflected generalized feelings that NGO workers in India were doing the "real" work while academics (especially Indian academics based in the Western academy) were seen as merely theorizing armchair feminists. This works as a move to delegitimize particular kinds of academic heuristic methodologies and voices of critique that seek to move these dialogues beyond instrumentality and functions to silence particular kinds of questions. The politics around deployment of the discourse of subaltern autonomy in the service of invisibilized neo-colonial global hierarchies—through decentralization and neoliberalization—lead to further precariousness of the subaltern individual. In resituating the NGO space as activist and in opposition to a so-called unified academic space, the NGO can be more clearly positioned to receive funding from governments that require an elision of caste or race identity politics and histories in the way they work to create supposed spaces for individualized subaltern autonomy. Human rights struggles and discourse begin to work within anachronistic frameworks of essentialized identities that in turn feed into the production of digital algorithms, law, and public policy.

Thus, the pressure for NGO workers and corporate social responsibility (CSR) organizations to move beyond "petty" academic feminist politics is part of the move toward the neoliberal appropriation of the idea of women's empowerment and is situated in a complex interplay of market economy logics. This results in increased shouldering of debt by women and the recruiting of women from the informal sector into the modern waged labor force. The contest is over who "empowers"—with the word empowerment coming to refer to moments of mainstream access and individualist autonomy of women only to the extent that they become recognizable economic and consumer subjects within neoliberal modernity.

Twenty years ago, though, when I was writing with an NGO worker, this was also a moment when transnational feminists and women of color in Western countries were amplifying their protest against the exclusionary politics of liberal feminisms and white/Western feminisms. Thus, what my NGO coauthor (who since then has moved into being an academic herself) was saying resonated with me on another level. On the whole, though, the simple performative binary of academic versus NGO field worker served as a useful rhetorical and methodological tool. Based in her location of negotiating for the livelihood of communities in a rural context, my NGO worker coauthor viewed feminism as exclusionist in its definition.[74] This moment thus signals a reading of feminism in some NGO spaces based more on entry points into the NGO space than on a generation/age-based "postfeminist" response to feminism even though some of the language resonates with postfeminist accusations regarding feminisms in the 1990s.

This moment is characterized in the history of Indian feminisms also by the increasing NGOization of women's movements, which has resulted in "an ontology of relatedness (a 'relational ontology', Go 2013) that makes it difficult to posit the local, nation, home and self as stable categories outside of the global and transnational."[75] In fact, what we see is an emergence of "woman as theater," commented upon by Spivak in reference to the 1995 United Nations Fourth World Conference on Women in Beijing. Transnational nonprofit organizations, Global South NGOs, and westernized corporate philanthropy organizations, for instance, put "women's empowerment on display."[76]

"Gender empowerment" as a term is mobilized by Global South NGOs and various development organizations (with "gender" referring to cisgender women only) in order to access funding from international NGOs and philanthropic organizations, since the narrative of the oppressed third-world woman carries a certain accepted valence in a continuing neocolonial framework within such settings. This sort of gender empowerment also serves to elide issues around race, caste, sexuality, and transgendered identities and makes "women's issues" an acceptable framework for extreme right-wing political formations as well, where the empowerment of women has symbolic power and autonomy for women only within a particular caste hierarchy.[77]

The engagement of the idea of "empowerment" is also recognizably more complex in contemporary times. No longer does it suffice to ask if empowerment happens. We need to ask if empowerment is sustained and also ask at whose expense this individual empowerment occurs. While some NGO and corporate social responsibility–based women's empowerment projects are shaped around so-called women's empowerment as an end goal, activists and vocal feminist academics in online and offline spaces are not shy about being vocal about the contingency of this very particular kind of reportable empowerment as end-goal.

CONCLUSION

In this chapter I mapped concepts and literature relevant to discussions of digital feminist activism in the Indian context. While chapter 1 discussed the ghar/bahir framework of postnational and postcolonial Indian and Indian diasporic women's movements, this chapter focused on discussions around "digital streets." Chapter 6 is a dialogue interlude that serves to push against and nuance while also elaborating on the frameworks from both chapter 1 and the present chapter.

NOTES

1. Radhika Gajjala, "'Third World' Perspectives on Cyberfeminism," *Development in Practice* 9, no. 5 (1999): 616–19, http://www.jstor.org/stable/23317590.
2. See Radhika Gajjala, ed., *Cyberculture and the Subaltern: Weavings of the Virtual and Real* (Lanham, MD: Lexington Books, 2012); Radhika Gajjala, *Online Philanthropy in the Global North and South: Connecting, Microfinancing, and Gaming for Change* (Lanham, MD: Lexington Books, 2017).
3. Sujatha Subramanian, "From the Streets to the Web: Looking at Feminist Activism on Social Media." Review of Women's Studies, *Economic & Political Weekly* 50, no. 17 (April 25, 2015): 71.
4. Aradhana Sharma, *Logics of Empowerment: Development, Gender, and Governance in Neoliberal India* (Minneapolis: University of Minnesota Press, 2008).
5. Relevant scholarship includes: Trishima Mitra-Kahn, "Offline Issues, Online Lives? The Emerging Cyberlife of Feminist Politics in Urban India," in *New South Asian Feminisms: Paradoxes and Possibilities*, ed. Srila Roy (London: Zed Books, 2012), 108–30; Sonora Jha, "Gathering Online, Loitering Offline: Hashtag Activism and the Claim for Public Space by Women in India through the #whyloiter Campaign," in *New Feminisms in South Asian Social Media, Film, and Literature*, ed. Sonora Jha and Alka Kurian (New York: Routledge, 2018), 63–84.
6. Kandukuri, personal communication with author, 2018.
7. Marwan M. Kraidy, "The Body as Medium in the Digital Age: Challenges and Opportunities," *Communication and Critical/Cultural Studies* 10, nos. 2–3 (2013): 286, doi: 10.1080/14791420.2013.815526.
8. I thank my colleague Michaela Walsh for listening carefully to my incoherent description of earlier versions of this chapter and for raising these points.
9. Radhika Gajjala and Sofia Ashraf, "Cyberfeminism and Content Creation," by Ian M. Cook, *Online Gods*, no. 6, podcast audio, March 2, 2018, https://www.stitcher.com/podcast/online-gods/e/53542877.
10. Clifford Bob, *The Marketing of Rebellion: Insurgents, Media, and International Activism* (New York: Cambridge University Press, 2005).
11. Elizabeth Losh, "Hashtag Feminism and Twitter Activism in India," *Social Epistemology Review and Reply Collective* 3, no. 12 (2014): 18, http://wp.me/p1Bfg0-1Kx.
12. For discussion of reformist, welfarist feminist politics, see, Nandini Deo, *Mobilizing Religion and Gender in India: The Role of Activism* (New York: Routledge, 2015); also see: Rajeswari Sunder Rajan, *The Scandal of the State: Women, Law, and Citizenship in Postcolonial India* (Durham, NC: Duke University Press, 2003); Devalee-

na Das, "Resisting Sexual Violence and Thinking beyond Due Process" (paper presentation, National Women's Studies Association, Atlanta, GA, November 9, 2018).

13. Brittney Cooper, *Eloquent Rage: A Black Feminist Discovers Her Superpower* (New York: St. Martin's Press, 2018), 195.

14. I do sometimes switch from Dalit-Bahujan to Dalit and vice versa—depending on who's work I am quoting from and how they use the terms—but in general I have tried to stick to the hyphenated form of Dalit-Bahujan. For explanation of this usage, see Valliammal Karunakaran, "The Dalit-Bahujan Guide to Understanding Caste in Hindu Scripture," *Medium*, July 13, 2016, https://medium.com/@Bahujan_Power/the-dalit-bahujan-guide-to-understanding-caste-in-hindu-scripture-417db027fce6.

15. Ayesha Vemuri, "After Nirbhaya: Anti-Sexual Violence Activism and the Politics of Transnational Social Media Campaigns" (master's thesis, McGill University, 2016), http://digitool.library.mcgill.ca/webclient/StreamGate?folder_id=0&dvs=1521324901089~502; Pallavi Guha, "Mind the Gap: Connecting News and Information to Build an Agenda Against Rape and Sexual Assault in India" (PhD diss., University of Maryland, 2017).

16. Guha looked specifically at coverage in the *Times of India* and the *Hindustan Times.*

17. Guha, "Mind the Gap."

18. Pallavi Guha, personal correspondence with author, 2018.

19. Kraidy, "The Body as Medium in the Digital Age: Challenges and Opportunities." *Communication and Critical/Cultural Studies* 10, nos. 2–3 (2013): 285–90, doi: 10.1080/14791420.2013.815526; Ramesh Srinivasan, "Bridges between Cultural and Digital Worlds in Revolutionary Egypt," *Information Society* 29 (2013): 49–60, doi: 10.1080/01972243.2012.739594.

20. David Wolman, "Cairo Activists Use Facebook to Rattle Regime," *Wired*, October 20, 2018, accessed December 7, 2018, https://www.wired.com/2008/10/ff-facebookegypt/.

21. Somini Sengupta, "Acquittal in Killing Unleashes Ire at India's Rich," *New York Times*, March 13, 2006, accessed December 7, 2018, https://www.nytimes.com/2006/03/13/world/asia/acquittal-in-killing-unleashes-ire-at-indias-rich.html.

22. Richa Nagar, "Mujhe Jawab Do! (Answer Me!): Women's Grass-Roots Activism and Social Spaces in Chitrakoot (India)," *Gender, Place and Culture: A Journal of Feminist Geography* 7, no. 4 (2000): 341–62, doi: 10.1080/713668879.

23. Veronika Novoselova and Jennifer Jenson, "Authorship and Professional Digital Presence in Feminist Blogs," *Feminist Media Studies*, published electronically February 23, 2018, 1, doi: 10.1080/14680777.2018.1436083.

24. Zizi Papacharissi and Maria de Fatima Oliveira, "Affective News and Networked Publics: The Rhythms of News Storytelling on #Egypt," *Journal of Communication* 62, no. 2 (2012): 267, doi:10.1111/j.1460-2466.2012.01630.x. Emphasis in original.

25. Zeynep Tufekci and Christopher Wilson, "Social Media and the Decision to Participate in Political Protest: Observations from Tahrir Square," *Journal of Communication* 62, no. 2 (2012): 363, doi:10.1111/j.1460-2466.2012.01629.x.

26. Gajjala, ed. *Cyberculture and the Subaltern*, 104.

27. While this is reported as suicide – several Dalit activists I spoke to have noted that they consider this institutional murder. I have tried not to name Rohit's death as suicide out of regard for the points they make even as the references I link to will describe it as suicide.

28. The event invokes the words of Nivedita Menon when she wrote in 2015 that "[n]ew identities continually . . . [arise] from different contexts, forcing recognition on our part that all political solidarities are conjunctural and historically contingent." Yet, given Nivedita Menon's role in the *Kafila* statement against "the list," there is some irony in this. See Nivedita Menon, "Is Feminism about 'Women'? A Critical View on

Intersectionality from India," *Economic & Political Weekly* 1, no. 17 (April 25, 2015): 38.

29. Also Dalit feminism dates even further back.

30. Padmini Ray Murray, "Writing New *Sastras:* Notes towards Building an Indian Feminist Archive," in *New Feminisms in South Asian Social Media, Film, and Literature,* ed. Sonora Jha and Alka Kurian (New York: Routledge, 2018), 110.

31. Timothy Loftus, "Dalit Feminism as Postsecular Feminism," in *Postsecular Feminisms: Religion and Gender in Transnational Context,* ed. Nandini Deo (London: Bloomsbury Academic, 2018). Kindle.

32. Arpita Chakraborty, forthcoming, p. 5.

33. Radhika Gajjala, "When an Indian Whisper Network Went Digital," *Communication, Culture and Critique* 11, no. 3 (September 2018): 489–93, doi:10.1093/ccc/tcy025.

34. Adrija Dey, *Nirbhaya, New Media and Digital Gender Activism* (Bingley, UK: Emerald Publishing Limited, 2018).

35. See also their article on "What Is Missing In the #MeToo Movement?" at https://www.epw.in/node/153269/pdf

36. At this point I was tempted to branch off into a discussion connecting with Nancy Fraser's work in *Fortunes of Feminism,* but that will have to wait for the next writing project.

37. Srila Roy, Twitter exchange with Radhika Gajjala, March 2012.

38. Mitra-Kahn, "Offline Issues," 109.

39. Ibid.

40. Ibid., 109.

41. Ibid., 110.

42. Losh, "Hashtag Feminism," 11.

43. Sonora Jha, "Gathering Online, Loitering Offline: Hashtag Activism and the Claim for Public Space by Women in India through the #whyloiter Campaign," in *New Feminisms in South Asian Social Media, Film, and Literature,* ed. Sonora Jha and Alka Kurian (New York: Routledge, 2018), 64.

44. Vemuri, "After Nirbhaya," 8.

45. Ibid., 9.

46. Guha, "Mind the Gap," 88.

47. Kraidy, "The Body as Medium," 286.

48. Including very vocal activists such as Christina Thomas Dhanaraj and Divya Kandukuri, in addition to Raya Sarkar, and a few others who prefer to remain anonymous.

49. Pramod Nayar, "The Digital Dalit: Subalternity and Cyberspace," *Sri Lanka Journal of the Humanities* 37, nos. 1–2 (2011): 72, doi: 10.4038/sljh.v37i1-2.7204.

50. Dalit Diva is the Twitter handle of Thenmouzhi Soundarrajan, a Transmedia artist and Dalit activist.

51. Gayatri Chakravorty Spivak, "Can the Subaltern Speak?," in *Colonial Discourse and Post-Colonial Theory: A Reader,* ed. Patrick Williams and Laura Chrisman (New York: Harvester/Wheatsheaf, 1994), 66–111.

52. Dalit Diva, Twitter Thread, May 30, 2018, 3:53 p.m., www.twitter.com%5Cdalitdiva.

53. Varsha Ayyar, personal correspondence with author, 2018. See chapter 4.

54. Partha Chatterjee, "History and the Domain of the Popular," *Seminar,* no. 522 (February 2003): n.p., http://www.india-seminar.com/2003/522.htm; Partha Chatterjee, interview by Javed Alam, "Subaltern Studies: No Dalit Movement so No Dalit Question Part 1–4," YouTube video, 16:23, posted by Dalit Camera, June 30, 2012, https://www.youtube.com/watch?v=67m-UuI9268.

55. Alf Gunvald Nilsen and Srila Roy, "Reconceptualizing Subaltern Politics in Contemporary India," in *New Subaltern Politics: Reconceptualizing Hegemony and Resistance in Contemporary India*, ed. Alf Gunvald Nilsen and Srila Roy (Oxford: Oxford University Press, 2015), 13.

56. Ibid.

57. See for instance the Twitter accounts of Dalit Diva, https://twitter.com/dalitdiva; and Prakash Ambedkar, https://twitter.com/Prksh_Ambedkar.

58. See Balakrishna Ganeshan, "Rohith Vemula 2nd Death Anniversary: Prakash Ambedkar Among Activists Invited to Speak," *News Minute*, January 15, 2018, https://www.thenewsminute.com/article/rohith-vemula-2nd-death-anniversary-prakash-ambedkar-among-activists-invited-speak-74766.

59. Nayar, "The Digital Dalit," 70.

60. Ibid., 72.

61. Jillana B. Enteen, *Virtual English: Queer Internets and Digital Creolization* (New York and London: Routledge, 2010), 19.

62. For definition of digirati, see Srinivasan, "Bridges between Cultural and Digital Worlds," 52.

63. For analysis of Black Twitter, see André Brock, "From the Blackhand Side: Twitter as a Cultural Conversation," *Journal of Broadcasting & Electronic Media* 56, no. 4 (2012): 529–49, doi: 10.1080/08838151.2012.732147.

64. Aaron Smith, "African Americans and Technology Use: A Demographic Portrait," Pew Research Center, January 6, 2014, http://www.pewinternet.org/2014/01/06/african-americans-and-technology-use/.

65. Brock, "From the Blackhand Side," 530.

66. Angshukanta Chakraborty, "Bhima Koregaon Violence: Why Indian Media Can't See Caste," *Daily O*, January 3, 2018, https://www.dailyo.in/politics/bhima-koregaon-dalits-media-tv-twitter-maharashtra-bjp-modi-brahmins/story/1/21524.html.

67. See Gajjala, *Online Philanthropy in the Global North and South*, for discussion of subaltern stagings on philanthropy websites; observations about Dalit individualism come from Twitter exchanges with Srila Roy and Sonja Thomas.

68. Laura R. Brueck, *Writing Resistance: The Rhetorical Imagination of Hindi Dalit Literature* (New York: Columbia University Press, 2014), 2.

69. Gyanendra Pandey, "The Subaltern as Subaltern Citizen," introduction to *Subaltern Citizens and Their Histories: Investigations from India and the USA*, ed. Gyanendra Pandey (London and New York: Routledge, 2010), 1.

70. Nishant Shah, "Thrice Invisible in its Visibility: Queerness and User Generated 'Kand' Videos," *Ada: A Journal of Gender, New Media & Technology*, no. 8 (2015): n.p., doi: 10.7264/N3VD6WRR.

71. Ibid.

72. See Srila Roy, "Women's Movements in the Global South: Towards a Scalar Analysis," *International Journal of Politics, Culture, and Society* 29, no. 3 (2016): 289–306, https://doi.org/10.1007/S10767-016-9226-6; Victoria Bernal and Inderpal Grewal, eds., *Theorizing NGOs: States, Feminisms, and Neoliberalism* (Durham, NC: Duke University Press, 2014).

73. Radhika Gajjala and Annapurna Mamidipudi, "Cyberfeminism, Technology, and International 'Development,'" *Gender and Development* 7, no. 2 (1999): 8–16, http://www.jstor.org/stable/4030445.

74. Gajjala, *Cyber Selves: Feminist Ethnographies of South Asian Women* (Walnut Creek, CA: AltaMira Press, 2004), 123.

75. Roy, "Women's Movements," 294.

76. Radhika Gajjala, Jeanette Dillon, and Anca Birzescu, "Networked Affect in Online Philanthropy," in *Online Philanthropy in the Global North and South* (Lanham, MD: Lexington Books, 2017), 84.

77. See Tanika Sarkar, "The Woman as Communal Subject: Rashtrasevika Samiti and Ram Janmabhoomi Movement," *Economic and Political Weekly* 26, no. 35 (August 31, 1991): 2057–62.

Chapter Six

Dialogue Interlude

Extending the Nuancing the Framework

Radhika Gajjala in conversation with
Debipreeta Rahut and Damini Kulkarni

RG: Based in the iterative dialogue process that I use and to see if I am providing a "plausible account," I went back into chapter 1 after our last set of intense conversations with each of you and incorporated some observations.[1] I noted that in some instances, the body tweeting or blogging is in physical domestic space and in some instances the body is in physical streets. But the corporeal body and the affective/ subjective body seem out of sync and split (even "disembodied") because of the ways in which our preconceived ideas of dualities and binaries are spatiotemporally static. Implicitly we view the body in place as corporeal, tactile, and physically tangible; on the other hand, we view the subjective as moving through aspirational, thinking, and imagined space. Over here, I would like us to elaborate with specific examples through dialogue performed with both of you.

For instance, in a recent conversation with me, Debipreeta, you noted: "Digital activism taking place among urban young Indian women is true, it is visible all over social media. But calling such activism a part of feminist activities is something that I have reservations about. We can't call it feminist, at least not all the digital activism."

141

While it was not my intention to characterize all digital activism as feminist, I understand that you mean we can't call all activism related to women's autonomy as feminist. Can you elaborate please?

DR: Thank you ma'am for giving me a chance to enter into a dialogue with you. It's been a learning experience for me via this rich participation. Let me start by giving you an example: In the case of the Nirbhaya incident (that your text talks about), people all across the social media were showing their rage and anger at the barbaric act (that was a result of cumulative media coverage and discourse of the event by the prominent media organizations and indeed the grassroots work of some activists or activist organizations, which ultimately led to some changes in the law). The incident actually sent shivers down my spine. Acquaintances (batchmates and seniors at my masters' program at the University of Calcutta) and relatives expressed their fear and rage at the incident, were vocal on their Facebook pages, and seemed to be fully in support of the girl. But in many personal encounters with me, they said that the fault was with the girl because she went out late at night with her male friend, and took a public vehicle in Delhi, which is notoriously unsafe. They remarked on her lifestyle and the kind of clothes she was probably wearing. But, on their Facebook pages, they expressed solidarity with the girl by using hashtags. And I am talking about educated urban women of a cosmopolitan city like Kolkata. Another recent incident: The Supreme Court here in India legitimized homosexuality by scrapping some parts of Section 377, which criminalizes sexual intercourse between people of the same sex. Many of my friends expressed their support for the verdict online. However, I recall that in my earlier interactions with some of these friends, they had expressed disgust at the idea of love transcending all barriers of gender, caste, and other social contexts here (in India). Thus, the activism in the digital sphere is very diluted. People are different on social media platforms, and that identity is not an extension of their real selves. They might support certain causes championed by the media and some activists, but only superficially.

RG: Debipreeta, this is an excellent unpacking and problematizing of how we tend to homogenize social media participation in campaigns as users—through sharing and liking—as representing a larger ethos of activism offline. What you are alerting readers to is the fact that not all digital acts of sharing and liking coalesce toward a common message about how society needs to respond to the event being protested.

We clearly know, for instance, that our likes and shares contribute to increasing the ratings of usage and the revenue toward social media platforms—regardless of the point of view of the person sharing, commenting, and "liking." Thus, the platform itself as a technosocial "actor" maintains an amoral stance. But what you are pointing to is that the features of social media platforms such as the "share," "like," "forward," and "retweet" do not necessarily reveal the rationale behind their use. It is the offline discussions and debates (or perhaps even the comments and discussions online) that reveal and explain motivations.

Would you say it is difficult to "dilute" activism in offline space? Can you share more thoughts regarding this difference?

DR: Yes ma'am, it is difficult to "dilute" activism in offline spaces. For example, recently, a couple of college-going youngsters leaning on each other during the rush hour in the Kolkata metro provoked a violent reaction from some middle-aged people. These people thought that their actions were against "Indian culture," and began taunting and abusing the couple. The boy was beaten and thrown out of the compartment when the metro stopped at a station. When the newspapers followed some of these older people (because their faces were visible on the CCTV cameras) on their Facebook pages, their profile displayed a completely different persona. But their thoughts and actions were different from what their online identity indicated. And it is their offline life that brought forth their real mentality. This incident shows that people's thoughts coincide with their actions in their day-to-day offline life.

RG: So what you are saying is that there is a virtual/real divide in how these people perform their identity online versus offline. The physical space inhabited by the corporeal body activates certain behaviors consistent with the social approval of their peers in these physical spaces. Similarly, in the social media spaces that they inhabit, they are careful to perform identities that blend with what they see as majority behaviors in social media space: behaviors that are also likely to be visible outside of Indian/local social space. In a sense, they are treating the physical offline space as more of a "home" space where they are "protecting" (controlling) women of the middle class/upper caste by forcing them into a further physical "ghar" space, and in the digital publics they are perhaps performing what they might think of as a "Westernized" modernity.

DR: Let me point toward an incident. In the Queer Parades in Kolkata, only those who actually feel for LGBT rights and are sympathetic toward the cause (irrespective of their age) participate. They might, or might not, be vocal about it on their Facebook pages, but they participate in parades only because they wish to express solidarity with the LGBT community. Online, people perhaps create an image that will be liked by everyone in the virtual world, in the hope that they will be accepted or popular. But interactions with these people offline points toward their thought process and real personality.

As far as hashtags are concerned, people are catching on with this trend, thinking it to be "cool." But they just don't understand the concept of hashtags. Even for the #metoo campaign, people actually came forward with stories of abuse and exploitation because the hashtag was in vogue—used by some popular people, and followed by the media. People felt the pain and anger of those people who came out with their stories, and they added to the chorus of voices online because social media was providing them with a platform. But in real life, they didn't take any concrete measures to fight for the cause.

RG: So what you are pointing to throughout this dialogue interlude is that there is not always a consistency between online behavior and offline behavior. Yet my question to you is this: Do you think it's only online and offline that these sorts of differences happen? Is it possible that online the people you have observed function within a particular social world and peer group and offline in another—and that this could explain the difference in their behaviors in both these social spaces?

DR: It has been seen that in the online community, you reach out to more people, via friend requests, likes, shares, pages, groups, etcetera. And you interact also through these online activities, sometimes even with strangers. But offline, you might not like the idea of befriending a stranger that easily. So there's this change of behavior and attitude of a person in online and offline space. I feel that online, we want to connect with more people with shared interests. But offline, we are more guarded, and probably like to connect only with closer people.

RG: Damini, now I turn to you and how you've been pushing against some of the ways I've been conceptualizing ghar and bahir by nuancing the concepts through examples. I was hoping you could start by responding to examples that DR brings up and then we can take it further into some of the other points we discussed.

DK: Thank you so much for including me in this, RG. I see the point here, especially when it comes to the rape of Nirbhaya, because it was stunning to see how people's online selves contrasted vividly with their offline presence. But as I was pointing out to you during our conversations, it seems that often, we perform our idea of an "ideal self" online. I know several people who speak about social issues very eloquently on Facebook. They cannot do so in their everyday life for several reasons, but that eloquent, activist version of them is their ideal self. Perhaps, if we peel past the apparent hypocrisy of the difference in their online and offline selves, the dialectic points to negotiations that people, especially middle-aged people I know, are carrying out in their own private spheres. To put it very simplistically, they want to be woke, and they are performing that ideal self online, but they are unable to practice those ideas every day, and that leads to the tension, and the split that has been pointed out in this dialogue interlude.

I feel, that more than online or offline spaces per se, any circumstance of social flux causes people to reveal their personal politics and this split (or hypocrisy, depending on your viewpoint). I see so many popular personalities contradicting themselves merrily on Twitter (Director Vijay Agnihotri is an example). The nature of the medium helps you to identify their "true colors," because it calls people out on "digital streets" (the way you have conceptualized it here). As the political situation in India has transformed and shifted in the past four years, so many people with terrifying social and political opinions have become more vocal in both online and offline spaces. They are "climbing out of the woodwork" as one of my colleagues pointed out, emboldened by the discourses that are currently taking root. Their personal politics was revealed in both spaces because of a change in the dominant sociocultural narrative. (I am reminded of Noelle-Neumann's conceptualization of Spiral of Silence here).[2]

It's also interesting how social media (the Me Too movement, in particular) helped people identify the harmful gaps in the private and public selves of so many people. I know women who discovered that men close to them, even ones who apparently seem to champion feminism in a public space, had sexually abused or harassed women. The case of Shamir Reuben, who claimed to be a feminist poet but harassed several women, is an example. So in many ways, social media becomes the site for the manifestation of the tensions in the definitions of "ghar" and "bahir," and the differences between them.

RG: DK, when you say social media helped identify gaps, can you say more: I know you point to an example, but in what way does that reveal those gaps?

DK: As we speak, a massive churn is under process in India, with several women coming forward to name comedians, media professionals, journalists, actors, and filmmakers who have abused or sexually harassed them. In a manner of speaking, this began with actor Tanushree Dutta reiterating the comments she had made in 2008 regarding actor Nana Patekar. When Dutta spoke up then, she was silenced and summarily replaced. However, when she spoke again in September 2018, several actors came forward to support her on Twitter, which opened the floodgates for many more women to speak about powerful men who had abused them.

Most of the men who have been named, such as comedian Utsav Chakraborty and actor Rajat Kapoor, were known for their liberal and "woke" politics. Twitter and Facebook have become the primary sites of this discourse, allowing space for women to "out" these men. This is not to say that they are "safe" spaces for women, because they are not. But I am attempting to demonstrate that Twitter, as a platform, helped to demonstrate cracks in their public and private personas, in that "split," or hypocrisy.

RG: Very interesting . . . in the context of this public/private split in social support for causes and what we were earlier wondering about— in our Skype conversation in a reference to Goffman, which did not make it into any of the chapters—in terms of Goffman's onstage and backstage behaviors and through examples that DR brought up for instance, what you are saying adds a different nuance.[3] Thinking about this in relation to publics and counterpublics, it's interesting how in social media space both coexist. Any more thoughts?

DK: I believe that the current wave of the movement offers examples of how so many publics coexist in online spaces. It is evident in the ways that these publics are engaging with women outing men, and the counternarratives that these calling outs are generating. Perhaps it would be helpful to look at publics and counterpublics on online spaces as resting on a continuum instead of a strict binary: it opens up ways of looking at how their navigations with technology cause different forms of anxiety among women who have spoken about their experiences of trauma.

For instance, there is a public on social media which is asking women to stop posting their experiences on social media, and file complaints in the "real world" so that action can be taken. There is another public that doubts the veracity of their complaints and claims that women are seeking fame, attention, and new job offers. It is curious how one public completely delegitimizes social media, while the other validates it to the extent that they believe it will single-handedly help women build their careers. Both these reactions are triggering very different kinds of anxieties in victims.

RG: Continuing this dialogue, I want to return to your responses and contributions to the discussion following my lecture during the GIAN lecture series at Savithribai Phule Pune University, where I talked about this book and its framework along a faux binary of "ghar/bahir."[4] Those discussions in our seminars were generally very insightful. In fact, even as I was giving the talk I began to make mental clarifications to what I had written in those chapters of this book.

I want to start out by asking you to articulate your response to what you heard as a ghar/bahir binary in relation to digital space occupied by women living in India and South Asian women in diaspora who connect with each other through the internet and other wireless tools. I suspect our conversation will allow me to unpack my faux binary (which is more a conceptual binary than an actual divide that defines what digital tools are used or digital social modes are inhabited).

DK: I have always called myself technologically incapacitated, because I believe that I cannot operate digital technology with ease. It doesn't come naturally to me. So while I feel comfortable in the digital domestic (parts of which I wouldn't see as "domestic," partially because I have internalized a great deal of the negative discourse around the word, and shedding it is still a work-in-progress), I dither on the digital streets.

I feel that the strategic/faux binary you draw itself sits on an extremely uneasy and precarious pair of terms. While creating a dichotomy between a "ghar" and a "bahir," we already associate "ghar" or "bahir" with highly diverse and varied signifiers, primarily because those two things mean very different things to different people. I often catch myself saying that I feel most "at home" near the sea, which is technically "bahir," depending on how we define the term. The slippage is natural because ghar and bahir are in no way analogous to public and private, and there will always be a tension between the physical space of ghar and bahir and the many symbols and icons associated with them.

For instance, I have been speaking to women about how they consume content on online streaming platforms, and one of them told me that watching content in her home makes her feel very uncomfortable. She had her reasons, but she preferred to take her device into her "bahir" to watch a show.

RG: So what you are saying is that ghar as a physical place is not a "safe" space—and yet isn't that the point though about a feminist inter-rogation of ghar and bahir? That in conventional patriarchal ideologies "ghar" is supposedly a space that protects women—yet women are controlled there; and, as in the case of the woman who prefers to consume streaming platforms outside of her physical home, it is a space that actually protects patriarchal structures and therefore the woman seeking autonomy is forced outside—and "bahir" then becomes her space of autonomy. Thus the strategic faux binary still works for me as a space to question the ideology of the home/ghar as a safe space for women as articulated through upper-class/upper-caste social norms. What I appreciate about this dialogue interlude with you is that it's helping me clarify and articulate the nuances: ghar and bahir are still conceptual boundaries that define women's oppression, women's place in society, and women's struggles for autonomy in a variety of ways. I look forward to more elaborations (and further push back as well) from you. As we proceed let's also think on this quote from Preeti Mudaliar:

> Massey notes that spaces rarely have unique specific identities and are susceptible to conflicts and difference that dictate how they are experi-enced and by whom [43]. Writing on the nature of public spaces, she notes that given their unregulated nature, it is often left to the population to socially negotiate and determine who gets the right to access these spaces in the absence of explicit rules. The outcome of these negotia-tions is predicated on the often unequal social relations between differ-ent groups of people that can exclude or weaken the right of presence of groups such as women who experience lesser power in relation to others [42, 43].[5]

What I began to realize during our earlier conversations in Pune and also during conversations with Preeti Mudaliar and Jasmeen Patheja while visiting Bangalore in 2018 is that in the draft version of what is now chapter 1 that I shared before September 2018, I had not clarified the differences between the concepts of "digital domesticity" and the conceptualizing around "ghar/bahir." I had allowed a conflation be-tween digital domesticity and "ghar," while I was slipping into conflat-ing digital activism as a "bahir" space. Yet the issue is not that clear and unmuddied is it? The issue of how autonomy and neoliberal indi-vidualization allow for the privatizing of digital publics and of physical publics (as in your example of your interviewee who prefers viewing Sacred Games in Starbucks alone rather than at home where others in the home space might censure her for doing so). She is indeed using a bahir space as a safe space—yet this is not unique, is it? Women and other marginalized groups have always negotiated oppressive household spaces controlled by patriarchal and class/caste/race hierarchies and norms by finding private enclosures in "outside" or "bahir" spaces or by forming community support in secrecy away from the surveillance.

This is done by creating domesticity-based enclosures around knitting groups, sewing circles, women-only puja rituals—and even in rituals of going out for their morning ablutions.[6] While these instances of shared autonomous spaces might lead to potential conscious raising and resistance, they also lead to comfort zones and outlets. The spaces of struggle, however, are sometimes in relational space within the spaces where the structural hierarchy is visibly reinforced. Thus, a living room where a debate around a movie might lead to conflict might reveal more possibility for structural shifts in the way the family unit—in the ghar—moves than if the woman kept her views outside of the home space. Are we seeing women managing to negotiate autonomy for themselves in spaces without actually shifting structures and hierarchies—is that part of the "neoliberal moment" in feminism? Yet these dilemmas and negotiations are not new.

NOTES

1. Kathy Charmaz, *Constructing Grounded Theory: A Practical Guide Through Qualitative Analysis* (London: Sage, 2006). I use the phrase "plausible account" in an academic move that is similar to what Charmaz notes in regard to "constructing grounded theory": even in this sort of interpretive method employed to build theory—interweaving qualitative interviews and immersion in online contexts—one cannot say that this process is one of data verification.

2. Elisabeth Noelle-Neumann, *The Spiral of Silence: Public Opinion–Our Social Skin* (Chicago: Chicago University Press, 1984).

3. Erving Goffman, *The Presentation of Self in Everyday Life* (New York: Doubleday, 1959).

4. Radhika Gajjala, "GIAN Programme: Studying Gender, Digital Labor and Globalization: Theory and Method" (lecture, Savitribai Phule Pune University, Maharashtra India, July 2018).

5. Preeti Mudliar, "Public WiFi Is for Men and Mobile Internet Is for Women: Interrogating Politics of Space and Gender around WiFi Hotspots." *Proceedings of the ACM on Human-Computer Interaction* 2 (November 2018): 4, doi: 10.1145/3274395.

6. Diane Coffey and Dean Spears, *Where India Goes: Abandoned Toilets, Stunted Development, and the Costs of Caste* (Noida, UP, India: HarperCollins India, 2017).

Chapter Seven

Dialogue Interlude

The Digital Queer Question

Radhika Gajjala in conversation
with Smita Vanniyar

The focus of this chapter is on queering the digital with two specific
views into queer digital space. One (represented by Radhika) is an
"outside" view from a heterosexual and older-generation perspective,
observing processes of queering the digital; the other is from a younger
generation Indian, queer point of view (represented by Smita). In this
dialogue we hope to convey a sense of queerness through our respective entries into these spaces and also a sense of the spatial and temporal nuances in queer digital spaces as they connected to Indian digital
diasporas.

THEN

Entering/Moving Out into the Internet

RG: My first user-end interaction with personal computers began in the
late 1980s in India. As a student of the humanities and social sciences I
had never actually worked with computers until then and my knowledge of them was from books, science fiction, and from brothers who
were engineers. Thus, while punch cards lay around the house sometimes near some engineering books, I had never worked a computer.

Therefore, it was in the late 1980s in India that I entered the space of computers with a vague aspiration on the one hand to gather the necessary credentials to find part-time work in the United States (where I was headed with child, following a spouse who had reentered graduate school), and with an avid curiosity to see if the software programs I was learning could indeed produce creative works or could be used in the creative education of five-year-old children, on the other hand. In a sense then, my entry into the digital of the pre-internet was a bridge from the private to the public and an implicit and aspirational move toward financial self-sufficiency driven by socially endorsed heteronormative domestic/relational encouragement—a reaching/stretching *out* beyond the binary of home and the outside (ghar and bahir) that an upper- to middle-class India allowed to educated heterosexual married women when there was potential salary to justify it.

My entry into the internet has its origins in the 1990s when I acquired an email account as a university student in the US, a little more than a year after I arrived in Pittsburgh. The modem and PC initiated social connections. Work emails were few and far between. But Usenet, email lists, MOOs, and the synchronous talk features of the early text-based internet days opened up my social space. Even while my access to the physical outside was never restricted in the US, the opening up of several outsides by access to the internet potentially allowed me multiple and comparatively diverse social interactions. The physical outside allowed me to understand my surroundings and freedom in certain ways—while the internet-mediated outside allowed several different kinds of outsides. Through the internet I was simultaneously "here" and "there" even while the computer itself was housed in a physically bounded space. In Elizabeth Reba Weise's words,

> I could call forth a new, nonblinking cursor on my screen, a cursor that was no longer the door to my own solitary world, but to the outside world.
> I walked through it. [1]

My solitary mind space, my daily writing—which until then was mostly in my notebooks, diaries, and on my typewriter—became a communal and interactive space. This had both positive and negative ramifications in the long run, but in those early days this was an outside world—fairly secret and seemingly only mine because very few others in my family (either in the US or India) accessed it in this way. They could not access me and I could not access them through this world and that was okay. I loved them dearly, but having this outside to myself felt . . . well . . . liberating (however cliché that sounds now).

SV: The aspect of the internet which was liberating to you there, the fact that there is this space where few in your family could access you and vice versa, is what got a lot of queer people online. Here was a space where they finally dare be themselves and not worry about "real" life ramifications. This is especially applicable to queer women and gender-nonconforming persons. The cyberspace has given them a chance to problematize and play with gender roles, gender identities, sexuality, and sexual preferences, none of which are static.[2] This is liberating. This is empowering.

RG: The concept of queering and of performing selves via the internet in the 1990s inevitably overlap. Fluidity of identity, gender (gender-bending), experimenting by performing gender textually—these were normal practices of being digital in the 1990s whether one was gay, lesbian, queer, trans, or cisgendered. The 1990s internet was indeed a queer internet, as compared to the extreme heteronorms being produced and reproduced through contemporary internet, appified, and social media spaces. The internet and gaming spaces of the 1990s offered sexual experimentation, gender fluidity, and homosociality as clear options and norms even if access to the internet itself was exclusive and restricted (comparatively) in those days. The notion of "on the internet no one knows you're a dog" worked for gender-bending and also was instrumental in allowing safe spaces online for young LGBTQ people to come out of the closet into global webs.[3] Further, as Gross notes,

> [T]here's the disembodied, performativity of cyberspace, the place where no one knows you're a dog, or whatever you choose to present yourself as. Queer folk are past masters at this game, as nearly every one of us went through the training program during childhood. Even if we weren't singled out for special (unwelcome) attention as sissies, tomboys or other gender nonconformists, most of us survived society's sexual bootcamp—highschool—either by masquerading and passing, or living on the margins.[4]

The queering of the internet in this sense then precedes the racialization of the internet. Digital divides of the 1990s were clearly socioeconomic, and access for racialized bodies was clearly based in a global political economy of histories of access to capital and dominant forms of accepted literacy and practice.

In the early 1990s, therefore, my interest was both in finding immigrant South Asian women and also in searching for new writing spaces/ outlets where my creative work could be shared, where my intellectual abilities could be freely expressed. As it turned out, several familiar and unfamiliar issues of gender, nation, culture, and class emerged in South Asian Usenet spaces, which led to the reactive formation of list spaces such as the South Asian Women's network (SAWnet), which is a listproc that was started in 1992 by South Asian women living in diaspora. At the same time, queer-oriented women and men formed their own list spaces as well, such as the Khush-list from the 1990s.[5]

We were all aware that all this was possible through the privilege of internet access and the ability to enter/create textual English typing spaces online. These were not spaces that were comfortable to all who entered, however. But the communities were forming. These spaces came to affectively allow those living lives outside traditional heteronorms defined through dominant cultures and politics of nation-states to think of them as our own safe spaces, until the question of who belonged in these spaces erupted every now and then.[6]

SV: The research team that published the study *EROTICS: Sex, Rights and the Internet* speculates that queer communities might have been the first ones to actually use the internet to "socially network" given the lack of physical space afforded to them.[7] They lived out their otherwise secret queer lives online, organizing and socializing over cables that connected them to one another. The formation of this imagined community, based on a concept theorized by Benedict Anderson, was possible due to one very crucial element of the cyberspace: anonymity. Queer people in various countries with repressive LGBTQ laws have been using the internet to meet each other and form communities without actually being forced to come out and put themselves at risk.

After crackdowns on the popular gay cruising spots in India, the main means for gay and bisexual men to meet others from the community was through chatrooms on Yahoo, Rediff, etc., and dating websites like PlanetRomeo. Online groups like GayBombay played a big role here. In Egypt, the primary queer space is online given the dangers of openly being queer in the Egyptian society. Grant Walsh-Haines also looks at how the blogosphere can be used for the liberation of queers in Egypt and for collective activism.[8] Similar is the case in Beirut, and the list goes on, what with seventy-six countries having laws criminalizing LGBT relationships and/or "propaganda of homosexuality" like in the case of Russia and Lithuania.[9] In Malaysia, the police are secretly infiltrating queer forums and pages for collecting data on the members. In 2006, four men were arrested in Lucknow, India, under the charge of "conspiracy to commit sodomy" under Section 377.[10] The police actually created a trap for one of them after finding his phone number on his PlanetRomeo (then known as guys4men.com) profile. The queer movement in Lebanon would not exist if it was not for the ability to network online. The movement traces its roots to the ability to access online spaces where lesbians could meet anonymously and safely, to discuss issues from dating to rights.

RG: I note this affective dimension and formation of new relationalities from my early internet connectivity not as a form of self-indulgence, but as a way to remind readers that this is the kind of social/affective space of "outness" where queerness and cyberspace connect. Researchers studying the intersection of cyber and queer have noted how from the 1990s, there has been a tendency to couple these two terms as "cyberqueer."[11] Nina Wakeford and Kate O'Riordan separately take up the question of cyber and queer and the issue of cybersexual in their respective work. Yet as O'Riordan has noted, this feeling of safeness in coming out and the idea of fluidity and access to the world was constrained. Discursive spaces outside the local were also fraught with known and unknown dangers. Global discursive hierarchies unsurprisingly emerged that simultaneously reproduced the old hierarchies and recoded and reformed new ones as possible speaking positions allowed particular kinds of speech from the margins and subaltern spaces. The internet came into its own through stabilizing and shifting particular constructs of identity, ignorance, and accepted norms. And so, while

> [t]he ideal cybersubject . . . and the ideal queer subject as fluid, converge[d] in fictions such as Sullivan and Bornstein's and critiques such as Turkle's, there is more evidence to suggest that contemporary online queer communities are stratified into fixed identity hierarchies (Munt et al. 2002), and anxiety about bodily identity is a strong determinant in online queer formations.[12]

SV: It's interesting to note how the politics that exist within the queer community in physical spaces is reflected in online spaces. It is but a subset of how offline hierarchies and inequalities get translated and adapted into a new space, in this case, the World Wide Web. When in the heterosexual world, men and women have always held their individual identities; in the case of the queer world, gay men and lesbian women are often clubbed together solely based on the fact that both of them are attracted to their same genders. When they did come together to combat their shared adversities, which included discrimination and prejudice, their individual identities had to be kept aside for a bit for the sake of the "greater gay good."[13] In India, there was a slight difference. Here, when gay men and transgender persons fought for their place in the public sphere, lesbian women fought against invisibility and their imminent erasure.[14] And there is the ever-present misogyny in most spheres that include men, especially those who were brought up to believe that they deserve it all. Patriarchy in the gay community is even more baffling in some ways. One faces discrimination in a space that one otherwise considers safe.[15]

This extends to the ways in which virtual spaces are constructed for gay and bisexual men versus those for lesbian and bisexual women. The contrast can be seen at almost every step in the socializing spaces, starting from the way the space is built, to the questions asked to the patrons and their main motives for accessing the space. For example, PinkSofa, a dating site aimed at lesbian and bisexual women, has easily twenty-seven options under "Interests," ranging from Activism to Vegetarianism, Socializing, Spirituality, Writing, and whatnot. There is also a query on "Children" when you fill in your profile with a drop-down menu of options next to it. When I had first visited the site in 2012, there were four options. It has now expanded to nine options. The only place where a user can mention a preference for casual sex or one-night stands is via the "Casual encounters" check box in the "What are you looking for" section. PlanetRomeo, a very popular dating site for queer men, when filling in your profile, has about fifteen options under "Fetishes," and columns to fill in dick size with a check box for "cut" and "uncut," but no question on marital status, and limited options for "interests." Queer spaces that are online also end up conforming to heteronormative ideas of how "men" and "women" look at sex, relationships, commitment, etcetera. Are we really truly queering anything here then?

Entering/Moving Out into Academia

RG: My scholarly/academic interest in the internet of the early 1990s began to take form around the same time I began producing scholarship about the digital, the postcolonial nation, and gender, as I started my doctoral work a couple years later. Heteronormative gender clashes online were the most visible to me in those days. Issues of subalternity and the nation were repeatedly engaged in classroom settings and I began to see how diasporic populations were reconnecting and shaping home-nation politics through discourse and capital flows. Queer South Asian spaces began to surface as early as the late 1980s. Parmesh Shahani describes how the queer populations in India and the diasporic South Asian queer folk connected through the internet.[16] He notes:

> Parallel to the social scene, in the late 1980s and early 1990s, the city witnessed the growth of political and sexual health oriented activism . . . [that] grew in tandem with and often, in close interaction with diasporic south Asian groups like Trikone in the US and Shakti in England. . . . [T]heir sense of alienation and quest for a purely social interaction space, together with the fortuitous arrival of the Internet led to the birth of Gay Bombay.[17]

"Bombay" in the naming of Gay Bombay signifies a more urban and cosmopolitan space than much of the rest of India. Therefore, even this is a comparatively socially privileged social space. Indians from Indian metropolitan social settings, therefore, could access the internet in 1995; some of them connected with Khush-list, which had been started in 1992. The Kush-list is considered to be one of the oldest of queer digital Indian formations.

In the early 1990s when I was working with listproc founding and moderation through the Spoon Collective, SAWnet, Trikone, and the Khush-list were very much in my field of digital vision and intellectual conversation space.[18] Thus not very surprisingly, my entry into the digital was also my entry into the investigation of gender beyond just heteronormative, liberal equal access concerns that come from and were most vocally expressed in the 1970s in middle- and upper-class educated spaces in India. Heteronormative liberal feminist discourse became easily co-opted into right wing national politics and into neo-liberal individualization where some women's privilege—coming from heteronormative caste/class space—went uninterrogated. The queer spaces of the internet, however, were engaged in far more complex struggles and brought out further nuances and struggles around gender, nation, and subalternity. Yet in the 1990s, published academic scholarship about the South Asian and Indian digital was still mostly about the Anglophone world.

IN-BETWEEN

Becoming Webbed

RG: Between the now of social/mobile media, app-based digitality, and the then of the listproc and Usenet days, "the web" exposed us all to the world. Early World Wide Web days allowed even amateurs to code. Hypertext markup language (HTML; invisible and inaccessible from the back end of the java and various GUI software interfaces we engage in as we "build" our web presences in the present day) was comparatively accessible—at least to English educated global middle classes around the world. What changed? Typing and coding selves into existence has become a bit more separated than before. Even though complex backend coding had been invisible to the average user during the days when HTML was visible and accessible to amateur coders, the typing of the self into existence relied on some forms of coding. Typing the self into existence meant simultaneously learning a minimal amount of coding. Present day minimal computing movements try to take us back to the political economy of those days and make us aware of the inequalities made invisible in today's political economy of digitality. [19]

Jenny Sundén writes of the typing into existence that is a requirement for any sustained online identity. [20] However, while the action of *producing one's self* in such an environment is enacted through typing, the particular participant's *subject position* is produced through the act of typing combined with preexisting code.

However, the web shifted from the days when we had access to html coding in the 1990s to becoming invisibly algorithm driven in contemporary times. There began to be provided apparently seamless user/ consumer interfaces, the texting, typing, imaging, recording, and selfieing into being began to be separated from the cognition involved in semi-coding selves into being. The embodied actions and literacies required shifted to different combinations of preexisting offline/online sociality, requiring sociocultural and technical literacies based in various other external gadgets and hardware in addition to the visible circuitry associated with a computer of the 1990s.

Living in the United States as heteronormative female Indian immigrant/academic, I had not encountered direct India in relation to the internet LGBTQ flow until around this period. My reacquaintance with queer cyberspaces in web space came through following what was happening on LiveJournal and other weblog spaces.[21] "South Asia" often came to the internet with a dominance of Indians through the IT sector. And with the youth technology networkers came some openly gay presences from India. Next generations of graduate students from India to the US included several openly gay male students from India. By this time, my own son (a gamer, software engineer, and digital artist) was grown; and even in his generational circles of gamers, there was an acceptance of gay maleness. Suddenly, what we saw in the 1990s media as attempting to break taboos was real and around us. But the inclusions and exclusions were different, and the struggles were both the same as before and different. In such a period of internet time, I coauthored works with Rahul Mitra about the weblog presences of gay Indian men.

SV: I want to add in a little here about the importance of chatrooms for the queers in India around the same time, and also about what kind of queer persons had access to these chatrooms. The RediffMail, Yahoo, and Indiatimes chatrooms on homosexuality were mostly frequented by gay and bisexual men with very, very few women. One main reason for this is the fact that internet cafes, which were the primary spaces for accessing the internet in the 1990s, were not conducive for a woman to frequent by herself. Many of the queer women who were on the chatrooms were those in the US and Canada.[22] But the fact that there existed chatrooms for lesbian and bisexual women on these sites helped in visibilizing the otherwise largely invisible population of women-who-love-women. During an interview, "Though I was a closeted gay man, the possibility of a lesbian never entered my mind. This is more because I was thinking more about myself than anything else back then but still," said Harish Iyer, a prominent queer rights activist.[23] He added,

> Once I figured out that I knew nothing about them, I decided to speak to some and find out. For this, I made a female ID to chat with them on the lesbian and bisexual women chatrooms, like the one in Indiatimes. I spoke to quite a few of them in fact, many from outside India as well. I then came to realise that I had many more stereotypes about lesbian women from the internet and television than about gay men. You know, about how they are all butch and things like that.[24]

In the offline context, the movie *Fire* (Mehta, 1996), released in 1996 in India, is possibly still the most quoted movie on lesbianism and India. (I have some personal reservations on this.) The film (surprisingly!) was cleared by the Censor Board of Film Certification in India before screening and ran in full houses in most metropolitan cities in India before it came to the notice of Shiv Sena and Bajrang Dal, extremist Hindu right-wing political groups. They stormed and disrupted screenings of the film in Bombay, Delhi, Surat, and a few other cities. This was not unexpected. But what is interesting is the timing of their attacks. There were all women screenings held for *Fire*. It was only after two of these screenings ran full-house did the political groups get worried. The third screening was stopped. Patriarchy loves the invisibilization of queer women as long as it does not affect the pleasure of men. This had to be overcome in the World Wide Web as well.

NOW

Return of Repressed?

RG: In the contemporary moment however, the question of immersion in digital culture itself is not "one thing" anymore (if it ever was)—it is many things: many digital cultures, many languages and modes of expression. It is more than the internet and contains many located intersections weaving in and through cybercultures and material cultures. The situation is even more complex for LGBTQ persons in South Asia. Laws around homosexuality in India, for instance, did a wide pendulum swing, first leading to a victory for the LGBTQ community in 2009. Then in 2012 and 2013, there was a return of the "repressed" right wing and opposition to the decriminalization of homosexual activity. This led to the 2015 rejection of the bill for the decriminalization of Section 377. At the same time as all this was occurring in India, gay bloggers were being murdered in Bangladesh.

SV: The influence of India and Indian laws and judgments on the other South Asian countries is sometimes underestimated. This is partially because of the sheer size and population of India, and partially because of the shared history and similar socioeconomic factors. For example, Section 377 exists in the same or similar forms in several former British colonies, including Pakistan, Bangladesh, Bhutan, Sri Lanka, and Maldives. A queer-rights activist from Maldives, at a human rights conference, said that when they try to bring up the reading down of Section 377 in Maldives, India's recent reinstating of the provision is often quoted back to them. Laws, amendments of laws, and judgments often rely on precedence. Any chance of that is removed here.

RG: The double-bind for queer populations in the Global South comes in the form of both local and neocolonial oppressions. While on the one hand local cultures and national law create outcasts of these populations, the global and Western spaces of so-called opportunities for coming out are based in "teleological investments [that] . . . have long been critiqued by poststructuralist theorists for the privileged (white) gay, lesbian, and queer liberal subjects they inscribe and validate."[25]

Digital queer therefore must be taken up by researchers and named through a continuum that takes into account immersion in both digital and physical spaces of work and play. The everydayness of being digital through leisure activities that are both highly competitive and immersive as well as playful and social, such as gaming, for example, means we do not look at gaming as something "outside" of routine life. Indeed, gaming or the use of social media in contemporary daily life is as habitual and seamless as turning on the television. Yet each of these are different activities of media engagement and demand different kinds of cognitive immersion and bodily engagement. They result in differing relational hierarchies of expertise and social capital with related gendering, racializing, and queering potentialities. In the 1990s while much of the Western (US centric) liberal democratic discourse/ world was focusing on noting things like gender-bending and inclusion of alternate realities through game space and cyberspace, very particular kinds of masculinities emerged that intersected with the idea of who can and cannot be a hacker and a gamer. By the 1990s US, television was very cognizant of inclusion and diversity—even when done uneasily and in forms of tokenization. The digital, on the other hand, became a space of actual relational experimentation and fluidity, even if it is disembodied in particular ways. (This disembodiment still differs, however, from our relationality with media that did not involve actual interactive contact with other people.)

SV: I could not agree more about social media and the digital space becoming a part and parcel of everyday life and living. The mobile phone, especially the smartphone, has taken this to the next level. It's not only used for networking or reconnecting with older contacts and friends, but is part of everyday communications and friendships and relationships. If you're queer, and in a physical space that may be unsafe, the mobile phone and the internet become your safe spaces and your support system. In recent times, social media spaces have also become the places where we document and archive our lives, and that of our community. There are several Instagram accounts that are retelling history through a queer lens. These accounts publish photos, stories, excerpts from underground zines, magazines, books, and so on from early years of the queer movement, subtly and not-so-subtly saying, "Hey! Guess what? We have always existed. You just didn't pay enough attention." This adds a whole new side to how the internet is perceived and used. Similarly, there are also feminist archives, black history archives, indigenous history archives, and those on Dalit history, among possibly many, many more.

The Lesbian and FTM Question

RG: In comparison to gay male presences online, the visibility of lesbians is different. In South Asian mass media lesbians are displayed for the hetero male gaze. As Rituparna Borah, a queer-feminist activist has noted, they are shown as "mushy" and as upper class, elite, and almost always as part of a couple.[26] Borah states that she is "fed up of the depiction of two women, who are so upper class, and beautiful together . . . with no issues in their relationship," and asks "Why won't you consider a lesbian just as an individual?"[27]

Social formations that take place in virtual spaces and form discursive communities impact our everyday materialities. In the case of India, they reproduce normative notions of "Indianness" and encourage specific gendered subject formations in online diasporic networks, as noted by various scholars since the 1990s. Virtual communities in a contemporary Web 2.0, social media era, however, are far more scattered and even spontaneous in how they form. They form around shared media clips, around shared selfies, shared thoughts, and so on. In looking at how queering through Indian space is made visible in online space, the comparative low visibility of looking at how "queering" of Indian digital and contemporary mediated diasporas occurs mostly through a focus on male bodies being queered. For instance, while Bollywood has a long history of making visible feminized male bodies (even if as "comic relief") it is less accepting of female bodies masculinized. We saw some feminist depictions of lead female characters performing masculinity in the 1970s—more than two decades before the digital erupted as a significant way to access and share Bollywood media in diaspora. Even then, the female character was often "subjugated" into a happy ending where she re-owned her inner woman. However, in contemporary digital cultures even this sort of strong woman—let alone a queer woman—is absent, even as images of transgendered bodies become visible. I am not arguing for a sexual binary recognition or the clear recognition of the trans and queer body as clearly "female/feminine" but instead I am pointing out that even transbodies are re-cognized in popular and public space more often as male to female rather than as female to male. The female subject position remains heteronormatively female and the queering of the Indian female body in media remains far more difficult, even in humor. The trans man is often depicted more as a sexualized female in men's dress to show off "feminine" biological attributes rather than to queer the subject position.

SV: It's almost become a cliché for non-queer actors playing queer roles to receive at the very least an Oscar nomination, if not an Oscar award. This is particularly true if the actor happens to be playing a transperson. In India, there is a curious obsession with male actors dressing up as female on the screen.[28] It is often quoted as the mark of the actor's acting prowess and versatility. In the Tamil film industry, all the major actors have cross-dressed on screen, some as serious main characters but more often as comic relief. When these performances are lauded, actors who play gay or bisexual roles often face subtle backlash. The depiction of same-sex attraction between two women is in itself very fascinating. *Fire*, possibly the most popular "lesbian" movie in India, shows two sisters-in-law in unhappy marriages falling in love. When one of them, Sita, played by Nandita Das, shows subtle signs of queerness, the other, Radha, played by Shabana Azmi, is depicted as a dutiful wife and daughter-in-law. Yes, sexuality is a spectrum and is fluid, I completely agree. But depicting that the two sisters-in-law fall in love because their husbands don't pay enough attention to them is extremely problematic. Another movie that showed same sex attraction between two women is *Girlfriend* (Razdan, 2004). This movie is driven completely by the trope of the psycho lesbian who is obsessive, jealous, and violent.

RG: Simultaneously, while this heteronormativity continues to be reinforced through ("benign" and explicit) violence against women, autonomous queer (Indian) formations are emerging online. However, as scholars such as Shah have noted, such autonomous queer zones actually further reinforce ghettoization and marginalization of queer bodies.[29]

SV: In 1985, Donna Haraway, in her iconic essay "A Cyborg Manifesto," spoke about the cyborg, a fusion of animal and machine that will transcend the restrictions placed by nature on culture.[30] This meant that technology could be used to counter things that are considered "natural" and hence permanent. Though she wrote this with regard to feminism and how women should use technology to fight patriarchy (which in turn gave rise to "cyberfeminism"), it rings true, if not truer, with regard to the queer, especially queer women, who have fewer physical spaces than gay men and transgendered people. The very act of creating a public profile on a social media platform or a dating website is an act of rebellion for a lot of queer persons. They are free to be themselves and identify as their true selves. The internet created this space, albeit with a lot of the old prejudices and discriminations. But we still have a chance to queer large portions of this space, and it's important to keeping pushing for this, a truly feminist and queer internet.

NOTES

1. Elizabeth Reba Weise, "A Thousand Aunts with Modems," in *Wired Women: Gender and New Realities in Cyberspace*, ed. Lynn Cherny and Elizabeth Reba Weise (Seattle, WA: Seal Press, 1996), ix–x.

2. Relevant scholarship includes Esperanza Miyake, "My, Is That Cyborg a Little Bit Queer?" *Journal of International Women's Studies* 5, no. 2 (2004): 53–61, http://vc.bridgew.edu/jiws/vol5/iss2/6/.

3. Bettina Heinz, Li Gu, Ako Inuzuka, and Roger Zender, "Under the Rainbow Flag: Webbing Global Gay Identities," *International Journal of Sexuality and Gender Studies* 7, nos. 2–3 (2002): 107–24.

4. Lawrence Gross, Foreword to *Queer Online: Media Technology and Sexuality*, ed. Kate O'Riordan and David J. Phillips (New York: Peter Lang, 2007), vii.

5. "The 'khush' mailing list," accessed March 22, 2018, http://www.qrd.org/qrd/electronic/email/khush.

6. Radhika Gajjala, "An Interrupted Postcolonial/Feminist Cyberethnography: Complicity and Resistance in the 'Cyberfield,'" *Feminist Media Studies* 2, no. 2 (2002): 177–93, doi: 10.1080/14680770220150854.

7. Jac sm Kee, ed., *Erotics: Sex, Rights and the Internet: An Exploratory Research Study* (Johannesburg, SA: Association for Progressive Communications, 2011), https://www.apc.org/sites/default/files/EROTICS.pdf.

8. Grant Walsh-Haines, "The Egyptian Blogosphere: Policing Gender and Sexuality and the Consequences of Queer Emancipation," *Journal of Middle East Women's Studies* 8, no. 3 (2012): 41–62, doi: 10.2979/jmiddeastwomstud.8.3.41.

9. "76 Countries Where Homosexuality Is Illegal," *Erasing 76 Crimes*, last updated May 19, 2017, accessed March 19, 2018, https://76crimes.com/76-countries-where-homosexuality-is-illegal/.

10. Vikram to gay_bombay list, "g_b Lucknow—update and suggestions (1)," January 9, 2006, https://www.mail-archive.com/gay_bombay@yahoogroups.com/msg06966.html.

11. See Kate O'Riordan, "Queer Theories and Cybersubjects: Intersecting Figures," in O'Riordan and Phillips, *Queer Online*, 13–30; Nina Wakeford, "Cyberqueer," in *Cybercultures Reader*, ed. David Bell and Barbara M. Kennedy (New York: Routledge, 2002), 403–15.

12. O'Riordan, "Queer Theories," 26.

13. Tyler Curry, "Gay Men, Lesbians and the Ocean between Us," The Blog, *Huffington Post,* January 30, 2014, last updated February 2, 2016, https://www.huffingtonpost.com/tyler-curry/gay-men-lesbians-and-the-_b_4688477.html.

14. Nishant Shah, "Thrice Invisible in its Visibility: Queerness and User Generated 'Kand' Videos." *Ada: A Journal of Gender, New Media & Technology*, no. 8 (2015), doi: 10.7264/N3VD6WRR.

15. Ibid.

16. Parmesh Shahani, *Gay Bombay: Globalization, Love and (Be)longing in Contemporary India* (New Delhi: Sage, 2008).

17. Ibid., 85.

18. "A Brief History of the Spoon Collective," accessed March 22, 2018, http://www.driftline.org/spoon_collective.html.

19. "Call for Presentations: Kickstarting the GO::DH Minimal Computing Working Group @ DH2014," *Global Outlook::Digital Humanities*, accessed March 19, 2018, http://www.globaloutlookdh.org/minimal-computing/kickstart-workshop/.

20. Jenny Sundén, *Material Virtualities: Approaching Online Textual Embodiment* (New York: Peter Lang, 2003).

21. The late-1990s and early-2000s—preceding the outbursts about and claims of newness through Web 2.0—saw the emergence of weblogs and pre-Facebook-like networks such as LiveJournal and Friendster.

22. RG Note: Smita's point here resonates with discussions I had with some other interviewees regarding the faux binary of "ghar" and "bahir"—some of which is fleshed out in my interlude with Damini. However, this specific point that Smita makes also clearly resonates with Preeti Mudliar's research (referred to in an earlier chapter: Mudliar, "Public WiFi Is for Men and Mobile Internet Is for Women.") that finds that cis male bodies occupy physical public space more easily, as they access the internet through internet cafes, but female bodies tend to access the internet through physically more protected spaces by setting up Wi-Fi zones through which to access digital publics. If we are to take Smita's point, then, trans and queer bodies also feel the need for a more protected/enclosed physical space from which to access the internet to participate in digital publics.

23. Harish Iyer, quoted in Smita Vanniyar, "To Mingle and Make Friends Online: Lesbians and Bisexual Women in India and the Internet as a Safe Space to Socialise" (master's thesis, Tata Institute of Social Sciences, 2015).

24. Ibid.

25. Jasbir Puar, *Terrorist Assemblages: Homonationalism in Queer Times* (Durham, NC: Duke University Press, 2007), 2.

26. Shelly Walia, "What Indian Lesbians Have to Say about an Advertisement Depicting Indian Lesbians" (includes commentary by Rituparna Borah), *Quartz India*, June 12, 2015, https://qz.com/425657/what-indian-lesbians-have-to-say-about-an-advertisement-depicting-indian-lesbians/.

27. Ibid.

28. There are some films where female actors dress as male but those are considerably fewer in number.

29. Shah, "Thrice Invisible in its Visibility."

30. Donna Haraway, "A Cyborg Manifesto: Science, Technology, and Socialist-Feminism in the Late Twentieth Century," in *Simians, Cyborgs and Women: The Reinvention of Nature* (New York: Routledge, 1991), 149–81.

Chapter Eight

Dialogue Interlude

*Reflections on Digital Mediation and on Becoming
and Being a Dalit Feminist Thought Leader*

Christina Thomas Dhanaraj in conversation
with Radhika Gajjala

RG: Dear Christina, as you know I've been following your public
writing for a while; then I started following you on Twitter and recently
we connected on Facebook as well. Thank you for agreeing to do this
dialogue interlude for this book. You have read some—if not all—
chapters of the book. This book started out as an exploration of how
gendered Indian spaces/voices/subjectivities were emerging through
the digital in contemporary times. I began this book actually before the
Nirbhaya protests that made the Indian feminist street activisms and
Indian feminist activist use of social media visible to global news media and other outlets. Prior to that, we know that access from India did
happen and young people from India were very much in internet-mediated spaces, yet the "cyberfeminist" angle became most visible post-
2000s—some researchers point to Pinjra Todd, Pink Chaddi, and others
as key moments for this visibility.

Yet, as I have learned, and you have known for most of your internet-mediated life, these have been Savarna-dominated movements.
Dalit feminist voices often get subsumed, wherein the Dalit women get
named distinctly as Dalit only when they are victims or are claiming a
distinct identity. It is almost as if Dalit feminist voice/subjectivity is

recognizable only through the naming; and so, "Indian" feminist movements—Indian cyberfeminisms—are implicitly centered around Savarna and middle- to upper-class issues (take for instance the issues of
"ghar/bahir," "loitering," and so on). Some of the dialogue interludes in
this book center around those issues as well. The Twittersphere, however, has some very strong Dalit voices, and I have been fortunate to
meet people like you, for instance, in this space.

Here, I want to ask you to talk about your writing life, both in digital
and elsewhere (yet I know that for someone of your generation, a lot of
your writing life is possibly mostly digitally mediated—whether or not
in social media space). I know I've already framed it because of how
the book is set up: for instance, this dialogue itself is occurring because
you emerge as a thought leader and significant voice online, which puts
you in the broad "category" of a digital activist linked to the Indian
context, whether you call yourself feminist, activist, or any other label—there is a way you are being externally identified by your readers.
Some of the themes I have introduced in other chapters of this book—
both in dialogue with several others and in conceptual frameworks that
I have articulated based on research—will undoubtedly shape our conversation.

To start us off, my first question here to you is about how you view
yourself: as feminist? As activist? Can you talk about your writing
journey toward your current point of digital visibility? You are a strong
digital presence; even if not a born digital person, you are in a generation socialized digitally. How do you see yourself as a digital activist:
do you see yourself as feminist (by naming yourself as Dalit feminist—
you are Dalit and feminist on Twitter)?

CTD: My struggle has not been with the feminist label; rather, I
don't want to be seen as a mainstream Indian feminist. Feminism in
India has predominantly been defined through the Savarna (dominant-
caste) lens. For instance, even the ghar/bahar binary you posit earlier in
this book could be a Savarna issue.

My goal, as a feminist, is to break dominant systems and hierarchies
to enable the validation of oppressed women's experiences and for their
socioeconomic mobility. My feminist models are not Gloria Steinem,
Virginia Woolf, or other visible Indian feminist leaders. I turn to the
likes of Black feminists—African Americans such as bell hooks, Audre
Lorde, and Angela Davis.

At present, I want to impact the prevailing discourse on Dalit and
feminist politics; as a Dalit woman I feel that is my strength. It has to

be done; it hasn't been done for so long. I do however struggle with being labeled as an "activist." I certainly partner with activists, but I do not consider myself one. I believe I could be an influencer and perhaps, eventually, a thought leader. My ability to continue to remain in digital publics as a potential influencer and a thought leader draws on the emotional resilience I have built over time—through circumstances, opportunities, and endurance.

I do think visibility should not determine the labeling of someone as an activist, because visibility could be a result of aspects that are outside of what the activist does. It could be because of privilege, for instance. I, as an English-speaking, educated Christian woman, obviously enjoy more visibility than activists who work on the ground. Activists on the ground don't always get digital visibility—at least not the Dalit activists that I know of.

Also, perhaps, I don't understand the popular definition of activism: I believe it is the work that activists do. Activists fight for people's rights, devoting significant time and effort of their lives. I feel more comfortable calling myself a potential thought leader than an activist, even in the digital space. To be honest, all I am really doing is speaking truth to power.

All my Twitter threads come from a personal place. But it is the world that politicizes me. For instance, when I write or tweet about mental health and Dalit women, my people would read it differently from the way Savarnas would. The latter would perceive it as a political essay, while my people would read that and go, "This is exactly what I have gone through. Thank you for putting that into words." This strengthens me. It helps me know that there's a fellow survivor who's going through something similar. So just because I put out my personal truths out there, which are being seen as political, it doesn't mean I'm an activist.

RG: So how do you come to be referred to as an activist? It's obvious you don't name yourself as such.

CTD: So I had to be part of a panel discussion in San Francisco for a discussion on the film *Fandry* (Nagraj Manjule, 2013). And that was the first time I had heard someone introduce me as a Dalit activist from India. I was not comfortable with that title at all. But that discomfort is not because I don't value activism—but I feel that all of what I do does not amount to what activists do. My work is not in any way less important, but it is not groundwork—for example, I'm not working enough with Dalit women survivors.

In India, if you are contradicting the mainstream way of looking at things, you generally tend to be called an activist, and I'm very mindful when I say I'm not the activist kind. The way you compared your work in the classroom, which is still transformative but not activist—I'd like to think that my work is similar to that: transformative, not necessarily activist.

RG: Returning to the point where you said that by even having that narrative of personal experience out there (seeing the personal as "political," right?), two things happen: others politicize it and those that identify with you read it as validation. In this context it became important to name your "Dalit-ness" so as to allow other Dalit women with access to reading literacies and to the digital space to feel validated in terms of their experiences of oppression and histories. Because even if non-Dalit women speak of similar seeming experiences, it's *not* the same because historically these women come from different trajectories. So, the Dalit identity naming is important for those women you talk of—who feel validated by what you write through your personal experience.

Can you now tell me a bit about how you started this writing journey?

CTD: I started writing when I was fifteen, about twenty years ago—writing to journals and magazines, feminist and political writing, on abortion, contraception, caste, and so on. In 2006, I discovered the digital space, when I was already a part of the diaspora and living in Singapore. I used Orkut and started groups there, and I also started a blog with a fellow feminist (who was actually a guy): we came up with something like "feminist fury." That blog and Orkut were two spaces where I could connect with people who read my writing. At that time, I wasn't writing with aspirations to be a thought leader or an activist; it all came from a personal space. I was just trying to tell people what my perspective was.

I went to a school where I wasn't treated so well. My college life wasn't great either. What I went through in these spaces broke my self-esteem. I wanted to be seen and heard and the digital space gave me that opportunity. I was not getting that recognition in my offline everyday life, but when I started to write, I started getting recognition.

After a hiatus, I started to write again in 2015. This time I was deliberately political in my writing. I feel like all my work these last three years has been incredibly important for me because it has also been a personal evolution. I've learned so much and I've also been able to connect with my Dalit sisters. I did not expect that my thoughts would have so much value.

RG: Thank you again for sharing so much information with me; it is clear that whether intentional or not, you are a thought leader and a social media–based Dalit feminist influencer. Yet, as you point out in our conversations earlier and now, what you write is not something recent: you've been thinking these thoughts for a long time. The digital tools did not "give you voice"—your voice developed through your personal life experiences and struggles that you have worked through.

CTD: My Twitter experience has taught me a few things. People are so oblivious to Dalit women and their unique experiences. The level of ignorance in mainstream communities is mind-blowing. I can't believe people aren't already talking of "inclusion" from the perspective of marginalized communities.

RG: There are questions about what "inclusive" means—the co-optation of the idea of "inclusion" for so-called diversity plans and so on. These have now become buzz words—continually used, but not redefined in relation to actual marginal communities and what comes from their experience. So in that sense what you're saying is very important. Do go ahead.

CTD: That's pretty much it as far as my evolution as a digital space-based influencer is concerned. Twitter has been a great space—even with its contradictions. This may not be true for all thought leaders, activists, or Dalit women, but I do feel that on Twitter I don't have to wait for a magazine or an editor to decide what I get to publish.

RG: So what you are saying is that the gatekeeping is reduced if you have particular forms of social and technical literacies. We still don't have enough formal offline/print outlets for the kind of writing you do for instance—and digital formats such as Twitter, *Medium*, and blogging allow you to bypass that sort of formalized infrastructural gatekeeping. Yet this works because you've trained yourself to write formally and to public audiences, even prior to the digital featuring heavily in your writing and self-expression. In that sense you are not like the "born digital" person who may have started most of their writing publicly online.

CTD: Just to be clear, there is a lot of language on Twitter that's extremely crass, and those in dominant social locations get away with it—they don't feel the need to self-police. But when a person from a marginalized location dares to call out or use crass language, they get blocked from these social media spaces. So I will contest your point on cultural capital and socio-technical literacies.

RG: Yes, please do. I want you to push back on the point about cultural capital and how people engage on Twitter because the point I made is potentially based in an elitism that privileges a particular sociality.

CTD: The only contention that I had to that point is that I think there are a lot of right-wing people who may not be lacking cultural capital in the larger Indian society, but their language is not in any way indicative of any social and cultural training/education. There are people on Twitter that do get away with extremely crass language, too. And yet, they don't get the treatment that a Dalit woman Twitter user gets.

RG: And the onus for people from marginalized positions is to have double the cultural understanding.

CTD: That's something my partner keeps reminding me of, too. In fact, Michelle Obama said to Stephen Colbert: "We couldn't afford to make mistakes," in a recent interview with him about her experiences in the White House. [1] And that's not only because she happens to be on a pedestal, but also because of her race. And it's a very similar experience. Like because of my social location, I cannot afford to be crass. Many times, I'm tempted to swear, but of late, I have deliberately stopped myself from using a certain type of language.

RG: I noticed.

CTD: I don't want to: (a) lose this opportunity; and (b) I don't want to lose out on the opportunities I have with my people who are maybe looking up to me. And for that I'm completely okay not being able to use Twitter as a venting platform—if the reward for that is that I am able to have access to my people and influence the right things.

It is sad that Dalit women are supposed to engage in a self-filtering sort of mechanism when they are writing, because one misplaced step can backfire.

All of the articles I have written over the past one year or so were mostly commissioned. But if I were to spend a significant part of my time putting out tweets on sex and penis and masturbation, I am pretty sure I would not be enjoying the same kind of "visibility," at least not in a positive sense. These are some of the things that are working against me within the Twitter space.

There is of course the usual backlash. Even today, someone had said, "Hey your name is Christina, how can you be Dalit? Are you going to apply for your OBC certificate?" My partner was like, "Wait till they know what was in your precious certificate." You see I don't have a caste certificate. I came under open competition—competing strictly on merit and nothing else.

This kind of trolling, it happens all the time. And sometimes it is hurtful; sometimes it's terrible. But I also see that in perspective because unfortunately I am very well informed of the kind of struggle and violence that my women go through. And whether we want to accept it or not—I do believe there is magnitude to suffering. I do believe there is a scale to violence, and therefore I want to place this kind of digital-based violence in contrast to the kind of violence that my women are facing on the ground. I can always log out of Twitter, I can always block these trolls; I can always delete my Twitter account. There is a way for me to protect myself from this violence.

RG: Yes, yes; there's a difference between discursive violence and there's even a difference between physically present emotional abusers in your everyday life and discursive violence.

CTD: Exactly. Unless there is actual violence that follows from these threats.

RG: Does the potential for being stalked increase through digital visibility?

CTD: I would not say that's the biggest thing acting against me. The things that are acting against me are things like the fact that I can't be completely myself. But there is also caste-based slut shaming and trolling. Once I got called a very horrible caste slur, but these are also things that have happened to me all my life. It is just a digital iteration of what is happening in the real world.

RG: They are micro-aggressions.

CTD: Yeah. I think as part of my Twitter thread, I did talk about this particular ex-classmate of mine, who tagged me and a few other lawyers, asking what section I needed to be booked under. That was a scary situation.

I have to keep reminding myself about my ultimate objective—what I really want to do within this digital space. Over the past year or so I have kind of focused more on Twitter in the digital space rather than Facebook. So I want to use Twitter more constructively and I do believe the space has a lot of potential for Dalit women. Not just in terms of putting our thoughts across, but also in terms of giving visibility to the ground-level activism that goes on every day.

Other Dalit women activists do this, too. This is potentially a huge opportunity for us. It would open several avenues and doors for us for solidarity, partnerships, and collaborations, even internationally. It also gives us an opportunity to cover the kind of work that we do within UN and other human rights mechanisms, as well as other international feminist spaces that we are part of. For example, we were part of the Association for Women's Rights in Development (AWID) conference in 2016. I was part of the United Nations Human Rights Council and the Universal Periodic Review that happened in 2017.[2] For all of this work that we are doing, I think Twitter has huge potential for us—both in terms of exposure and visibility as well as sustaining and creating partnerships. These are things that are working well for me as well as the movement that I am attached with. And I will continue to use this space because, like I said, I am not dependent on any editors or writing spaces that will decide on how good my work is or not. Sometimes I feel like my Twitter threads get more visibility than my articles do.

RG: Yes. That's because of the way in which people read nowadays.

CTD: I am absolutely okay with it and I compile it into moments and I have a repository of all the thoughts that I am putting out there. And sometimes, this is precisely what I want to do. I want to be able to—for lack of a better word—I want to do inception on people. I want to break their ways of thinking, their mindsets. And I am learning how to do it and I am learning how to do it more effectively and be more impactful. Not necessarily in a manner that will make them defensive, but in a manner that will really change them.

RG: Somebody else might describe themselves as an activist for doing all this work, right? It's because your work is beyond Twitter. You are networked in spaces that kind of move agendas forward. And again, we have all this discussion around why somebody might not want to use the word activist or not. So, let's leave that. Let's pause that. It's something to be explored further at length.

It's lovely that you also talked about the fact that you had the Orkut group. It's evidence of the fact that Indian women and women from Global South or other places not in Europe, the UK, or the USA didn't suddenly appear and become global. It's not like an Arab Spring. Well even Arab Spring wasn't an Arab Spring, right?

So, it's not like suddenly you have found yourself because of Twitter. You have been negotiating different spaces to access writing spaces. This is why your points are so rich—your writing self moves according to the technologies for writing available and according to how digital publics open up within each technology, so to speak.

So, for example, we had gatekeeping in newspapers that was different—the infrastructures and hierarchies of gatekeeping in contexts of print publishing were, and still are, far more oppressive. Shedding that gatekeeping and writing through *Medium* or Twitter, it does different things. What you said that was very valuable is that even there, you kind of policed your voice so that what you say is not thrown away. You did not want what you are saying to be made disposable or frivolous.

And so you are still working within a certain code of behavior that is implicitly defined by particular hierarchies. And you are also pointing—which I agree with—to the fact that when you are a liberal white feminist or a liberal Savarna feminist, you resort to these seemingly rebellious behaviors that have a different valence in relation to perceptions of Dalit women's bodies.

Your points about Dalit women on Twitter and the extra self-policing expected have also moved us now to a discussion of Dalit women's bodies being seen as exploitable and disposable (to use your own words in our conversations). You also mentioned some points in regards to this in the article "Swipe Me Left, I'm Dalit."[3]

CTD: Dalit women and expression of sexuality is situated in a different power hierarchy—just talking about what might be considered to be sexually blatant on Twitter, for instance, cannot be sexual liberation for us. Rather it has to be established that Dalit women are not sexual objects and that our bodies are not sexual by default.

RG: Yes. Because Dalit women's bodies are already on the streets, so to speak (as Divya was also noting in her dialogue for this book).

CTD: Exactly. And I try to touch upon this as part of my "Swipe Me Left, I'm Dalit" article on dating. The article was very much inspired from how black women have been stereotyped as Jezebels and Sapphires and Mammies. Melissa V. Perry talks about this in *Sister Citizen: Shame, Stereotypes, and Black Women.*[4] I think she is just amazing. *Sister Citizen* is a seminal piece of work. I think Dalit women face very similar stereotypes.

I have articulated similar stereotypes where Dalit women are seen as promiscuous women, as victims and as aggressive. I think that Jenny Rowena's article on Silk Smitha is also amazing—she writes about how the movie got made, *The Dirty Picture* (Milan Luthria, 2011) and how Vidya Balan acted in it.[5] And of course, she talks about several things, you know: how Dalit women's bodies are typically seen as exploitable and therefore disposable and all of it. But when Vidya Balan performs the role, she literally just dons this Dalit woman thingy and then post-movie, she goes back to being a sacred woman. She has briefly been sexualized for the purposes of commerciality—for commercial purposes. And then she just steps out of that whole mask. And it's very interesting to think about it because when such movies get made, like, what are they ultimately saying? They are basically reiterating and regurgitating the same old stereotype that we have been trying to fight for so long.

RG: Yes, and so there's a gentrification that kind of redeems Silk Smitha?

CTD: Exactly, exactly. And only as determined by the Savarnas and accepted by them. So, it's implied that only if there is this scaffolding that's constructed by Savarnas can Dalit women live and function.

It's the minds of Savarnas as defined by Savarnas, right? And so most of our articulation, if I am right, has been only from the perspective of liberating ourselves from these stereotypes. So as part of my work, at least hopefully in the next two years, I will be able to articulate and pen a piece on what it means to be a Dalit woman and give yourself the freedom to be sexual.

Like, what does sexuality mean? My expression of liberation and feminism cannot touch upon aspects of sexuality, and it has still not.

RG: This problematizes even movements like Why Loiter, wouldn't you say? I know that's what Divya says.

CTD: Yeah, exactly. And so I want to be able to write that piece, and the digital space is the way to do it. Because I remember writing two pieces of poetry. Actually, there was this Italian researcher who got in touch with me and another person named Maari. And she wanted to publish a book, an anthology of poetry, and one of the themes that she gave—I mean, she had several themes to pick, and I picked—Eros. I wrote five poems on sex and sensuality and erotica. I mean you can call it erotic pieces of poetry. And two of those I read as part of a poetry reading, both in Bangalore as well as in Beijing. And it's very, very caste-heavy poetry. Both are erotica and caste heavy.

So, I want to be able to get to a point where I am able to leverage the opportunity the digital space has given me to write about these things. Maybe I am wrong, but I don't remember anyone talking about—any Dalit woman talking about—sexuality and freedom and liberation, the way that mainstream feminists do.

It is something that is not spoken about, and I see digital space as a good opportunity for me to be able to talk about it. I won't talk about it now but at some point.

RG: Thank you so much.

CTD: Thanks; have a good day.

NOTES

1. *The Late Show with Stephen Colbert*, "Full Interview: Michelle Obama Talks to Stephen Colbert," YouTube video, 27:52, December 1, 2018, https://www.youtube.com/watch?v=jXwaQXquA7E.

2. "Universal Periodic Review," United Nations Human Rights Council, accessed December 11, 2018, https://www.ohchr.org/en/hrbodies/upr/pages/uprmain.aspx.

3. Christina Thomas Dhanaraj, "Swipe Me Left, I'm Dalit," *GenderIT*, April 14, 2018, https://www.genderit.org/node/5082/.

4. Melissa Harris-Perry, *Sister Citizen: Shame, Stereotypes, and Black Women in America* (Harford, CT: Yale University Press, 2013).

5. Jenny Rowena, "The 'Dirt' in *The Dirty Picture*: Caste, Gender and Silk Smitha," *Savari*, June 17, 2012, http://www.dalitweb.org/?p=736.

Chapter Nine

Further Dialogue Interludes

This chapter is presented as a series of conversations between various actors invested and active in digital streets practices and activism. Each conversation is presented separately in order to maintain the internal composition and flow of dialogue between the coauthor and myself as this chapter moves from one theme to the next. There were several other interludes begun between March and July 2018, but we were unable to complete them in time for the final book manuscript submission deadline. We hope to continue these conversations in other formats and in continuing collaborations.

ON FEMINIST DIGITAL STREETS

Dialogue Interlude with Pallavi Guha

RG: Pallavi Guha and I pooled together our research understandings of digital feminist activism in a dialogue. Pallavi recently completed her doctorate in journalism from the University of Maryland. Her research examines the role of news media and social media in building an anti-rape and sexual assault public agenda. In her research, she examined the influence of both news and social media platforms in anti-rape and sexual assault feminist activism and interviewed sixty-five feminist activists and journalists. I had interviewed her several times in the process of writing this book—first as a South Asian woman living in the United States who uses digital tools personally and then as I heard her present her research in various conference venues. Now we come together as co-researchers to discuss what each of us is seeing through the research we have each done and how this manifests in relation to what I am referring to as the Indian digital (feminist) streets. The conversation here focused mainly around rural feminists in relation to digital publics and in relation to policy change—micro and macro.

PG: Based on our recent conversation, I have identified nine interrelated themes listed below. Radhika and I will attempt to briefly address these themes (not necessarily in a linear order, as the themes will connect up in conversation) here in dialogue and raise questions while also narrating examples. The themes are:

1. Hierarchization of feminist activism in India: I couldn't meet the field officers of a feminist organization because the director decided to call off our meeting, and I was not allowed to speak with the field officers in the absence of the leadership. Yet another feminist activist, who is well quoted in the media, told me she only does face-to-face interviews or conversations, and asked me if I would travel to India for the interview.
2. Process, resource differentials, gatekeeping in feminist activism in India.
3. Clustering them rural and urban; English-speaking upper-class and Indian-language-speaking lower-class activists.
4. Digital feminists want to influence public agenda and awareness. Rural feminists go a step forward and try to bring small changes by engaging with law enforcement and policy makers. For instance, they negotiate with law enforcement to take action so that the young women can go to college without getting harassed by the boys.
5. Problematic when bigger feminist organizations have strong ties with international organizations: become involved in branding, co-opting the hashtags to promote. Based on Facebook curation.
6. Rural feminist activists were much more involved and dispassionate about their work. Most of them said: ask me whatever you need to know. Some of them said they didn't even have the necessary resources to go from one village to another to do dharna—some women/girls would sometimes skip breakfast or lunch to save money to travel.
7. Assumptions of identity politics in feminist activism: struggles of activism.

8. Community and localized feminism: example of Raya and rural feminist activism.
9. The role of feminist organizations aligning to political party.

RG: Pallavi, thank you for that very helpful listing of themes from our Skype conversation in March 2018. With your permission I recorded the conversation, and we have now replayed it several times so that we might unpack the themes a bit. Your excellent dissertation work points to the differences in process and resource differentials in regard to rural feminists and metropolitan feminists. In talking to other collaborators and feminist startup founders such as Riddhima Sharma and Japleen Pasricha, we also came to see that there are differences in resources even among feminist startups and nonprofits in terms of funding and access to skilled and voluntary labor and know-how as well. As we chatted, we realized that we had in fact interviewed some of the same people among the groups of self-identified digital feminists. I, however, have not had the opportunity to interview rural feminists, and my understanding of their feminism comes from ethnographic visits to rural areas in India and from reviewing literature—including your research. Can you say something about how rural feminists see the relevance or don't see the relevance of access to social media for their activism?

PG: Rural feminist activists understand that social media platforms are the way to go to reach out to people outside of their communities. Possibly that's the reason most of them have been venturing into the digital space—setting up Facebook pages, posting photographs and videos, and networking with journalists through WhatsApp. But their main focus is still community-level activism, where they try to influence policy making and support girls/women against violent perpetrators. Most rural feminist activists are quite open about their struggles and challenges on digital platforms. Initially they would seek out help within the family, but some of them have now ventured out to smaller digital media strategy firms. The anti-rape rural feminist activists are also very open about their work and strategy, unlike the urban activists.

RG: So, what do you mean by community level? Isn't that what metropolitan feminists also do—advocate for policy change in relation to specific problems that arise?

PG: By community level, I mean very localized issues, such as young women trying to go to college who have to face street sexual harassment (eve-teasing). And there are other incidents such as domestic violence, use of toilets, and caste-based violence against women for whom the rural activists work. They are looking forward to resolve the issues for their community and within their community; whether it results in policy change or not, they want a change in the circumstances. They are trying to create safe spaces, but going head-on with the issues; if the cops tell them to adjust, they don't take no for an answer—they start picketing and networking with the journalists to make them listen and do their job. This does not bring about any policy change—a bill or something—but it brings about a change in the attitude. Gradually the law enforcement officials start to cooperate—which is their job anyway! The rural activism forces them to go back to basics. The rural feminist community tries to bring about a change within the community and awareness in the people. By looking at the small picture, they are trying to influence the bigger picture. In my understanding, metropolitan feminists are looking to bring about policy changes such as the Verma Commission, and they deal with the bigger picture only.

RG: Pallavi, I'd like you to take a look at the dialogue interlude with Shilpa Phadke (chapter 3) and return here to talk about some of the key points you make above if you don't mind? I think you might have something to say. Feel free to quote from that interlude.

PG: It was empowering to read about #Whyloiter, and the points that Shilpa made reiterate what I have also gone through as a young woman in India. Loitering, or as it is said in Bengali, *rock r adda* or *rockbaj*, is a prerogative of boys or men. Whenever girls roam around, it is looked upon and discussed with disdain! And so #Whyloiter is a great initiative, but, again, to me it is only possible for urban, city-based women with access to the internet. Rural women are equally reclaiming public spaces. In my interviews with some of the rural feminist activists from West Bengal, they said that they meet up at the chatal (an open public space in the village) at 6:30 p.m. a few times a week, where all the women of the village meet up to talk about sexual violence and other violence. There are no invitations, but everyone in the village knows that it's the time when the women meet up to talk about anything they want. They don't hashtag; they just spread the information by word and engage as such. And this in itself is a movement, where they have claimed a public space in the village to discuss their issues, including violence. I see it as being similar to a chat room or a hashtag movement. There are more examples of claiming public spaces, such as the *dharnas* the rural feminist activists would engage in.

Dialogue Interlude with Pallavi Rao

RG: Pallavi, thank you very much for agreeing to converse with me about Indian digital feminisms and your observations as you continue to do work on caste and media spaces. Could you start us off on the conversation with your preferred point of entry? I will then ask further questions—you have read some of the previous interludes and a draft of the chapter on digital streets, so you can feel free to question/critique my approach to this issue as well.

PR: Thank you. I have been thinking a lot about conversations I've seen in digital spaces about the term "'Savarna feminist." The response by Brahmin-Savarna women has been to treat this term with suspicion, keeping it in quote marks and continually referring to it as something *others* term *us*. I cannot recollect more than a handful of instances, where Savarna women have either accepted their Savarna positionality or addressed it when discussing caste.

What does it mean to term someone a "Savarna feminist"? Is it an epithet? Is it an ad hominem argument? Can we put into words and thoughts what it means when we're called "Savarna feminists"?

In my own work, personal actions/reflections, and activism, I take the term quite seriously as decentering my lenses and filters applied to the world of patriarchy. It continually destabilizes what feminist critique has been so far in my life, like questioning something like #YesAllMen. Or agonizing over whose empowerment and liberation I talk about when I say "women's lib." I constantly run the questions, "Which women? Whose liberation?" in my head as a refrain, as a reminder.

However, it seems that digital feminist media and feminist media scholarship have yet to pause and rethink these possibilities. The old caste-ignorant approach persists, and I find myself increasingly aggravated by pop culture discourse on the internet.

RG: In thinking about location and in unpacking ideologies of knowledge production, how might we move forward in this critical work?

PR: I don't have a blueprint to follow, so I find that I have to make many of the mistakes myself in order to learn. With mistakes, they can paralyze you. Or they can galvanize you to do better, and so I have

found two particular ways in the very personal realm where the galva-
nizing has felt really productive.

One is the dismantling of the long-held biases, assumptions, and
ignorance of my immediate family. This is almost a pedagogic exercise, and my brain goes into teacher mode for this intervention. This is
also uneven and not always consistent, but it works. I have slowly been
training my parents to go beyond casteist WhatsApp forwards, or that
polemical Brahminism in the workplace, and to go to Google, to look
up stats, facts, and records to educate themselves—and to not perform
empathy in this particularly South Asian way where we revel in con-
descending pity or savior-like smugness, but to have a genuine empathy, where they can imagine what it must be like in the places of the
marginalized. If the personal is the political, then the political has to be
made personal, so I do the work of bringing caste power into the family
dinner table talk. One sneaky way that *really* works is when I make my
mother—who is fluent in Tamil and Marathi—translate Periyar and
Phule for me, as I don't read either language. She is herself surprised
by how much she ends up sympathetic to their politics. Radicalizing
my parents just that little bit has already given me a little feeling of
freedom from caste-patriarchy, and I know they sense a feeling of our
relationship having opened up more. These are small feelings and small
moments of success, but I hold on to them until I can ensure there's a
next one.

The second way I approach the issue has been more complicated. I
am deep into this slow process of unlearning socialized caste practices,
and a lot of it has come from reading and writing, from immersing
myself into histories, polemics, and analytics authored in multiple
places. This is already reeking of privilege—to say that I'm doing a
PhD in unlearning, to spend hours on end tracking down an obscure
document of Ambedkar's, to access this entire world of scholarly literature about caste locked up in American ivory towers of academia. To
present reading and writing as labor when it's also a deep pleasure and
self-indulgence bothers me. But it has undeniably been an epistemic
shift and valuable in the way that perhaps diary writing is. I think about
the blog space I have on *Medium*, for instance, and about three of the
posts that came from reading Ann Stoler's *Carnal Knowledge and
Imperial Power* and coming to the idea that a Brahminical politics of
the home and the bedroom is loaded with power. That style of informal
yet analytical critical writing is something I keep wanting to perfect
every day; on days when I write a perfect sentence that manages to say

just everything that needs to be said, it feels like a breakthrough. I also seek out other essays I want to write, like Katie Schmid's "Why Would Anyone Ever Want to Be a Wife?" which made me pick up my laptop and start writing sentences in the hope that even one would turn out as lovely and lucid as Schmid's.[1]

So, for me at least, the immediate outward turn and the immediate inward turn are where the critical work clashes least with location and still feels like it's radical and interventionist. The larger projects of building solidarities, interventions, organizing, and documenting histories I keep working on through whatever associations and networks I can find that are led by Ambedkarites and anti-caste activists.

RG: Thank you for sharing a small bit of your struggle toward this journey of unlearning our privilege. In talking to various others as part of a feminist iterative process of cowriting in this book, I have begun several dialogue interludes—over and beyond the many interviews I've done and exceeding those that are actually being included in the final published version of this book. Unfortunately, this iterative process contains mostly exchanges with young women from locations such as yours. Those that have written with me in this manner are either within the academia in India, in Europe, or in the United States. I had interviews and Twitter DM exchanges with several Dalit activists and twitter influencers – and who form part of the phenomena of what Washington Post[2] refers to as the "Dalit Twitter." A few of them are in the various interludes in this book – such as Raya Sarkar/Steier, Varsha Ayyar, Divya Kandukuri and Christina Thomas Dhanraj

If you have any last words to say to wrap up our dialogue, I'd love to include them here.

PR: I think we have to acknowledge that the global flows of capital—material and sociocultural—benefit transnational elites first, and they have staked out spaces in digital feminist platforms or initiatives. But also, rather than make that purely pejorative, we can talk about the inevitability that global/transnational spaces are designed to have been occupied by transnational elites prior to anyone else—the global village has always been conditionally accessible to things like knowledge of English, crossing digital divides, and infrastructural lack.

I also want to say that as much as the feminist project is to smash the patriarchy, too few Brahmin-Savarna feminists center caste ideology in analysis and activism. Caste is a regional episteme in South Asia through which many other identities are mediated: class, gender, sexuality, ethnicity, language, and so on. However, when one encounters discussions of contemporary urban feminist activisms, caste, which is critical to analysis, is minimized. For instance, does popular discourse understand that rapes are a function of caste (even those of Brahmin-Savarnas, Nirbhayas, and Tehelka journalists)? How does decriminalizing Section 377 (i.e., homosexuality) news commentary understand caste, which is essential to constructing norms of heteronormativity and the "deviance" of homosexuality? How do "loitering" or "Pinjra Tod" as feminist praxis pay attention to divisions of caste? While these issues are acknowledged, any Bahujan voices or critiques in these spaces are somehow not prioritized. Becoming radical with caste will therefore have to mean:

1. Not paying lip service by mentioning "Dalit women" as an anonymous collectivity but to name, recognize, and acknowledge who we are engaging with;
2. Not inviting token Dalits to events and conferences as "add-ons" (as Christina Thomas Dhanraj pointed to on Twitter) and instead centering their critique of caste-patriarchy as the most acute analysis of the system we are trapped in;[3]
3. That the problem of caste cannot be the problem only of Dalits, and so it means emphasizing that there are stakes for all women in dismantling caste, which shapes the particular forms of the patriarchy they experience.

And so caste, as it features in their lives and spheres, should be an urgent issue for all South Asian feminists.

So, when we talk about Third World women, the binaries of colonizer/colonized/ or Western/non-Western or North/South simply do not do justice to the violence women face disproportionately across South Asia. The postcolonial native is not unitary. The subaltern woman is not unitary. In our hurry to critique neoliberal white feminist discourse, we cannot presume that our participation in other forms of elite feminist networks is innocent or our neglect in addressing it is "not so bad."

These binaries have always been muddled by the graded hierarchies that the elites and the colonized bourgeoisie have occupied, and historiography, cultural studies, sociology, and gender studies are only now unravelling the muddy territories we have taken for granted. I am thinking, for instance, of Ann Stoler's focus on the middle-class whites who were subject to colonial regimes of conjugality and sexuality when they moved to the colonies.[4] These gradations of whiteness in imperial bureaucracy are matched by gradations such as caste or ethnicity in the colonies, complicated along class lines and racial boundaries, and rather than elide or reduce them through binaries, a nuanced topography of how they have transferred into digital spaces (and remain pertinent in the non-digital medium) is necessary.

RG: There's a lot more discussion we can have of course following this supposed "wrap up"—but I'll wait for continuing projects to unfold clearer strategies that produce ruptures in how postcolonial feminisms, South Asian feminisms, transnational feminisms, and/or Third World feminisms have thus far engaged these issues. An important difference between previous decades of attempts and contemporary modes of disruption to me is the increasing internet visibility of Dalit feminist viewpoints in global, transnational, Anglophone, discursive, and activist spaces. As I've noted in the introduction (and in past research) and as various scholars and activists have also noted, digital activism occurs in a neocolonial ethos. Further, in regard to social media as a facilitator of social justice movements, the mainstream, West-centric celebrations of "Arab Spring" protests set the stage for the ways in which Indian digital activism is generally talked about, even by some activists themselves. This is perhaps because of an inadequate exposure to the history of internet connectivity, and hierarchies of connectivity have already set the stage for digital publics and how they are received. As Ramesh Srinivasan notes, "A public narrative has surfaced of fearless youth activists, working in tandem with the masses to unhinge dictatorial power, armed with cellphones, Twitter feeds, and Facebook groups"; in actuality, these visible activist feeds are but a tip of a small percentage of the larger movements that have a larger presence spatially, temporally, and technologically, but often remain invisible to mainstream audiences.[5]

Thus what is visible now in the digital as a calling-out through contemporary Indian public spaces and digital publics has had a long history of struggle. Only in the recent past, with a shift (however slight) in the demographics of India's Western-educated, English-speaking/ writing, and mobile gadget–bearing diasporic populations do we see an emergence of these voices from the margins in digital publics. Yet it is these very voices that now play a strong role in pointing out how institutionalized academic and feminist spaces engage in tokenism of the sort you point to. Some of the remedies suggested—in the list above—for the exclusion of Dalits in mainstream activist or academic spaces are similar to points made by Black feminists. In fact, even postcolonial and transnational feminists themselves have made such points in relation to ourselves in Western academia. The mode of engagement through digital publics in contemporary call-out cultures serves both to reveal and rupture hierarchies, but it also works to invisibilize the long histories and nuances within these struggles.

It will be interesting to see how postcolonial/transnational/Third World feminist formations—themselves fairly recent in the history of what is narrated as "feminism" (through a Eurocentric lens)—will respond to having the fissures and ruptures revealed. Pallavi, do you want to add any final words here from your location generationally as entering global digital publics in a post-Twitter and post-Facebook ethos?

PR: Yes, I agree, my own position as a Brahmin woman in American academia is entrenched in certain epistemic privileges that are undeniable, as are the choices I frame as feminist and empowering. Therefore, I take meticulous note of how and when I can claim the status of a "woman of color." Digital online spaces are often where big reminders are often driven home for me, and it's where I have had exchanges that are both fruitful and moving. The challenge of where this fits into "movements," rather than existing as cyberspace ephemera, is what I would continue to unravel.

ON #LOSHA

Dialogue Interlude with Ayesha Vemuri and Raya Sarkar (who is now Raya Steier)

Note: Although Ayesha and I Skyped with Raya a couple times and also recorded the conversations with their permission and transcribed much of it, we are reconstructing the dialogue here in three distinct voices with all three of us speaking to each other, rather than characterize what Raya said in third person.

Soon after I finished one rough draft of the main chapters in this book, and following several Twitter exchanges with fellow South Asian feminists in our own little Twitterverse of discussion around writing projects and feminist debates around "the list" and so on, Ayesha Vemuri offered to get in touch with Raya Sarkar so we could talk in more detail about the process of putting #LoSHA together, the backlash, and so on from Raya's point of view. We had two long Skype sessions with Raya: Raya gave generously of her time and patiently explained the reasons, the process, and the methodology behind #Lo-

SHA. Ayesha and I then worked together through email and Google Docs to select parts of our dialogue with Raya so as to elaborate with commentary and thoughts of our own in relation to the idea of [feminist] digital streets laid out in chapter 5 of this book. The goal here is to reveal a process involved in the digital activism of the crowdsourced list, which we feel is different from some other digital streets activisms such as the dissemination of feminist opinion pieces and activist voices through blogs (such as kafila.online *and* Ladies Finger*); feminist startups with their dissemination of feminist messages and information through Twitter, Instagram, and Facebook (such as feminismindia and FemPositive, for instance); and movements such as #whyloiter, #girlsatdhabas, #pinjratod, and online activism related to the Delhi rape. What follows is a dialogue between Ayesha and me in conversation with some selections of the transcript of our conversation with Raya interspersed.*

RG: Ayesha, as you probably sensed, this morning I had a bit of an "aha" moment following our conversations with Raya yesterday and a few days ago. Raya, I feel you belong to a different wave of digital activists than those using social media for putting messages out.[6] The activism you initiated instead offers to do a large portion of the invisible work (whether it was offline or through digital connectivity). The work was done within and through the digital with a lot of victims of sexual harassment connecting with you through their everyday-life digital sociality. The digital was a safe space for them to connect with each other and to call out their harassers in public through the digital. In chapter 7, Smita Vanniyar notes how the digital became a safe space of coming out of the closet for many LGBTQ youth since the 1990s. This release of the list it seems to me is in a similar vein; it also allows border crossings because it's a transnational space rather than bound down by local academic hierarchies and—more importantly in your case, Raya—also local (and brutal) caste hierarchies that silence young women from naming their harassers.

AV: Interesting, I hadn't thought about it in that way before, but I agree that in Raya's case, the digital space is both intimately known, through everyday social life, and also a kind of safe space, in that it offers these young women an opportunity to name their harassers without being subject to scrutiny and disbelief or worse. Raya, you spoke several times about the accessibility and transparency of digital spaces, and that those were some of the main reasons you chose to post the list on Facebook. In terms of accessibility, by posting the list on Facebook, you and the other survivors were able to bypass the gatekeepers of "traditional" spaces, and gain quick and easy access to public-facing posts (even though the list was not intended to be this viral phenomenon it became). In terms of transparency, Facebook allowed them to be transparent about the particular academics who had harassed or abused women without needing to be beholden to the often silent and secretive spaces of university harassment committees and so on. In many ways, the list was a response to the fact that outside spaces—the offline world—are normally unsafe, especially for the young women who contributed to the list. The list was like a proposition to help make those spaces slightly safer; it therefore functioned as an exercise of warning one another, of looking out for one another. So, although it provided a kind of safe space—albeit a very fragile one—it was also a space of feminist praxis in that the women were believed, their stories were heard (by Raya, I mean), and they were supported. And this, of course, is often one of the major things both lacking in traditional court systems, as well as what so many survivors say they need in order to begin the process of healing.

   RG: Anyway, before we proceed, I want to say thank you again to both of you. Ayesha, thank you so much for mobilizing this connection and the generosity with which you offered to make time to connect me to Raya. Raya, thank you for your generosity. As busy as you are in your personal life at this time and as much time and emotional energy as the backlash around this list has taken from you, you could have said no. But you did not, and I very much appreciate this. So to continue . . . Raya, can you tell us what digital space means to you?

   RS: I would like to first explain what the digital space means to me and why I chose to disseminate data/whistleblow about alleged sexual harassers through it. The digital space is where one may develop a presence independent of beneficial kinship arrangements and beneficial privileged networks that one needs in real life to develop a similar presence. Even though only around 30 percent of the Indian population has access to the internet, the space is still more accessible than social spaces in real time. Information is accessible, and you don't have to physically be in spaces that are inaccessible to large swaths of the population, such as conferences, lectures, classrooms, or judicial arbitration rooms to access knowledge and information. You can not only access information, but also engage with it in digital spaces, and this is why I chose to disseminate a list on my social media profile through which I am connected to many people. Digital spaces demand transparency; for example, people often bring up old tweets made by famous figures reflecting one opinion that clashes with their latest tweet. I feel this extent of transparency is scary to many people, especially to those who in the past got away with saying one thing behind closed doors and doing the opposite in praxis. Because of this culture of transparency in the digital space, I decided to post on my social media—whoever wanted to access it could do so by going to my profile.

AV: The other thing that I was struck by, as we discussed in our Skype session with you, Raya, was your detailed and sincere description of the *process* of creating the list. Oftentimes, those reporting about the list or commenting on it tended to present it as something that was somehow a childish or thoughtless act. Many—both those who criticized you as well as those who supported you—left out the thought and process behind the list.

RS: Since a large number of women approached me to share their experiences of sexual harassment at the hands of academics, I decided to process all of it through a comprehensive methodology. I looked up case laws on sexual harassment in India like *Visakha v. State of Rajasthan*, among others, to understand what the courts have said about sexual harassment. I added the accused's name to the list only when their alleged actions were within the scope of sexual harassment decided by the Indian courts. Many women presented me with tangible evidence like damning emails, texts, phone records, and complaint reports that substantiated their testimonies. I think women collect all forms of damning evidence because they fear they may not be taken seriously otherwise. It was a very long and taxing process because I was not merely collecting data but also engaging with persons who have been through trauma and who deserve sensitivity and a space where they are believed and not aggressively interrogated. The emotional labor took a toll on me, too, because reading so many instances of sexual harassment was quite triggering.

RG: So there was a lot of work—invisible offline and online labor, so to speak—that went into this moment that seemed to some to be a whim and a fancy. It seems as though it was spontaneous in thought and idea, but driven by sincerity and a detailed process.

AV: Raya, when you shared this process, I was struck by two main things. First, the intense labor you clearly undertook and the thoughtfulness with which you conducted the process of creating the list. Throughout this process, you were aware of the ways in which women are regularly revictimized by formal systems and sought to avoid doing further harm by actively caring for them, and doing that emotional labor of bearing witness to their stories and experiences. But at the same time, you also did the other labor of examining the legal system, the definitions of assault and harassment that already exist in the courts and in university or workplace sexual harassment committees. And finally, you also performed the labor of collecting evidence. As you reminded us, you are, after all, a lawyer by training. And that's the second thing: so many media reports and online conversations mentioned this fact in passing, but didn't really seem to examine more deeply how this affects and shapes your activism. By creating the list, you are not automatically dismissing due process or the law. In fact, as you mentioned, you asked all the survivors if they were interested in filing a formal complaint, and also offered to help them with that. And I think the fact that so much online debate elides this completely reveals how little we are willing to engage with nuance and admit that digital activists, like any other activists, are also drawing on other kinds of knowledge.

There is an assumption that digital activists, or "fingertip activists," as Nivedita Menon so dismissively called it, are less authentic, more naive, and more childish than "real activists."[7] Yet, the use of digital tools is merely one obvious step in activist praxis—as activists have always used the media and technologies at their disposal in doing their work. I see digital activism of this sort to be as sophisticated, as well as full of errors, as any other activist media practice in the past.

RG: The irony here, of course, is that those who are dismissing the work of the list have themselves been pioneers of a sort in the digital activist space. Prior to the Arab Spring, the Egypt uprisings, and the Delhi rape activism that all went viral through social media such as Facebook, and Twitter particularly, there was the idea that the digital tools should be used for citizen media. This started as early as 2003— through the blogosphere. *Kafila.online* was one of the first groups to get online into this sort of space through blogging. These were not what we would call "digital natives," but they certainly were willing to use their fingertips and believed in the power of connecting to the global through the dissemination of local news and activist content via the internet. There also was much invisible labor in digital space that goes beyond the names highlighted in the blog posts. Again, to reiterate points I've made earlier in this book (in other dialogue interludes and in chapters)—to bring them back into this conversation—I see there are different iterations of how the digital is mobilized in the service of activism. In our dialogues with Raya, I don't think we raised these points, but, Ayesha, perhaps you'd like to comment? I know you have done extensive research on feminist activism in your excellent MA thesis and have interviewed several of the activists in relation to the Delhi rape of 2012, for instance.[8]

AV: I think a *lot* of different kinds of online behaviors are grouped together as digital activism, and it's worth spending time to tease them apart. As you mentioned, Radhika, my MA thesis was interested in the idea of how campaigns concerned with gender-based violence go viral, and with their widespread reach can inform perceptions of gender (including violence and activism related to gender) both in India and abroad. However, the different tactics that are used, as well as the reasons for creating these campaigns at all, are widely varied. Digital platforms, as Sarah Banet-Weiser notes, are double-edged tools.[9] Although I think she was talking about the potential for the proliferation of online abuse as well as supportive, radical love, I think it also applies to the profit-making potential of these platforms alongside their potential for change making and community building. I know this is slightly tangential to what you were talking about, Radhika, but I think it is important to acknowledge that sometimes the umbrella term of "digital activism" also includes those whose work is geared toward marketing and profit, even when it concerns a social issue like gender-based violence. In this case, I think the labor and sharing of information is about increasing the social capital of an organization or individual toward the end of it translating into monetary or other profit. On the other hand, you have the kind of affective labor like that of Blank Noise (hat tip to Elizabeth Losh's amazing article on that!) and #LoSHA, which has other aims—pedagogical, community-building, solidarity-inviting forms of labor. And of course, you have all the different variations in between. These include, for instance, organizations, especially NGOs, who work in the gendered violence space and primarily use social media to promote visibility about their work, as well as those who primarily exist online, and engage with users through their online work, like blogs and new media sites like *Ladies Finger* and *Feminism in India*.

And I think what's also important in all these forms of activism is *how* the issues of gendered violence are represented, by *whom* and on *whose behalf.* While it can be easy to discern some of the more obvious profiteering attempts from activism, issues of unfair or extractive representation and debates about authenticity continue to be a problem even in self-avowedly feminist spaces. For instance, *Ladies Finger*, Feminism in India, and Youth Ki Awaaz—all feminist sites—have recently come under scrutiny for writing about Dalit women and oppressed communities, but not hiring any Dalit writers. Therefore, there's an accusation that they are profiting and building their own social capital by writing about these issues, but not actually doing the work within their own platforms of increasing access and representation of these voices. I think these same tensions come up in feminist activism, and who is seen to be an authentic activist, and who has the right to speak: there is a sense of gatekeeping and maintaining strict access by those who are seen to be "legitimate" activists versus those who are not. And much of it is about going through the correct channels and staying in line. Raya, did you feel that there was a similar dynamic in your experience of the list?

RS: It was not possible for me to decipher the caste of the survivors who contacted me because caste is complex and many caste Hindu last names have been adopted by Bahujan communities. I refrained from asking them their caste when they were sharing their experience of sexual harassment because many persons do not want to be "outed" as Bahujan and I did not want to add to their trauma. Dalit Bahujan, Adivasi, and Muslim women do feel very alienated in real-time spaces where they are an oppressed minority—even in "upper"-caste feminist spaces within institutions. When redressal systems are run by people who are "upper" caste and those who have entrenched caste biases, minority women are less trusting, as they should be. The panels are similar to an all-white jury with a token person of color occasionally added to the mix: how can someone trust redressal systems where the system's oppressor plays the role of the juror? Savarna ["upper"-caste] feminist spaces, too, are alienating for minority women for the same reasons.

AV: Rather than involving the communities in the conversation and giving them credit as being experts on their own condition, this sort of activism speaks for them. And I think that goes to what you were talking about in terms of social media providing the space where more people are able to also get their voices heard. I mean, obviously there are still some power differences and so on, but I guess it provides a little bit more space for communities that have long been silenced to come out and have a voice about themselves, on their own terms. It provides them a platform to speak on their own behalf without necessarily having access to those academic spaces or journalistic spaces, which tend to be still very upper-caste dominated.

RS: Yeah, and also another thing that's important is that Bahujan people are also calling these different hypocrisies out through these channels. There's a higher call for transparency essentially, and it's easier for Bahujan activists to do it through social media, which is free, relatively more accessible, and you don't have to quit your day job to do it. If you have mouths to feed at home, you don't have to be somewhere else, you don't have to be in socially hostile places to disseminate information and do your activism. The digital space provides, despite the online trolling and vitriol, communities that have been silenced for so long another platform to get their voices heard and validated. The digital space is where Dalit Bahujan and Adivasi persons can speak on their own behalf unlike in academic and journalistic spaces that are "'upper"-caste dominated—where it is difficult to do the same without being spoken over.

AV: Yes, absolutely, and I think what we're witnessing now is the power of these alternative opinions and perspectives: these voices are reverberating in important ways across many power-entrenched spaces. While I definitely don't think that we're at the point where "traditional" spaces and institutions are responding in a meaningful way, I think what *is* meaningful is that the challenge to these spaces is more visible than ever before, and that is a necessary first step.

Dialogue Interlude with Inji Pennu

RG: Dear Inji, thank you for agreeing to this dialogue interlude. Can you start us off by talking about your overall activist motivation and different projects both offline and online? Also, could you describe the process of your work with Global Voices and the rationale behind why you do this work and so on?

IP: Though I was working in technology, and computers were core to my existence on many levels, I came to the social community world of blogging, etcetera as pure leisure. Having lived in rural areas of the United States, I wanted to feel and touch the Indian in me, and other than the occasional long drive of two hours to visit an obscure Indian store, I didn't have much to connect with the Indian woman in me. Having to regularly maneuver through a white male system at work—being in the technology field—and facing displeasure and social rejection from housing to even at a doctor's office, you want to stand in front of a mirror and feel a little good about yourself and the skin and hair you are covered with. So, these occasional escapades to search for the Indian in me landed me obviously into Indian food stores, then took me to frequenting the web, and later on even writing about food, though I hardly knew anything about cooking. Slowly, I entered into web communities and the virtual spaces, but privacy has always been a concern as a technologist, too.

I don't have any capacity or any merit to be called an activist. But I was forced into many situations to raise my voice. In the offline world, there are many procedures to address an issue, but interestingly, the virtual world did not and still does not have any procedures or process-es to address the violence; and most importantly, being gendered fe-male, you are on the receiving end of this violence, even just for having a strong political opinion. Internet communities are still fairly new to everyone, the corporations and the users. It is a Wild West zone. I would say that is propagated and advertised as "freedom" by the white male power structure, where in fact it is instead a colluding place to set back time and erase the many struggles marginalized communities and people have been fighting for on the ground for many years.

At first, I was generally working against the Hindutva hatred that was propagated at that time, when we all had the "comforting" percep-tion that the hatred was contained to the US—until the Gujarat geno-cide happened and later Modi placed himself as the proponent of the increasingly violent Hindu right wing.

Later, as more women came into the arena, women's rights, or even a voice to speak, had to be sought for—including her rights to her work once a lot of women's work was stolen by Yahoo India, Inc. During this time, I got in touch with Global Voices. It has been an enriching experience working with some of the stalwarts and the dedicated set of journalists and writers, most of them champions of human rights. It was a place where it was easy to be understood, to get mentored and mentor others, to participate in virtual news rooms, and be at the cutting edge of digital journalism and innovation. It was a good match for a woman equally interested in journalism and technology—I would say it was one of the best matches I've made. I have been extremely fortunate to have some wonderful editors who changed my world perception of editing and reporting. And they do it with the utmost mutual respect and dignity.

RG: Can you talk a bit about how you see caste activism happening (or not) through digital space?

IP: I remember specifically some ten years ago, in heated arguments for affirmative actions, everyone asking around, where the Dalits and Adivasis were in virtual spaces. Now, you can observe how those communities have etched out their spaces and assert their identity, demand their dignity, and lead and shape everyone else's politics. For me, I would say it put me in my place, asked me to shut up and reflect introspectively on my privileges at multiple levels. My feminism, especially, has been shredded into a million pieces, deconstructed, and reshaped.

RG: I know you were very moved by the work Raya was doing with #LoSHA—would you like to say a bit about that?

IP: Two years ago, one of the closest persons in my life was sexually assaulted on a prestigious campus. I know her only as a feminist, yet it took her a while to realize the impact of the sexual assault. Male spaces are advertised as liberal campuses, and rampant sexual violence is encouraged.

So, when Raya's list started to evolve, as I could count all the doors that were shut for my friend, I jumped right in, because I knew we had to make noise. That list, to me, is the placard of a protest that eventually I believed would turn into a process to mitigate the gaps of the due process and more importantly make everyone believe in the victims. Because, as I experienced firsthand, sexual harassment was always suspected and dismissed as if it didn't exist.

Raya, during the making of the #LoSHA process, in every post, would say that they believe in every victim. Bingo. Raya touched the crux of the issue with just their words. But it was not easy. Listening to stories of sexual violence is not easy, and every word reminds you of your own trauma; at the same time, you have to support a total stranger and instill hope even while knowing the helplessness of the situation.

Then came the criticism of it by people whom you thought would guide you, the hate after that, broken friendships and trust, the legal threats. But I would say Raya created history and I am glad I could watch it unfold in front of me.

Dialogue Interlude with Mirna Guha

RG: Mirna, as a follow-up to our intense Facebook exchanges, I'm inviting you to share your thoughts about #metoo and Indian digital (feminist) streets.

MG: Hi Radhika, thank you for inviting me to share my thoughts. The thoughts I shared in our Facebook discussion have been circulating in my mind since #LoSHA. In particular, in response to the feminist backlash regarding an emphasis on due process, and comparisons between #LoSHA and "mob justice" by prominent feminists I started to think about the burden on victims of violence to "narrate" and contextualize what has happened to them. There is an implicit suggestion that it might be simply not enough to name the abuser, but that details must be provided for it to be seen as a narrative worthy of recognition, sympathy, and feminist approval, even. These thoughts have resurfaced in light of the #Indianmetoo movement which is being embraced in the mainstream to an extent greater than the reception of #LoSHA—in media, and by feminists who condemned #LoSHA.

I think what I see as the distinguishing feature between the two is the role and centrality of the "survivor narrative" that I speak of above. Those who are posting on Twitter as part of #metooIndia are providing these—not simply screenshots but narratives that tend to evoke public sympathy to a greater extent. And one cannot deny the voyeuristic element too. #LoSHA was remarkable in many ways because it removed the need for survivors to provide graphic details of their abuse and firmly placed the onus of "explaining" and "contextualizing" the abuse on the abuser—there was a starkness of just having a name added to a list without a long, heart-wrenching story of how the abuse happened and what form it took. I think that was much harder for people to get behind than what is happening now, which models itself on the #metoo movement in the United States, led by narratives of abuse followed by naming the abuser.

This makes me think again about "survivor narratives"—what role do they play and why do we need them so much? And what does it do to those narrating intimate and horrific details of their personal experiences at the cost of "contextualizing" abuse—the burden of providing this narrative and being up for scrutiny but also for sympathy? I see the women posting on Twitter now being cross-examined and accused of lying, and I also see sympathy and support for the narrative. Yes #LoSHA had narratives, but the "naming" seemed to me to be more powerful than the "narrating," and I cannot help but wonder if that is playing a big role in how the two were publicly received.

And of course, there is an element of power, too. The ways in which people consume narratives and the balance of power between production and consumption of narratives. In some sense, a victim naming an abuser is an act of power, but having to provide the narrative in exhausting detail and being up for scrutiny removes some of that power. Whereas anonymously simply naming someone, as #LoSHA rendered possible, is an act of power without apologizing for it or contextualizing it. The former produces perhaps a form of victimhood that is more palatable—the many women sharing their narratives as part of the #metooIndia movement are public—their identities, images, stories, and lives—and perhaps that all of this is up for consumption, including the allegation, makes them more fit for mainstream embrace? #LoSHA, if you remember, was mostly anonymized.

I should mention here that I come to this conversation with my own experiences and journeys of producing (and consuming) narratives. I started working within a youth group that was supporting survivors of child sexual abuse when I was nineteen, in Kolkata, the city I was born in and lived in for twenty-five years. The desire to work with the group and on the issue of child sexual abuse stemmed from my own experience as well as that of a close friend in school. At that point, twelve years ago, this issue was shrouded in silence. There was a sense of power in speaking up, in speaking about what had happened to us, and to use that to connect to others. Our narratives felt disruptive and powerful: to speak of our experiences was to shatter the myth that child sexual abuse does not happen in urban India, to highlight the prevalence of this issue, and to speak our truth. So much has changed, I feel, in the last decade—conversations on violence, especially sexual violence have become so public, so visible, so mainstream even.

RG: And as feminist academics, we recognize and validate personal location and experience and how it shapes the knowledge we produce. Meanwhile, when you say "power of speaking up": what is it about the present moment that you think is highlighting this power?

MG: I think what's powerful about #LoSHA but also with #metoo is that the abuser is being named. In some instances, they are doing so without necessarily providing a narrative of abuse and remaining anonymous (#LoSHA); in others, they are identifying themselves as victims in the public eye but *also* explicitly naming the abuser (#metoo). I am familiar with victim-led narratives of abuse having worked with those who have experienced sexual abuse and gender-based violence in India over the last decade. But at the point when I started, although we did name abusers, there was a trepidation, a fear of consequence, and of course the lack of a public platform like Twitter where one could name and expose their abusers to millions in a blink of an eye. I am not trying to say that victims don't fear consequences anymore; if anything, naming abusers publicly brings with it more scrutiny. But the way I see it, narratives seems to have changed from "this happened to me/I am a survivor of [insert form of violence]" to "XY did this to me." In *Speaking Freely: Unlearning the Lies of the Father's Tongues*, Julia Penelope writes about this, about how the language we use and the ways in which we construct sentences about the performance of violence affect our perceptions of the violence being perpetrated. [10] She uses a standardized example, "John beat Mary," and then looks at how that can be reframed as "Mary was beaten by John," and then "Mary was beaten," and eventually "Mary is a battered woman." At the last stage, the perpetrator is eventually invisibilized and the burden of the narrative of the abuse—what happened, why, how, and so on—rests on the victim along with the actual effects of the violence perpetrated against them. And it is here that I think the power of #LoSHA in particular lies—the onus is on the accused abuser to explain what happened, to "give a statement," rather than the victim having to contextualize the violence they have experienced and then being vulnerable to scrutiny and cross-examination. And this shift in responsibility is monumental, I believe, and is strengthening the ability and power to speak up.

ON MAINSTREAMING AND ACADEMIC CO-OPTATION

Dialogue Interlude with Tarishi Verma

RG: Dear Tarishi, thank you for agreeing to this dialogue interlude. Can you start us off by talking about your overall motivation and feminist approach to journalism: how you developed your feminist voice both offline and online? Also, could you describe the process of your work with the newspaper industry in India as more and more readers seek their content through social media?

TV: It's difficult to pinpoint that moment when I thought, bingo, I need to switch my feminist voice on. It's been an incredible process, and that's what makes it so enriching. I think the beginnings were in my internship with the *Deccan Herald*. I'd only been in Delhi for two years and this was before the 2012 incident. It was an unpaid internship that required me to work long hours. More often than not, I'd be spending late nights in Gurgaon, which has been deemed unsafe since forever. Being a woman in journalism itself was a big step. At that time, I would do women-related stories that may or may not be so necessarily revolutionary, but I definitely tried to do something. I remember doing a piece on bra size and my mom going, "Haww, why are you talking about this?" It was hilarious, even though I rolled my eyes at my mother. I tended to talk about "women's issues" every now and then.

In my next internship at *The Week*, I didn't have much choice in selecting topics to report about so I couldn't bring in a lot there. Similarly, with *Hindustan Times*, I did not have a choice of selecting topics. Throughout this time, I was studying, moving from an undergrad degree to a postgrad degree, and enhancing my understanding of feminism.

This knowledge I took to my new workplace, which was not an internship but an actual paid job. It was definitely intimidating at first because the workplace had all men in leadership positions and the work that the women did was either nothing or not valued. I remained quiet for the most part in the initial first weeks—until the Jisha case happened. Later, a conversation with a second-level boss about the rape of a Dalit woman sparked my first ever piece for the *Indian Express* (online). While my boss argued against using "Dalit" in the headline, I did not feel up for debating with him. So, I poured it out in my article instead.

It sort of started from there. I think it came to everyone's notice quickly that I worked on certain specific issues. From then on, it became easy to suggest any topic. The more men increased around me, the more it became imperative to write on more issues. Besides, right in front of me, I could see bias in how women were treated or even how they behaved or projected themselves. There was a clear division between who handled the important things and who handled the unimportant things. I could bring in my feminism in the articles I wrote for them. This eventually translated into my inclusion in the #GenderAnd series of *Indian Express* (IE).

RG: Thank you for this. I'm curious about a #GenderAnd series for a mainstream newspaper. Coming from the 1970s generation myself, I find it quite amazing to see that these issues are actually being welcomed in mainstream press! Can you tell me more about your work for *Indian Express* and this move not only to feminist content that you participated in but also the move to online content on the part of mainstream national newspapers in India? I know I'm asking a lot, but whatever you can say.

TV: It surprised me too, considering how only a few weeks before #GenderAnd was launched, I had asked for a separate section on gender itself. My request wasn't a short-term special but a larger section that could track gender-based stories on a more regular basis. I was denied at first, with the editors saying that it is not something that can be implemented—it'll cost money, and so on, even though what I suggested probably didn't require anything more than a few thousand. It became possible because Neha Dixit spearheaded it.[11] However, just because she was an award-winning journalist did not mean it was easy for her. In fact, they probably questioned her more. She gave me a lowdown on how the meetings between her and the then-CEO—who, it had already been established, was clearly nowhere near understanding gender issues (it's a whole different story)—went, and it was not a pretty picture. She had to fight tooth and nail for the #GenderAnd section and the stories that went into it. For example, in a story about women CEOs, Neha suggested we have a story on Dalit women who have reached that position. However, the IE CEO suggested that if one is doing a story about women CEOs, we might want to focus on what to wear and what not to wear because "*humein pata toh hai* [we know] women are CEOs now." Neha eventually left the office—I don't know about the reasons—but a second season of #GenderAnd happened, too, with another head. Said CEO had left before the second run.

#GenderAnd started online and has remained so. It was a hashtag, after all. The story (just one) published in print did not fare as well as the stories published online only. I'm not sure what happened with it in terms of analytics, but there was a much more diverse set of stories the second time around. My honest point of view is that it is also a little "trendy" (quite a play on the word because of Twitter trends) to do these stories now. It's more of a business decision that "oh, you know, maybe the #MeToo movement is happening, right now we'll get most hits on these kind of stories." That is also me being cynical. I'm sure this is a step in a positive direction, but then why do we need to do "specials"? There is a "special status" for gender stories. If they could just implement it in the ways they report, or in the newsroom by changing who gets to be in the hierarchy, or just treating their employees equally, even that would be implementing feminist values in some way. Additionally, because of this special status, not everyone wants to contribute to it. All women are/were a part of the #GenderAnd team at IE and the men weren't even expected to participate. The male leads were in fact extremely dismissive of the section. They did not say as much of course, but other nonverbal communication made it pretty clear. Just the interaction of one of the leads with Neha reassured me that the workplace wasn't going to change—and this was an interaction between an award-winning journalist (Neha) and another one who had no credentials to his name, none. There is no basic respect.

As far as the move to online is concerned, that shift started happening a while ago, but no one took it as seriously earlier as in the past three to four years. We not only track the website, but also the app. Both are not so integral to how the paper fares because the online has sort of a separate image to maintain. With *Indian Express* specifically, it had a niche audience with its print version primarily because it doesn't report like or look like the more popular *Times of India*. The online component struggled to take off because of this. The then-CEO moved toward more entertainment stories (read: sex-based content) then. The revenue increased dramatically with that change, but what decreased proportionately was the quality of these stories. One example: an article was published on the website that was simply just provocative pictures of Sunny Leone (a former porn star who is now a Bollywood actor). It was also specifically published late at night only for a specific audience.

I think there is effort to increase readership by changing the content thematically. What I personally felt was the need for a dynamic change—in terms of more interactivity and content beyond text/words that made the online component more interesting. *Hindustan Times* (another national daily) is in fact doing extremely well in that aspect. It has done a string of stories meant specifically for posting online, with interactive content and interesting subjects. Once again, gender-based issues only come out as specials, but they do have more relevant specials that are more contemporary. Not a broad gender series, but they have highlighted specific aspects. For example, they focused on online trolling faced by women, and used the interactive format to actually give a lowdown on how much and how bad the trolling is. Of course, their revenue is not that great. I mean, it is a chicken and egg story.

In any case, the move is imperative. More people access news on phones and Twitter. If they don't adapt their content to online platforms, their content will not reach anywhere. It is actually interesting to see the lack of literacy in the country but at the same time, the high use of mobile phones. While I firmly believe that newspapers won't go away in India anytime soon (the use has drastically decreased in the US), the online platform will also have to do equally well.

Dialogue Interlude with Arpita Chakraborty

RG: Arpita, we connected on Twitter around discussions of #LoSHA in fall of 2017. Since then we have had many discussions and I know you are writing on the topic as well. So, thank you for agreeing to engage in a dialogue around the issue of Indian feminist activism through "digital streets." To start off, I want to give you an opportunity to frame our conversation since you've read some of the chapter drafts in this book. What points would you like to take up in this short interlude?

AC: Thank you so much Radhika for making me a part of this. The other interludes are indeed a very important intervention in the discourse on cyberactivism, especially post #LoSHA. However, I would like to take our conversation beyond #LoSHA to another aspect of cyberactivism: the role played by cybernetworks in contemporary academia. In the current times of transnational academic migration, connections through social networks, and in fact exclusive online academic spaces and networks, I think #LoSHA also pointed toward the need to focus our attention on the effects of these changes on academic experiences, especially for younger academic-activists.

RG: Arpita, can you elaborate a bit more please? Also, as you elaborate, we are now one year away since #LoSHA and #metooIndia have burst forth. Any thoughts?

AC: What I meant by changes in academic experiences are two things: first, I see the way transnational academic connections are transcending traditional barriers like seniority, distance, a difference of cultural capital, and so on. Simply said, it is much easier for younger researchers to get in touch with senior scholars and engage with each other's opinions on contemporary issues on a regular basis through platforms like Facebook and Twitter. While this puts scholarly engagement under more scrutiny, it has taken academic engagements beyond the boundaries of the classroom. There is an almost seamless production of academic performance on the part of all the parties engaged— and I use the word *performance* here consciously in the sense Goffman had used it.[12] There are both positive and negative effects of this, the most concerning of which for me is the vulnerability of younger academic-activists and the power equation in such interactions.

This is the second change that performance of academia has seen: the increase in interactions has also exposed young researchers to myriad forms of exchanges beyond the confines of classroom interactions.

These are ill-defined, and often the boundaries are blurry for both sides. With changing forms of interactions, we need new discussions around codes of conduct and what is to be considered acceptable in informal interactions. Here, the Ronnell case has shown us that even while we have created newer channels of communications successfully, we have not been able to create feminist discussions around them as necessary.[13]

#MetooIndia is easier for academics to respond to because as of our writing (October 10, 2018), it has been confined to the media industry. I would like to reiterate here again my concerns about unequal social and cultural capital as hindrances to #LoSHA. The support provided by mainstream feminists to #metooIndia were sparse when #LoSHA came out. The differentiation of presence of evidence in the case of #metooIndia and its absence in #LoSHA reeks of the same misogynist rhetoric that we have been trying to counter for decades. But #metooIndia has shown the power of Twitter as a tool for transformative change at the same time. It is important that we remember the role played by #LoSHA in initiating this change and also enforcing consequences for the offenders named by survivors. Survivors should remain central to the feminist concern, and the accused who have been proven guilty (Lawrence Liang being the first) should face consequences. India cannot expect to change its situation on gender violence if its feminist politics choose to believe survivors selectively. And caste remains one of the central concerns in this selective framework.

RG: Thanks, Arpita. A lot packed in there. As you said these interludes are a different form of writing, and we will leave several points unfinished and without unpacking here, as in other interludes. But I want to follow up and ask elaboration on two points.

Your reference to Goffman? Say more! And, how do you see caste as central? Could you elaborate?

AC: I mentioned Goffman in connection to his ideas of the presentation of self. With the expansion of barriers of traditional classroom-confined interactions, the performance of the academic self is extended both temporally and spatially. Academia is now spread across spaces like Facebook groups, Twitter DMs, and Instagram pages. In the words of Goffman, academics are on stage more and more, and the borders of academic life and private life are much less marked now.[14] This makes social interactions much more difficult to typify, and scholars have more and more access to each other's private lives. During #LoSHA, what remained much less spelled out in words was the discrepancy between such public- and private-lived politics—which exasperated and disillusioned survivors to a great extent. There is an urgent need to talk about how the dissolution of this boundary is affecting not only academic relations but every sphere of life where a previous differentiation between formal and informal existed.

We have seen caste come up again and again in the discussions around #LoSHA as well as #metooIndia. The caste identity of feminists who opposed the list was seen as a marker of their privilege, and being called "Savarna" was seen as an insult in turn by the former. We both are aware of the now-famous alleged split between feminists—the allegation of "Savarna" had a big part to play in that split. Being an upper-caste feminist, I find it crucial to voice that I do not find the term "Savarna" to be an insult. I do find it making me uncomfortable, primarily because it makes me cautious about my own privilege even while participating in the same struggle. But feminism never promised us comfort—it was never about making us snug in our positions of caste and class privilege. I think what Dalit feminists were pointing at was the upper-caste, urban position of privilege of those who were oblivious of the real face of "due process" in Indian academic spaces. And to take that as an insult is, for me, missing the point: that we are indeed privileged. The fact that I am typing this interlude is the very evidence of a certain sociocultural capital. It is immaterial whether Raya is Dalit or not for the larger politics of #metoo or #LoSHA; but by raising questions about the authenticity of their Dalitness, the upper-caste nature of the Indian feminist movement and its uneasy reflection on its own ontological position is made clear.

RG: Arpita, thank you for your contribution. As you know these dialogue pieces are "interludes" and are by nature incomplete—they open up different angles on the issues discussed in relation to contemporary gendered Indian digital publics. I have also enjoyed our small "South Asian Twitterverse"[15] since we connected around discussions of #LoSHA last October (2017).

AC: Our Twitterverse is an excellent example of the positive aspects of the transnational dissolution of barriers in academia. I have also thoroughly enjoyed the thought-provoking engagements that we have continued to sustain. These interactions will hopefully help in solidifying our own understanding and enhancement of digital performances of academia.

ON NONPROFIT ORGANIZING

Dialogue Interlude with Riddhima Sharma: FemPositive

Riddhima Sharma is the founder of an online feminist startup called FemPositive (http://fempositive.org/). I connected with her to interview her for this book sometime in 2017. While with Feminism in India, I continued my relationship through contributing writing (https://feminisminindia.com), and with Genderlogindia I continued my relationship through curation of Genderlog in Novembe, and then in December 2017, with Riddhima I developed more of a research relationship. In what follows we dialogue around the resource differentials for feminist startups and digital street activism and the kinds of labor that such organizing and implementation requires. In doing so, we draw on my prior interviews with other feminist startups and connect with my previous and continuing research on NGOization and ITization.[16]

RG: Riddhima, thanks again for Skyping with me. Can you talk about your work—why you founded FemPositive and so on?

RS: So, my cofounder, Chirag Kulshrestha, and I founded FemPositive in September 2014 after I spent a year at the Research Centre for Women's Studies, Shreemati Nathibai Damodar Thackersey (RCWS, SNDT) Women's University, pursuing a certificate course in Women's Studies. This course, for the first time, introduced me to Indian women's history and feminisms and gave me the opportunity to dive deep into this subject. FemPositive was born with the idea to be a space where people who want to learn about Indian feminist herstories, and women can come to access valuable information in easy-to-understand and shareable visual formats. This was particularly intentioned to be for people who aren't engaged with these subjects academically or in other ways (keeping in mind this was after Jyoti Singh's case and there was renewed energy in India to engage with women's issues). Since neither Chirag nor I had any real experience with the nonprofit or feminist space and add to that I was still pursuing my studies (I was in law school) and Chirag had a full-time job, we decided to first start a page on Facebook—a social media space where a lot of political conversations were buzzing at the time.

From a small Facebook initiative, FemPositive has grown immensely in the past three years to include a long-term digital feminist archival project: Feminist Reads; offline workshop modules on online violence,

sexual violence, and laws around it, etcetera; various collaborative projects with other nonprofit organizations; and a feminist reading group.

RG: Riddhima, you so casually said two things I'm really anxious
for you to elaborate on! First, if neither of you had experience in feminist spaces—also what do you mean by that—then what was your
motivation? Second, you mention that Jyoti Singh's case renewed energy in India to engage with women's issues. Say more please!

RS: Okay, so in 2014 I was still in law school, and the only engagement I'd had with some sort of nonprofit work was through a student
organization called Model Governance Foundation that I was heading
and running the blog of. At the same time, Chirag had been working for
a TV production house with a degree in media and communication,
with absolutely no grounding in the nonprofit sector or feminism. We
both basically had never worked with or observed the work of any
feminist NGO in India except for my one-year stint at RCWS, SNDT
with their women's studies certificate course. Whatever we know now
in terms of our politics, work ethos, ideas, and collaborations are all
what we've built through trial and error with FemPositive.

About the second thing, in the aftermath of Jyoti's case, the protests
online and offline, the conversations online and offline, and the discussions after the Criminal Amendment Act, 2013 (which was also motivated by Jyoti's case), a lot more Facebook pages, groups, and NGOs
were formed that wanted to talk about or work on issues of women's
rights and feminisms. (Side note: Feminism in India and Safecity were
both post-Jyoti Singh organizations.) Of course there were feminists
and NGOs working even before this, but it was just that this was sort of
a watershed moment that brought these issues into what is called "the
mainstream" where people like me, who had probably never really
learned about or engaged with feminism, were reading a lot more about
consent and definitions of rape, and so on, not from a legal perspective
(the way I was learning in college), but from a feminist standpoint.

RG: You and I have conversed several times over Skype since I
first interviewed you for this project. It's been lovely getting insights
into the process of not only your own feminist awareness through your
everyday interweaving of online and offline sociality but also of how
you were motivated to start this feminist project. Yet I know you, as
much as several other feminists doing these sorts of startups, struggle
with issues of labor and access to other sorts of resources to maintain
the projects and move them forward. Can you say a bit about these
issues please? We recorded our interview, so it would be easy for me to

objectify you and characterize what you said (as I have done in the chapters preceding these dialogue interludes), but I would like to include your own telling here, since you agreed to do the interlude with me.

RS: Yes, it is absolutely true that young feminist organizations or groups face a lot of struggle in the process of finding their footing. The nonprofit sector is sometimes not very welcoming and it is important to learn how to navigate the space effectively.

One of the chief concerns for young feminist organizations is funding. It is tough for NGOs to get a decent amount of funding if you are still figuring out your niche or expertise, if you don't have a concrete project proposal or a solid team or partnerships to work with. The lack of flexible funding and the many formalities and stipulations of registering an NGO and procuring some sort of funding means that NGOs must either get creative with their limited budgets or limited labor. (There are a few organizations like FRIDA [https://youngfeministfund.org/] that do offer flexible funding to feminist groups/organizations that are unregistered, too.) Some of the reasons why we haven't yet formally registered or actively applied for funding are: the FemPositive team never expanded beyond Chirag and me; we had seen how funded feminist organizations were sometimes tied by their responsibilities toward funders/donors that required strict monitoring and evaluation, clear, limited goals, and subjects to work with; and we mostly worked online, were self-sufficient (since we were both working for a good part of the last three years), and at other times, were partnering with other organizations for space and resources for workshops and reading groups.

Of course, the lack of funding and a formal structure also meant that we were limited by our own time and capacities and have been unable to expand our work/team despite immense potential in the areas in which we are working. We had to watch several opportunities pass us by because we weren't registered, but that was also a price we were willing to pay, because in some way this meant that we kept all the control of what we do, who we associate with, and who and what politics we support.

RG: I remember thinking—as you were telling me about how competitive the struggle for visibility and for resources is in this feminist startup scenario—that what you are telling me is very similar to what I observed as I was doing offline ethnographies of NGOs in development work. I wrote a bit about this in my last book *Online Philanthropy in the Global North and South*. In that book my coauthor, Jeannette Dillon, and I wrote about how some post-dotcom entrepreneurs shifted toward startups that focus on content and services connecting digital givers from more well-to-do populations to digital borrowers from the relatively poorer populations of the world. I also wrote about the NGO-ization of development work based on collaborations with NGO workers in India. You have read some of this work, I think. Feminist activism in the digital streets draws from a mix of these issues we raised in that book as well. Do you see those connections? Any comments?

RS: Yes, I do see these connections. The struggle for visibility and strong digital presence becomes a very necessary component while applying for international grants or fundraising through various digital platforms. But one more interesting thing we see is that international organizations or companies are increasingly collaborating with NGOs in developing nations through awards, grants, competitions, etcetera, and additionally, international organizations are setting up their own social enterprise in various countries (for example, Teach for India and Breakthrough).

There is obviously an edge one can have if you have resources to beautify or make your work look deep and impactful through various modes of content creation, videos, testimonials, and so on, from the people and communities with whom you work. But questions of ethics, confidentiality, and the safety of these people, as we have discussed at length during our Skype interview, are always things one battles with. Is it okay to allow funders—foreign or local—to document or record young people, women, or communities in low-income neighborhoods? Is it okay for you to project these communities as vulnerable in order to showcase your work as some sort of philanthropic initiative? White people coming and observing or shooting poverty in developing countries, rich or upper-middle-class people taking pictures or videos when they go to an orphanage or old-age home on their birthday or some other festive occasion and posting on social media—in this time of putting the nonprofit sector on the social media map, these are still some issues one might want to think about.

RG: My dialogue interlude with Pallavi Guha is about rural feminists and their process of outreach to media and the world at large in the contemporary feminist scene. Our discussions focused on a post-2012 timeline—since 2012 signifies a major shift after the Delhi rape protests, and smart phones/WhatsApp became comparatively more widespread in use since about 2014. Can you compare your experience with Pallavi's and comment on what you might know of rural feminists?

(Incidentally, when Pallavi and I talked and compared notes, we, of course, found out that she and I had interviewed several of the same feminist activists and founders of feminist startups.)

RS: I'm not entirely sure of who might fall under the category of rural feminists. But one thing I have observed and understood in my very limited experience is that the way we function in academia and urban feminist spaces is perhaps in need of a complete overhaul. When a feminist movement rises organically, through organic leadership from within the communities, where the issues are to be raised, that is when a movement can really succeed and be empowering. One sees that when we see the spectacular history of work of Dalit, Bahujan, Adivasi, and Muslim feminists most recently evidenced by the Chalo Nagpur March last year and the Maha Dalit Mahila Andolan in Haryana on March 22nd, led by and participated in by local women.

Conversely, an urban feminist approach, not completely, but to some extent, is somehow focused on researching or uplifting those we consider underprivileged in some way—for instance, a panel discussion on women's studies where feminist organizations are invited to present their work, bring along a couple of women with whom they worked in a nearby village. They narrate their stories to the participants in Hindi/Marathi/Gujarati (any non-English language) and are subjected to becoming spectators in a discussion conducted purely in English on their lives and experiences when they don't understand the language. Is this practice of theorizing their lives by strangers in a language they don't understand justified in their presence? Intersectionality and true inclusive feminist praxis still seem to be a distant dream.

RG: And I wonder about caste issues in digital activisms? Have you, for instance, had any opportunities to collaborate with Dalit activists in digital streets?

RS: I have to really thank digital activism and documentation for the lessons and information that I wouldn't have otherwise had the opportunity to learn or come across. Coming from a Brahmin family and growing up learning mostly Brahminical history and behavior, I was absolutely oblivious to so many important issues.

Following the work of and reading so much on platforms like Dalit Camera, Round Table India, Savari, Adivasi Resurgence, Dalit History Month, Velivada, and TransVision that are run by Dalit Bahujan Adivasi (DBA) folks made me rethink my feminism, go back to the start, reread Phule, Ambedkar, and Periyar and develop a much more conscious politics. I truly believe and support the idea of collaborative work, of promoting the work or writing on these platforms without appropriating their work, life stories, or struggles. Transforming our work as more of allies at FemPositive was really important for us. In turn, we want to direct our work and content to privileged folks who need to sensitize themselves, to talk to more people about intersections of feminisms, caste, trans inclusiveness, LGBTQIA issues, etcetera.

The most important and revolutionary work that is currently happening (and has historically happened) is through the work and efforts of DBA and Muslim feminists online and offline.

Connecting the above points, it is also important to note that the most well-funded, recognized organizations are those composed of upper-caste feminists that occupy the most space in the mainstream media.

RG: Thank you again for giving so much of your time to my writing project—both through repeated interviews and through this writing for the dialogue interlude. I'm sure we will talk more in other projects and collaborations. For now, I think the dialogue interlude will be useful in elaborating points raised in other chapters and in the other interludes.

Dialogue Interlude with Noopur Tiwari: Genderlogindia and Smashboard.org

RG: Dear Noopur, thank you for agreeing to at least a brief note in answer to my question about your overall activist motivation and different projects both offline and online, like the process of starting @genderlogindia. I have indeed benefited from our Skype meetings and talks since October/November 2017, but since those were not recorded and I only took notes to incorporate what I learned from you in the overall book—and you were at that time more of a "research subject"—I just thought to include your voice here in this interludes chapter with a few brief paragraphs.

NT: Dear Radhika, thanks for inviting me. I'd say my overall motivation is quite simply my lived experience in our patriarchal world. Like all other women, the choice I have is to resist or turn a blind eye to what's around me. I also want to find ways in which we can find new ways to communicate and get organized. I was in Valencia on the 8th of March this year (2018). And I was walking with Spanish women who turned up in huge numbers for "la huelga feminista," at which women were striking to ask for their rights. It was very invigorating, of course, to see women beating drums, shouting slogans, and swarming into the streets. But I also feel that there is no one in particular to whom street protests can now be addressed. They no longer threaten or dismantle power in the way in which they probably could some decades ago. We are unable to hold political leaders accountable anymore, and therefore we can't really expect them to "listen" either. We need critical thinking. And technology may have some answers. What digital projects can do is harness tech and social media to streamline and regroup us to focus on specific actions. I want to be able to exploit that for creating feminist spaces and tools.

I joined the Genderlog team because I felt it was a good way of forming a community around a Twitter handle. It's a crowdsourced handle that invites one new guest curator every week, so there is no one voice from the pulpit, as it were. You have a bunch of people talking about diverse things. Most curators come back to us and say they have been able to learn much. All this while people reading their timelines are learning from them. There's an active exchange of ideas happening, and by speaking from a group handle, the curators get a certain cushioning and a certain authority at the same time. I like the dynamics of such a handle.

The current project that I am working to launch is called Smashboard—A Tool to Smash Patriarchy (https://smashboard.org/). We are going to be using this to build several digital projects for women and run mostly by women. The first one will be a platform against sexual harassment. It will allow victims of sexual harassment to communicate, organize, and act efficiently in a safe environment. It will minimize all the risks and barriers related to speaking out against sexual harassment.

RG: Smashboard . . . hmm . . . ambitious indeed! Do you mind telling us more about the digital projects you are planning and also how you figure out funding these projects and the labor toward them?

NT: We are living in a patriarchy and there is a huge deficit of technological innovation to enable those who are fighting this structural problem. We use tech to make all kinds of work easier, so why can't we do this for those battling all the violence unleashed by patriarchy everywhere? That's why we want to build Smashboard—the first-ever feminist social network and "digital ally" especially designed for the purpose of making this everyday battle against patriarchy easier. The platform seeks to empower all women with access to the internet and their allies (regardless of their gender) with three basic functions: stay informed, communicate securely, and seek/provide the right kind of support. The idea is to treat feminist conversations as mainstream and to simultaneously develop a kind of digital solidarity.

As a "digital ally," Smashboard works on the assumption that women are courageous, but it will not make impossible demands on them to take extra risks and push themselves to take action before they are ready. This basically means that we will make sure that the tech allows ample room for anonymity and confidentiality for victims and survivors if and when they need it. In order to respond to the crisis they face, women first need to be cared for and they need time to build support. In the real world, victims and survivors asking for support often have to: reveal who they are; face invasive public scrutiny; and push themselves to fit into the "good victim" mold or lose out. Smashboard will circumvent some of these rigid barriers by expanding the support base. We will have hubs built in, so that people can find the right kind of journalists, lawyers, and mental health care experts without having to run from pillar to post.

Smashboard will also have syndicated feeds of news from various feminist portals and will generate original content from locations the platform is being used in. We also want to see more data and research around feminist issues on our platform. One of our unique features is an insurance—the idea of mutualizing risk. So, subscriptions will be a bit like paying insurance premiums.

For the funding of these projects, we are participating in an "Initial Coin Offering" (ICO) as a not-for-profit startup. So, the labor will be remunerated as we raise funds. As for the choice of this method: billions of dollars are being raised via ICOs for all kinds of businesses, so, why should a feminist project not benefit from this kind of thing? We are not apologetic about making an entry into a zone that is mostly populated by hardcore financial projects. We need funds to build this project and we are confident of its worth. So, investors should be able to see that.

Also, conventional methods of seeking investments tend to give investors the power to interfere in governance. If we allow patriarchal corporate sector investors or institutions to have a say in how this project is built, we will be undermining its primary goal. Remember, our tagline is "a tool to smash patriarchy."

The world of fintech [financial technology] needs more gender diversity. At the same time, we are not fans of shiny, corporate feminism. Nor are we just another feminist promotional gimmick that aims to enrich a handful of women CEOs. In fact, in the long run, we want to be able to focus on research and development aimed at developing simple digital tools that can help women who don't have the fancy devices that many of us own.

Last but not least, it's about women and technology. If the blockchain is all set to change the way we will be doing things in the near future, as women, we should be "early adopters" to mold it to serve us. So, at Smashboard, we are also trying to do that.

RG: What you're attempting then highlights a fact of our contemporary social ethos. That even while some people still characterize the "digital" as somehow outside of our everyday, the digital is now actually part of our everyday infrastructure for existence. This has implications for how we develop potential globally reaching, yet locally situated legal and emotional support systems and safe spaces. Do you want to elaborate on these points a bit?

NT: You are right. Digital universes are indeed part of our lived reality and no longer external as such. Smashboard's social network will serve as a digital community that will power nodes and clusters that function as hubs for those trying to reflect upon problem resolution and seek and offer support to one another. It will try to create the right kind of conditions for survivors of sexual harassment and abuse to communicate, organize, and act efficiently in a safe environment. It will minimize some of the major risks and barriers related to speaking out against sexism and sexual harassment and abuse.

The platform provides an infrastructure to women, gender minorities, and their allies with three guarantees: stay informed; communicate securely; and seek/provide/build support along with allies and experts. The idea is to treat feminist conversations as mainstream and to simultaneously expand feminist digital spaces into areas of active support and solidarity.

As a "digital ally," we hope that some of the interactional biases can be circumvented or minimized in two ways: we are trying to create a space that is especially designed with the awareness that victim blaming and patriarchal biases seep into our relationships with people we "really" know; and we will foreground and address the needs of the victims and survivors (whether they are facing micro-aggressions or full-blown abuse) rather than focus on who they are.

The tools and services make it possible to:

1. Stay connected to global and local feminists communities

2. Find and communicate with journalists, lawyers, and mental health care experts
3. Store and share evidence
4. Ask questions
5. Benefit from an insurance policy

For instance, Smashboard's premium subscription will pay for:

1. An insurance policy for legal and mental health care coverage
2. Access to preliminary advice from a panel of lawyers, mental-health care experts, and community members
3. Unlimited access to global feed of news and views
4. Special discounts on online feminist courses and webinars

These subscriptions are not purely commercial as they also aim at mutualizing the "risks" of social injustice and the resulting loss of access, privilege, and power we encounter in our daily lives. In a sense, defining, measuring, analyzing, and building defenses against these risks will also mold the perception of patriarchy as a concrete and common problem rather than as something abstract or something only feminists amp up as "issues."

Interlude with Sohni Chakrabarti

RG: Sohni, thank you very much for agreeing to this dialogue interlude! I am so excited. As you've been one of the excellent supporting team members and fellow writers in our little Twitter support group that now also has a secret Facebook group to work as a writing support group, you know what this project is. I also interviewed you in 2017 when I saw you were one of the @genderlogindia curators. When I started to curate that handle, I got a lot of mentoring from you on how to conduct the curation. I've enjoyed our exchanges so far, and it's great that now we can write together in this form. To start us off, can you tell me about your experience of digital activism—either as an activist yourself or as someone who is on social media a lot and is exposed to digital activist spaces?

SC: Thank you for having this dialogue with me, it is a real pleasure to have this dialogue interlude. To be honest, I have never imagined myself as an activist because I believe that activism requires a certain kind of passion and tenacity that I lack. However, having said that, my experience with digital activism has evolved since I started being more active on Twitter. I think that Twitter is an excellent space for online activism because of its public nature, as it is a micro-blogging site; hence, it allows the scope to reach out to a wider audience about issues and causes. More recently, Twitter allows its users to post multiple tweets together in a thread, making it a very interesting mode for digital activism. The interesting thing about Twitter is the networks that you can form online and find people who share your causes and concerns. It is also a great way to connect with people, navigate multiple spaces, and interact widely with people from different communities. In terms of digital activism, Twitter offers boundless possibilities—you can choose to engage only with a select audience, you can choose to tailor your threads according to your causes, you can choose to maintain a distance and observe different handles, or you can be aggressive with Twitter and use it as a space to voice your opinions. It is also interesting to see how access to online spaces differs; upper-caste, heterosexual, white, upper-class people tend to dominate these online spaces and have a wider network and wider target reach. Moreover, I have noted that people who face any form of structural disadvantages offline tend to be more active and more aggressive with their Twitter activity. I think that is a necessary part of the struggle because unless the marginalized and the disadvantaged fight back aggressively, they stand to lose their limited online space as well.

Since #LoSHA, there has been a huge amount of debate over "Twitter feminists," "internet feminists," and now more recently, "fingertip feminists," but what is ignored is the ability of these online communities to network, form allies, and mobilize themselves. It is possible to bring a lot more people together through social media to support your cause as opposed to the pre-internet generations. Also, I don't see it as much different from the sloganeering and propaganda of street activism in the earlier, pre-internet days; it is just that this can now be done online in a time-efficient manner. What has been even more interesting is to note that the ones who are accusing the activists/feminists of adopting digital modes of activism are also using the same digital mode (*Kafila* is a blog!) to voice their opinions. Hence, I think that social media in general and Twitter in particular has the potential to give voice to many, and it is interesting as a scholar and a feminist to see diverse voices emerging everyday online.

RG: Thank you for this Sohni. You and several of the other young women on Twitter and Facebook have been amazing in how you've been responding to this debate. As Ayesha and I were conversing with Raya (see interlude above) it was even clearer to me that this response came from a misunderstanding of the form and process of the crowd-sourced networking, labor, and activism of young women who are mostly "digital natives." In our Twitter exchanges, I remember we went over this point. Padmini Ray Murray particularly was noting this difference as well. Observing the discussions around #LoSHA began to give me insights into the differences between the blogging of feminists, which is not in and of itself activism, but a way to disseminate information about activist movements and issues as they emerge. Here, too, I learned that the movements initiated by #blanknoise and #whyloiter are also different (see conversation with Shilpa Phadke in chapter 3). Even though they rely on hashtags, and processes around digital dissemination are slightly different from the writing and dissemination of blog-posts, they are not digital in quite the way the #LoSha process was. I've said more on this in my interlude with Ayesha and Raya. Any thoughts on process?

SC: A blog post is not essentially much different from writing an op-ed in a print magazine or a newspaper, or even maintaining a journal. I think the most effective part of #LoSHA was that it was entirely a crowdsourced list making students aware of potential sexual harassers. It was extremely easy and shareable in its format, and hence, it effectively went viral. You are right that many misunderstood the labor and networking that goes into creating such a list that others can screenshot, print out, and share in order to be aware of potential sexual harassers on their campuses. Also, the list worked, because there were just that many stories within the whisper networks before and it provided many people with some kind of a tangible evidence to the rumors they had heard.

RG: Now share some thoughts on genderlogindia and your experience curating and so on.

SC: Genderlog is a very intriguing platform because it is crowd-sourced and follows the format of a weekly curation. Hence, there is an opportunity to give voice to diverse feminist discussions on the handle, but also, the weekly format allows the curator to be flexible and really tune the discussions as per the engagement that they receive. Of course, having said that, it is also a challenging handle to curate because you do not know which way the discussions will spiral after you have tweeted. It may go as per your plans, but it may also go in a whole different direction. However, it is often a problem to condense complex ideas into an easy, shareable, and tweetable format; sometimes, the nuance is lost in an attempt to make ideas tweetable. But overall, Genderlog gives you the opportunity to really engage with the audience, since it allows the audience the space to come forward and enter into an active dialogue with the curator. Hence, what is so exciting for me is that it is almost a live/real-time engagement with many people who challenge, critique, and contribute toward the curation.

RG: Sohni, several of us have also been talking about how in post-NGOization spaces, women's autonomy is framed as a "job opportunity." In my recent book *Online Philanthropy in the Global North and South*, for instance, my coauthors and I described various case studies where NGOization and ITization mobilize "empowerment" as a discourse that works to market their enterprise. There is another interesting co-optation of the #LoSHA moment happening now, wouldn't you say?

SC: I would say that post #metoo and #LoSHA, there has not only been a co-optation of the method of an online or digital crowdsourced list but also the wider anti-caste discourse. I have noted an increase in the anti-caste discourse coming from many mainstream as well as online media portals, and also, there has been a general increase in debates around inclusivity and intersectionality. Of course, there have been portals, such as Feminism in India (FII), that have been trying to address intersections of disability, caste, religion, etcetera from a gendered lens. More recently, there has been Point of View, Mumbai's Skin Stories, which was launched last year to tackle disability, sexuality, and gender, but post #LoSHA, they gradually forayed into narratives of caste-based discrimination and violence.

Even, for that matter, Genderlog had an onslaught of curators trying to weave the caste discourse into the variety of topics that they were discussing on the platform. The clear emphasis was on inclusivity, or as you have already mentioned "empowerment" for groups viewed as marginalized or oppressed. However, for most of these digital streams or portals, intersectionality serves as an additive categorization or compartmentalization, whereby, an implicit stress is placed on the identity markers of an individual rather than on the structures of power. There is also an impulse to make feminism more marketable, albeit, "intersectional"; hence, the central argument made by Kimberlé Crenshaw that women "are differently situated in the economic, social, and political worlds" is lost.[17]

Furthermore, caste serves as a metanarrative for much of the new media and digital feminist trends emerging from the Global South. I say "metanarrative" because there is a desire to go beyond the usual story of women's oppression and women's empowerment. Now, the main project is to showcase a brand of feminism that is profitable and more click-worthy. This ties in with what you have been saying in your book *Online Philanthropy in the Global North and South* about how there is a new impulse to get the "social and the financial" to work together or as a measure of utilizing the subaltern or the Other in the digital sphere to spearhead a philanthropic project.[18]

However, there have been some good examples of trying to give voice to those who are relegated outside the mainstream digital focus. One such example is Khabar Lahariya going digital in 2016, bringing the rural feminist movement into the urban, mainstream digital domain. Another great example of this is #dalitwomenfight, which brings Dalit Women's Self-Respect March/Dalit Mahila Swabhimaan Yatra into the digital limelight. Using an effective hashtag, the digital project helps mobilize urban and rural Dalit feminists and activists and their allies together both online and offline. Moreover, it is an attempt to subvert the limitations and marginality experienced within dominant cultural spaces of society through an embodiment in digital spaces. These hashtags and handles found new iteration through the #LoSHA moment, providing digital trends with a new wave of feminist championing for the cause of women's empowerment. Hence, the co-optation of #Lo-SHA is also a co-optation of the wider online anti-caste discourse. Post #LoSHA, the project of tackling sexual harassment in India became synonymous with the project of creating inclusive, albeit, "intersectional" spaces.

RG: You make some excellent points here. Can you say more about Khabar Lahariya and others and their activism? Pallavi Guha—with whom I have an interlude in this chapter as well—has researched the marginalization of rural feminists in national media outlets and makes a general observation based on her research that "digital feminists want to influence public agenda and awareness. Rural feminists go a step forward and try to bring small changes by engaging with law enforcement and policy makers. For instance, they negotiate with the law enforcement to take action, so that the young women can go to college without getting harassed by the boys" (see theme 4 in dialogue with Pallavi). What do you think?

SC: Khabar Lahariya, which is an all-female-run publisher, was founded in 2002 and since its inception has catered to five rural districts in the Bundelkhand region. Until 2016, it was running in print format in a region where literacy level is low, hence, its circulation was fairly limited. However, with the increase in smartphone usage even in the rural regions, they decided to do away with their print format and go fully digital. Going digital allowed Khabar Lahariya to increase their audience reach exponentially as well as connect the rural with the urban. In a sense, the subaltern made a direct entry into the digital world, and they use their own voice to create a space for themselves. With the use of smartphone technology, the internet and recording apps, Khabar Lahariya has been able to share stories from the villages on the internet. Similarly, dalitwomenfight.com, which trends across social media with the hashtag #dalitwomenfight, is another project that blends the rural with the urban. It helps showcase the Dalit Mahila Swabhimaan Yatra/Dalit Women's Self-Respect March to the wider world as well as generates funds via donations to hold tours, conferences, and so on around the globe. They are incredibly active on social media, especially Twitter, and often hold discussions on gender and caste online as well. There is also Dalit History Month, which runs on Facebook and Twitter with the hashtag #dalithistorymonth; the project aims to bring the forgotten history and untold stories of caste assertion on to the digital sphere.

Another notable mention here would be Ahmedabad Talkies and Navsarjan Trust's *Project Heartland*, directed by Pratik Parmar and Parth Jani, which is a YouTube miniseries that showcases stories of caste assertion from the rural areas of Gujarat.[19] The several episodes show the plight of rural Dalit women in Gujarat and their struggles for empowerment and emancipation from caste-based gender violence and discrimination. The docu-series is cleverly shot and edited using an ordinary DSLR and a basic editing software and then circulated widely on YouTube and other social media channels, hence, bringing the subaltern directly onto our computer monitors through a click of a button. Moreover, we get the opportunity to hear their stories from their own perspective, thus subverting Spivak's critique by giving the subaltern a history and a voice.[20] Prior to *Project Heartland*, Navsarjan Trust also shot *No More Now*, a full-length documentary, also directed by Pratik Parmar. The documentary focuses on the struggles of Dalit women in Gujarat and their fight against patriarchy and the caste system. While it was initially kept offline and screened at festivals and events, later on it was widely circulated on YouTube—again bringing the rural directly to the digital sphere.

What is most interesting to me is that all these different projects have gradually garnered ample attention in the mainstream social media spaces. They are widely circulated by internet users from different castes, classes, genders, sexualities, races, and nationalities. So, taking up from what Pallavi Guha has mentioned, small measures are being taken by these projects with the vision of a bigger and more collective social change. Furthermore, these projects are indeed philanthropic and do not aim to generate profit through the use of technology and the internet. Of course, the act of going digital definitely can be seen as an impulse to make themselves more marketable in the digital world, but this is an act of assertion and a way of reclaiming space in the mainstream digital sphere.

Note: At this point there was a bit of a time lag before we continued the dialogue.

RG: Now in October 2018, a year after #LoSHA, we were in a discussion on Facebook, your profile page, my profile page, and then on Twitter in response to #metooindia. I'd love to have you talk about your responses in this dialogue interlude as well.

SC: First and foremost, I, like several of us involved in the debate, have expressed online already that I am thrilled that influential sexual predators are being named and shamed publicly, and we are already seeing the outcome. Several predatory men have been forced to step down from their position until a thorough investigation is conducted. So, in one sense, what we are witnessing today is a cathartic experience for many who have been voicing our concerns over sexual harassment in India.

However, to say that India is now having its #metoo moment acts as a complete erasure of #LoSHA. It is interesting to see that many, like Kavita Krishnan, who considered #LoSHA an act of "blackening of faces" have come forward in support of the new movement.[21] The ones who felt the need to appeal for due process when #LoSHA emerged on the internet do not have any problems with the recent outpour of #metoo stories. I view the recent outpouring of survivor stories on social media as an extension of #LoSHA. Some women, such as Anoo Bhuyan and Sheena Dabholkar, urged survivors to direct message (DM) them with their stories, which they anonymously shared online. Hence, Bhuyan and Dabholkar provided anonymity to survivors who wanted to come forward and took on the burden of accountability upon themselves (unless of course, survivors wanted to name and shame publicly as many have done).

So essentially, it has been a step forward from #LoSHA where only the names of the perpetrators were revealed without disclosing any details of the assault. As many have said, what the new movement has done is provided more credibility to the claims as well as clarified the exact nature of assault. Also, as many have argued online, the reason for doing so has been the hard lesson that they learned from #LoSHA, where the credibility of the claims was challenged simply on the grounds that no further evidence was provided. Here women like Bhuyan and Dabholkar—by publishing on behalf of survivors—are providing that credibility: the claims can be traced back to them in case any of the accused wish to challenge the claims. And they have first-person accounts by the victims in case the victim or the perpetrator in question wishes to escalate the matter and seek legal recourse. Furthermore, the alleged perpetrators are given direct access to follow due process by filing a lawsuit.

I see this as a direct outcome of #LoSHA, which was a desperate plea for help by survivors who were repeatedly failed by the due process. What we see now is a stronger iteration that due process has repeatedly failed women in India. Furthermore, the recent act of collecting stories is itself an elaborate form of list making, where the name of the perpetrator is placed alongside the nature of assault they are alleged to have committed.

Hence, when feminists such as Kavita Krishnan choose to support a certain kind of narrative while erasing others, it raises a pertinent question: whose #metoo is this? What space do survivors from marginalized communities have in this recent #metoo? Also, what happens to the survivors without access to technology and the internet? Who will advocate for them online and how? How do we ensure that everyone understands that the stories we see today on Indian social media are at best a mere fraction of the #metoo stories that exist in India?

Here lies the fundamental problem with upper-caste feminists jumping in to claim this recent outpouring of sexual assault stories as #metooIndia. What it shows is that certain stories when told by a certain population of people are bound to be believed more than others. The same ones who criticized Raya's list have no problem believing that the recent movement is credible, and hence, due process is not needed. If due process was needed in the case of #LoSHA, and Raya was put on the spotlight to prove their claims, why are the women coming out now and the women helping them not charged with the same demand? Why is the recent movement being deemed as #metoo and a necessary measure to tackle the sheer scale of sexual harassment, when many conveniently discredited #LoSHA despite it showing the sheer scale of sexual harassment within academia? More importantly, why were we not listening when many of the victims who contributed to #LoSHA came out publicly and defended their claims?

What I noted with the new Indian #metoo is a hegemonic stronghold of privileged feminists who have deliberately erased the intersections of caste, class, race, sexuality, disability, and other genders. In an attempt to shed light on rape culture and sexual harassment, other interconnected systems of oppression are downplayed or ignored. While some of the women participating in the new #metoo have acknowledged Raya's #LoSHA as a catalytic moment that has led to the movement that we see today, however, many established feminists have chosen to ignore the importance of last year's #LoSHA. This shows the status-quo mentality of many privileged Indian feminists who only wish to dismantle patriarchy as long as it does not directly come into conflict with their caste, class, sexual, or gender networks. It is a convenient feminism that positions itself on selective outrage while erasing the voices from the communities most vulnerable to sexual abuse, harassment, and violence.

NOTES

1. Katie Schmid, "Why Would Anyone Ever Want to Be a Wife," *The Establishment/Medium*, February 19, 2018, https://medium.com/the-establishment/why-would-anyone-ever-want-to-be-a-wife-b48d81d097c4.

2. See "The new 140-character war on India's caste system" at https://www.washingtonpost.com/world/asia_pacific/the-new-140-character-war-on-indias-caste-system/2016/05/11/df3f38e8-299a-43b8-a313-fcce84055301_story.html?utm_term=.d2e8bffdf414

3. Malară sculat (Christina Thomas Dhanaraj), Twitter post, April 16, 2018, 6:56 a.m., https://twitter.com/caselchris1/status/985819301407051778.

4. Ann Laura Stoler, *Carnal Knowledge and Imperial Power: Race and the Intimate in Colonial Rule* (Berkeley: University of California Press, 2002).

5. Ramesh Srinivasan, "Bridges Between Cultural and Digital Worlds in Revolutionary Egypt," *The Information Society* 29 (2013): 50, doi: 10.1080/01972243.2012.739594.

6. Padmini Ray Murray, Twitter correspondence with Radhika Gajjala, 2018.

7. Nivedita Menon, "In the Wake of the AUD Report," *Kafila.online*, October 3, 2018, https://kafila.online/2018/03/10/in-the-wake-of-the-aud-report/#more-38051.

8. Ayesha Vemuri, "After Nirbhaya: Anti-Sexual Violence Activism and the Politics of Transnational Social Media Campaigns" (Master's thesis, McGill University,

2016), http://digitool.library.mcgill.ca/webclient/StreamGate? folder_id=0&dvs= 1521324901089~502.

9. Sarah Banet-Weiser, *Empowered: Popular Feminism and Popular Misogyny* (Durham, NC: Duke University Press, 2018).

10. Julia Penelope, *Speaking Freely: Unlearning the Lies of the Father's Tongues* (New York: Pergamon Press, 1990).

11. "Neha Dixit," Wikipedia, last modified September 26, 2018, https://en.wikipedia. org/wiki/Neha_Dixit.

12. Erving Goffman, *The Presentation of Self in Everyday Life* (New York: Doubleday, 1959).

13. "Avital Ronell," *Wikipedia*, last modified November 19, 2018, https://en. wikipedia.org/wiki/Avital_Ronell.

14. Goffman, *The Presentation of Self.*

15. This is basically a label a few of us who were discussing South Asian feminist issues gave ourselves, and it includes the hashtags we followed and the retweets and discussions we had.

16. For example, see Radhika Gajjala, ed., *Cyberculture and the Subaltern: Weavings of the Virtual and Real* (Lanham, MD: Lexington Books, 2012).

17. Kimberlé Crenshaw, "Mapping the Margins: Intersectionality, Identity Politics, and Violence against Women of Color," *Stanford Law Review* 43, no. 6 (July 1991): 1250, doi: 10.2307/1229039.

18. Radhika Gajjala, *Online Philanthropy in the Global North and South: Connecting, Microfinancing, and Gaming for Change* (Lanham, MD: Lexington Books, 2017), 13.

19. For more about *Project Heartland*, see: Aarefa Johari, "From the Heartland of Gujarat, a Soul-Stirring Web Series on Dalit Stories," *Scroll.in*, November 28, 2016, https://scroll.in/reel/822681/from-the-heartland-of-gujarat-a-soul-stirring-web-series-on-dalit-stories.

20. Gayatri Chakravorti Spivak, "Can the Subaltern Speak?," in *Colonial Discourse and Post-Colonial Theory: A Reader*, ed. Patrick Williams and Laura Chrisman (New York: Harvester/Wheatsheaf, 1994), , 66–111.

21. Kavita Krishnan, "'It's like blackening faces': Why I Am Uneasy with the Name and Shame List of Sexual Harassers," *Scroll.in*, October 25, 2017, https://scroll.in/article/855399/its-like-blackening-faces-why-i-am-uneasy-with-the-name-and-shame-list-of-sexual-harassers.

Afterthoughts

*Different Ways of Writing Together
and Unfinished Conversations*

Radhika Gajjala in Conversation with
Kaitlyn Wauthier

These afterthoughts are written in the spirit of revealing collaborations and support systems of writing and continuing the attempts at dialogic writing that I've put forth in the whole book with its various dialogue interludes—even as I acknowledge that it will remain uneven in what and who it represents and in how the various voices are framed. As can be seen in the interlude chapters, an attempt was made to bring in interviewee voices; this attempt to diversify the voices continued even as I was writing—thus chapter 9's interludes kept expanding based on who was willing to participate. As I was ending the final revisions and responding to suggestions and critiques by the anonymous reviewer for the book, I sent several messages to Natalie Bolderston about things like word count—in panic!—and then decided to finish the writing first and see how it played out. But of course there's no really truly "finished" product here—because as I was revising, several things happened across the globe in digital publics that impact what I have put together in this book.

Once I got the blind peer review of the first draft of this manuscript returned to me, I had to put this writing away for a few months because I had to travel to Indonesia and India on some funded projects. One of these was a teaching project funded by the Global Initiative on Academic Network (GIAN) with Dr. Madhavi Reddy at the Department of Media and Communication Studies of Savitribai Phule Pune University, where I presented some of this work as part of a seminar lecture. The dialogue interludes got extended. After the Pune trip, I went to Bangalore, responding to an invitation from Dr. Preeti Mudliar at the International Institute of Information Technology (IIIT). I had discussions around various topics, including a project on feminist infrastructure labs and on WhatsApp and fake news with members of Shristi Institute of Art, Design and Technology in Bangalore (including Padmini Ray Murray, Pooja Sagar, and Chinar Shah) and members of the Center for Internet and Society (including Puthiya Purayil Sneha and Sumandro Chattopadhyay). There has been considerable discussion concerning WhatsApp as fake news.[1] In July 2018, the WhatsApp company put out a call for proposals for a grants of up to $50,000 to help solve its fake news problem.[2] In future writing—bolstered by more data collection and collaborations—I hope to take this discussion further.

In the digital streets research, I tried different ways to reach out to various Twitter handles, and while some who agreed to dialogue interludes are visible in the social media sphere, they are not all visible in quite the same way. I am glad this is so. I would not be happy just interviewing those who have been most often noted in various feminist writings to date. While acknowledging their visibility, I also asked others who looked interesting and who represented other voices in terms of age and caste. Not all agreed. I cannot claim that the observations I make about social media activism are representative or conclusive. They are merely a part of continuing discussions and dialogues around the emergence of Indian activism in social media space—around women's autonomy mostly—and sometimes they are anti-feminist and/or anti-caste. As noted in the introduction, #metooIndia surfaced in October 2018—almost exactly a year after #LoSHA. There have been many heated debates around that as well. The implications of both these movements within gendered Indian digital cultures in relation to caste, class, media, various institutions in India, and so many other things will need to be unpacked. There is much work in this regard to look forward to in next projects. My collaborators and I have only just skimmed the surface in our dialogues.

These afterthoughts continue as a dialogue between Kaitlyn Wauthier—who has been reading my writing—and me, as I've been sending chapters to her for her expertise in Chicago-style formatting. Kaitlyn was assigned as my Research Assistant from the American Culture Studies program at Bowling Green State University (2017–2018), in support of the work I do with the Fembot Collective, and was therefore also an editorial assistant for *Ada: A Journal of Gender, New Media, and Technology*.[3] We are together engaged in the work of a feminist collective along with our colleagues at University of Maryland and Oregon University such as Carol Stabile, Eva Peskin, Shehram Mokhtar, Bryce Peake, Sarah Kember, and so many others.[4]

Kaitlyn will speak for herself, her location, the questions this project raises for her, and how it connects to issues in which she is invested in the dialogue that follows. We will both summarize what we think this book is about.

KW: As Radhika signals in the above introduction, I am currently a graduate student at BGSU, slowly progressing through my dissertation, which, like Radhika's work, is based in ethnography and personal narratives closely linked to my sociocultural location. My primary scholarship considers different understandings of disability and the ways in which disability is institutionalized through multiple locations. I draw a lot of connections, for instance, between my current project on Make-A-Wish and Radhika's previous book, *Online Philanthropy in the Global North and South*. Scholarly endeavors aside, my personal trajectory and life experiences differ in many ways from the women whose voices speak throughout *Digital Diasporas*. I have the privileges of whiteness, a knapsack of associated socioeconomic privileges; I am cisgendered, straight, and married; English is my first language; I am a citizen of the country in which I reside.

As the wife of a person in diaspora from the Global South, however, I see how my partner uses digital gadgets and platforms to stay connected to his home and his family in Iran in many of the same ways that your collaborators, Radhika, express. His family primarily uses the platform Telegram, which shares many of WhatsApp's features referred to in related work by you and Tarishi Verma, and functions as a way to connect those in domestic/ghar spaces with the digital streets, too.[5] In terms of its use as a tool of domestic labor, my spouse and I use Telegram daily as an instant messaging service, even if we are at home together. We share photos, files, Instagram videos, and many other visual media messages through the service. One of the benefits of the platform is that my husband or I can easily forward to his family the photos we take through the app—this is particularly important as I meet my mother-in-law's expectations as a daughter-in-law. Additionally, as my husband's family are effectively banned from seeing their son in person for the time being, Telegram is also a tool that his mother and grandmother use to care (i.e., perform emotional labor) for him—sharing cooking tips, words of encouragement, and advice for being a good husband.[6]

Recently, we also have seen how Telegram can work as a tool of digital streets activism, too. Telegram has been more visible as of early 2018 because the Iranian government shut down access to the app during the December 2017–January 2018 protests across the country, as reports circulated that protesters used the app to communicate and organize.[7] Many Iranians, however, use Virtual Private Networks (VPNs) to bypass such restrictions and to stay connected to their families in diaspora.[8] Telegram's potential as a tool of activism hasn't reached that of Twitter, by any means, but I am curious to see how its use develops in the next few years.

As a woman who works from home, too, the dialogue interludes by women working from home (chapter 2) strongly resonate with me. Many young people in Iran live with their parents until they are married, and men like my husband are often not asked or expected to take on domestic responsibilities. Furthermore, as he lived in an apartment in Tehran, he also never had experiences of home or car maintenance that I was taught living in a detached single family home in the US suburbs. As a result, I take on most of the domestic responsibilities in our partnership, which is very hard, as I simultaneously live with the loneliness and isolation of working from home on my dissertation. While my husband slowly makes progress in his at-home domestic labor practices, I also do a lot of care work to teach him many skills, while he also works to adjust his labor and social expectations as a recent immigrant to the United States.

RG: A lot has happened in gendered Indian digital diaspora spaces since I first proposed this book and signed a contract for it in 2014. In this book I have framed contemporary women's inhabitation of digital publics along a continuum and faux binary between home and the world ("ghar" and "bahir"). Obviously I haven't covered everything there is to cover. My own points of entry, sociocultural location, and access to the people in these spaces—online and offline—among other factors, limit what I have covered. In writing about digital diasporas in this present book, I organized my discussion through a (faux) binary of ghar and bahir that I have extended from earlier published research examining online "Hindu diasporas"—mostly by scholars situated in Western academe. The "ghar/bahir" binary and axis has been incorporated into Indian feminist articulations about the woman's role in society and is drawn from a dichotomy used to redefine gender roles within Indian nationalism in order to mobilize middle-class, dominant-caste women as political and nationalist agents. It has also been used as a variation of Western feminist articulations of private/public binary and axis. The use of this binary orients the work socio-spatially rather than geo-spacially, temporally (where histories of migration and the nuances would be emphasized) or towards the engagement of the complex nexus of caste, class, race, sexuality and (trans)gendering. But this binary orients the gendered use of digital technologies regardless – because this binary is also a hegemonic, structurally imposed binary on women. The private and the public, domesticity vs profession, home vs the world – these are the binaries deployed in relation to "family values" not just in the South Asian socio-cultural contexts but worldwide. Policy around development of material infrastructures and physical architectures for the planning of projects like "digital iindia" or "digital Bangladesh" and so on work to reinstate women in the home space while also extracting labor from them outside of home. This sort of extraction of labor from women outside of the domestic but by keeping her in the domestic is not new of course in the digital era – but it proliferates now and can be pitched as modern and empowering move for the enrichment of women's lives. Even software/platform algorithms are developed through such implicit spacially binary assumptions.

Yet, rooted as this ghar/bahir theorizing as a way to examine the women's question in India is in the Indian nationalist move to mobilize upper caste women's labor towards nationalist projects, it elides struggles faced by people marked as outside of the implicity caste, class and cis-gendered framing of this spaciality. Very few Indian and postcolonial feminists have engaged this problematic. The queer, trans and dalit hashtag publics in the past few years have been creating global awareness through their protest movements, everyday posts and strategic socio-political campaigns drawn from their offline organizing. Thus these digital publics serve to rupture not only the Indian women;s movement, but also postcolonial feminist theorizing around gender and subalternity. Thus I can quite surely say that a majority of even the critical, feminist and queer research on even Indian *digital diasporas* is more casteless than anticaste (including my own work) to date.

A more expansive and nuanced discussion of this is warranted in future work. As some of my activist interviewees reminded me – their communities have been protesting for a long time. The protest movements have longer histories than their twitter presences. They are – contrary to what several new media researchers might note – not "new." The twitter generation is younger and definitely disseminating and updating these movements, making them further relevant to next generations while also creating awareness in a global, transnational public sphere - the movements themselves have longer histories of offline strategy, politics and struggle.

This book did not set out to—nor did it—evaluate the authenticity of any form of activism or scholarship. Some debates and discussions of politics are taken up for discussion, and they are specific to particular spacio-temporal intersections that emerged as I was immersed in these spaces and as I was in dialogue with my interviewees. Although I describe certain events happening in the digital streets and engage in conversations around even the most recent #LoSHA—and my support for the young feminists who initiated this is clear—I have not written solely about that event.

I also have not elaborated on discussions and critical engagements around corporate and NGO-initiated digital movements around women's autonomy. These inevitably bleed into my next writing projects.

The interviews, conversations, and even follow-up in-person meetings offline that inform the writing in this book begin with an entry point that is digital. I entered my search for "Indian women" through the internet and of course I mostly ended up with an examination of Indian women in digital space. While I do have interviews of women and men from other South Asian regions—Sri Lankan immigrants to Norway, Bangladeshi women and men in Bangladesh and in diaspora, Pakistani immigrants in diaspora and interviews with Pakistani activists such as Girls at Dhabas—these do not form a critical mass of the collected data or ethnographic evidence that I draw from.

In my observations concerning gendered Indian digital publics, I also relied on interviews and supplemented them with insights from my participant ethnography and conversations with collaborators, some of whom are included in the dialogue interludes and as coauthors of chapters. The ethnographies and conversations include the following of an Indian digital feminist Twittersphere and engaging in activities such as curating the genderlogindia Twitter handle. In addition I looked at evidence of place making—traces of relational moments—that are left in online archives and that remain as (multimedia) texts.

Kaitlyn, as you were reading and supporting me through the writing of this book you had some critical insights. Would you mind sharing your thoughts on what you think we did in this book and how it resonates with you?

KW: I think this book has become two projects in one. The first project is the unpacking of the faux binary between ghar and bahir, like you mention. Your interviews and the resulting interludes, though, have informed a second project—a methodological intervention that reworks readers' relationships with the text and the ideas brought forth through your research and analysis. As you indicate in the introduction and as you've noted in talking about this project before, they belong together in order to reveal the (recent, de-linearized) historical timeline of feminist movements into the digital for both NRIs and feminists physically located in India. As a reader, the interludes force me to contextualize various feminist digital interventions as they pertain especially to issues of caste, gender, sex, and generation—something that I think could only happen by visibilizing so many diverse speakers.

In talking about the structure of the book in its entirety, I know you've gone back and forth about what to include and how to draw linkages across the book. In one of these conversations, I realized how, as a reader, I had started thinking about chapters. In an earlier draft, where you had included reprints of the previous chapters, "Placing South Asian Digital Diasporas in Second Life" and "WhatsAppified" with Tarishi Verma,[9] it was clear that the chapters in section I at that time were setting up the concept of digital diasporas in general through the exploration of two different technological interventions (Second Life and WhatsApp). But after spending time with those chapters, I realized, too, that they also implicitly introduced the concepts of ghar and bahir that interweave through the entire book, becoming central points around which the other conceptual investments circle. To me, those chapters respectively demonstrated how people can alternatively engage in the digital bahir while remaining physically located in the ghar and/or remain critically involved in the maintenance of the ghar while physically inhabiting the bahir. As those earlier drafts were reworked and reconstituted into what are now chapters 1 and 5, I think the concepts of ghar and bahir still anchor this project's analytical pursuit, but that you loosened your original structure to root the dialogues more firmly as the critical intervention of the project.

RG: So before you continue to talk about the second intervention that you see this book making, let me interrupt you to ask what you now see in how the chapters are reorganized since I also decided to remove the chapter reprints from 2011 and 2018 like you mentioned.

KW: To me, the focus of this project has clearly shifted to vocalizing the diversity of voices that speak to the inquiry into offline/online intersections at the digital streets—the multiple access points that your collaborators have tested, bended, and forged in their feminist, academic, activist, domestic, or otherwise personal and/or political practices. Therefore—and this is the project's second intervention—I also think *Digital Diasporas* illustrates your commitment to critical ethnography and its writing practices. As a reader, I feel that the dialogue interludes ask readers to engage differently with this book than they might with other academic texts they read. Not all of the individuals that have contributed to the writing of this book come from academic backgrounds, and therefore they broaden readers' understandings of what constitutes an academic publication. The book's composition and presentation of these voices, too, encourages reader to draw connections and linkages between themes and threads themselves. As an aspiring ethnographer-in-training, I really enjoy that your research and writing partners and your interviewees/coauthors express their ideas in their own words without your authorial hand shaping our interpretation as readers. This allows readers to build their own relationship with the project and will hopefully inspire some active discussions of the book!

Digital Diasporas definitely speaks to your other recent projects and your work on online philanthropy in particular. This book complements your analysis of the ways in which philanthropic organizations "stage" subjects located in or from the Global South online and instead shows what it looks like when these subjects speak for themselves.

RG: Thank you Kaitlyn. I have drawn energy from interactions with you and the rest of the collaborators in this book. There are still various unfinished dialogue interludes that I have not used—including one particular recording with Jasmeen Patheja and Riddhima Sharma that is transcribed and ready to script out as a dialogue interlude.

"Completing" this book feels like I have closed the door after a very long community gathering where we have all engaged with each other intensely, intellectually, and emotionally. It has been a great pleasure to struggle through the cowriting of this book. There are of course various threads opened up in this book that could potentially be elaborated on and examined more closely. I did not take up questions, for instance, of the complex and contradictory implications of call-out cultures or lists. I also have not foregrounded this book by recounting histories of Indian feminisms or the official versions of the Indian women's movement—thus there are some gaps in what academics might consider to be literature review, context, and elaboration. For instance, in the last couple days before sending the final version of the chapters to the publishing editor, one of the contributors asked a question that reminded me that while various chapters and dialogues address the fact of Savarna embeddedness of Indian feminisms and even of postcolonial feminisms, I have not taken up an extensive elaboration of this very important intervention of naming hitherto "Indian women's movement" as embedded in Savarna bias. In the context of my dialogue with Divya Kandukuri, she clearly states her view that Indian feminism as it is currently manifested is indeed Savarna.

As noted earlier, some of the interludes (particularly those in chapter 4 and chapter 9) serve to rupture the mostly Savarna narrative of digital access and of postnational and postcolonial Indian feminist frameworks. The question of whether "Savarna feminism" can or should coexist alongside "Dalit feminism" is similar to the question of whether "White feminism" can co-exist with "Black feminism." Merely removing the labels will not ensure that the complex negotiations, coalitions, collaborations and self awareness will occur. Exercises in "unlearning privilege," even while useful for introspection and for moving forward into collaborative action, cannot in themselves actually undo history. In the contemporary individualistic and neoliberal ethos there is a tendency to celebrate any sort of expression of autonomy on the part of "women" while portraying "all lives" as inhabiting a level playing field through an erasure of historical specificity. Oppression and abuse are positioned as individual issues rather than as communal, institutional, and infrastructural.

While these labels seem "equal"—white versus black and Savarna versus Dalit—we know that there are unequal infrastructural and historic conditions that gave rise to formations such as Dalit and Black feminisms as responses to the unnamed bourgeois dominant caste– or dominant race/culture–based movements. White and Savarna feminists were not named as such until the oppressed groups of women spoke up, noting how white and/or Savarna women have been complicit in their oppression. Thus, if posing the question, "Is Savarna feminism or White feminism always exclusionary?" the answer would be yes. But, could we see Black feminisms and Dalit feminisms as exclusionary in the same way? The answer would be no. As some of those I cowrote with in this book—and others I interviewed—have noted (regardless of their Savarna or Dalit locations—and most of these were women currently living in India), the Indian women's movement can now be seen as having been caste blind: we cannot *unsee* that anymore. Savarna feminism *is* exclusionary (Divya Kandukuri and Damini Kulkarni were quite clear in noting this openly). The following quote from Hazel Carby about the relationship between white feminism and black feminism can be seen as relevant in thinking about Savarna feminism and Dalit feminism as well:

> In arguing that most contemporary feminist theory does not begin to adequately account for the experience of black women, we also have to acknowledge that it is not a simple question of their absence, and consequently the task is not one of rendering their visibility. On the contrary we will have to argue that the process of accounting for their historical and contemporary position does, in itself, challenge the use of some of the central categories and assumptions of recent mainstream feminist thought. We can point to no single source for our oppression. When white feminists emphasize patriarchy alone, we want to redefine the term and make it a more complex concept. [10]

This is also a good place for me to end this book, with much more to be work—to be continued—in next projects.

"The End"

Postscript

"things are not getting worse, they are getting uncovered. we must hold each other tight & continue to pull back the veil." - adrienne maree brown [11]

NOTES

1. Elizabeth Dwoskin and Annie Gowen, "On WhatsApp, Fake News Is Fast—and Can Be Fatal," *Washington Post*, July 23, 2018, https://www.washingtonpost.com/business/economy/on-whatsapp-fake-news-is-fast--and-can-be-fatal/2018/07/23/a2dd7112-8ebf-11e8-bcd5-9d911c784c38_story.html?utm_term=.aad53549ea3c.

2. David Lumb, "WhatsApp Enlists Outside Help for Its Fake News Problem," *engadget*, July 5, 2018, https://www.engadget.com/2018/07/05/whatsapp-recruit-researchers-for-its-fake-news-problem/.

3. See Fembot Collective, https://fembot.adanewmedia.org/.

4. See *Ada: A Journal of Gender, New Media, and Technology*, http://adanewmedia.org/about/.

5. Radhika Gajjala and Tarishi Verma, "WhatsAppified Diasporas and Transnational Circuits of Affect and Relationality," in *Appified: Culture in the Age of Apps*, ed.

Jeremy Wade Morris and Sarah Murray (Ann Arbor: University of Michigan Press, 2018), 205–18.

6. See, US Department of State, Bureau of Consular Affairs, "June 26 Supreme Court Decision on Presidential Proclamation 9645," https://travel.state.gov/content/travel/en/us-visas/visa-information-resources/presidential-proclamation-archive/june_26_supreme_court_decision_on_presidential_proclamation9645.html; US Department of State, "Sanctions Announcement on Iran," November 20, 2018, https://www.state.gov/r/pa/prs/ps/2018/11/287500.htm.

7. "Iran Protests: Telegram and Instagram Restricted," *BBC News*, December 31, 2017, http://www.bbc.com/news/world-middle-east-42529576.

8. "Unblocking the Internet: How Iran's Protesters Use VPNs to Defy Govt Censorship," RT Digital (blog), *Medium*, January 4, 2018, https://medium.com/@rtdublindigital/unblocking-the-internet-how-irans-protesters-use-vpns-to-defy-govt-censorship-216fa763886f.

9. Radhika Gajjala, "Placing South Asian Digital Diasporas in Second Life," in *The Handbook of Critical Intercultural Communication*, ed. Thomas K. Nakayama and Rona Tamiko Halualani (Hoboken, NJ: Wiley, 2011), 511–33; Gajjala and Verma, "WhatsAppified."

10. V. H. Carby, "White Woman Listen! Black Feminism and the Boundaries of Sisterhood," in *Theories of Race and Racism: A Reader*, ed. J. Solomos and L. Back (London: Routledge, 1999), 110–28.

11. https://twitter.com/adriennemaree/status/751799298791211008?lang=en

Bibliography

Abraham, Rohan. "All You Need to Know about the Transgender Persons Bill, 2016," *The Hindu.* Last modified November 30, 2017. http://www.thehindu.com/news/national/all-you-need-to-know-about-the-transgender-persons-bill-2016/article21226710.ece.

Ahmed, Bipasha, Paula Reavey, and Anamika Majumdar. "Cultural Transformations and Gender Violence: South Asian Women's Experiences of Sexual Violence and Familial Dynamics." In *Gender and Interpersonal Violence: Language, Action and Representation*, edited by Karen Throsby and Flora Alexander, 44–65. London: Palgrave Macmillan, 2008.

Alcoff, Linda. "The Problem of Speaking for Others." *Cultural Critique* 20 (Winter 1991–92): 5–32. http://www.jstor.org/stable/1354221.

Ambedkar, B. R. "The Annihilation of Caste." In *Dr. Babasaheb Ambedkar: Writings and Speeches.* Vol. 1, 25–96. Bombay: Education Department, Government of Maharashtra, 1979. Available online at The *Annihilation of Caste* Multimedia Study Environment. New York: Columbia University, 2004.http://ccnmtl.columbia.edu/projects/mmt/ambedkar/.

Anderson, Benedict. *Imagined Communities.* London: Verso, 1983.

Appadurai, A. (1996). Modernity at large: Cultural dimensions of globalization. Minneapolis: University of Minnesota Press.

Arendt, Hannah. *The Human Condition.* Second edition. Chicago: University of Chicago Press, 1998.

Arora, Payal, and Laura Scheiber. "Slumdog Romance: Facebook Love and Digital Privacy at the Margins." *Media, Culture & Society* 39, no. 3 (2017): 408–22. doi: 10.1177/0163443717691225.

Ayyar, Varsha. "Caste and Gender in a Mumbai Resettlement Site." *Economic & Political Weekly* 48, no. 18 (May 4, 2013). https://www.epw.in/engage/discussion/caste-and-gender.

———. "Caste-Gender Matrix and the Promise and Practice of Academia." *Economic & Political Weekly* 52, no. 50 (December 16, 2017). https://www.epw.in/node/150602/pdf.

Banet-Weiser, Sarah. *Empowered: Popular Feminism and Popular Misogyny.* Durham, NC: Duke University Press, 2018.

Basu, Amrita, ed. *Women's Movements in the Global Era: The Power of Local Feminisms.* Boulder, CO: Westview Press, 2010.

Belkin, Linda. "The Opt-Out Revolution," *New York Times Magazine*, August 7, 2013, http://www.nytimes.com/2013/08/11/magazine/the-opt-out-revolution.html?rref=collection%2Fbyline%2Flisa-belkin&action=click&contentCollection=undefined&region=stream&module=stream_unit&version=latest&contentPlacement=2&pgtype=collection.

Bernal, Victoria, and Inderpal Grewal, eds. *Theorizing NGOs: States, Feminisms, and Neoliberalism.* Durham, NC: Duke University Press, 2014.

Bhatt, Amy. *High-Tech Housewives: Indian IT Workers, Gendered Labor and Transmigration.* Seattle: University of Washington Press, 2018.

Bhattacharjee, Anannya. "The Habit of Ex-Nomination: Nation, Woman and the Indian Immigrant Bourgeoisie." *Public Culture* 5, no. 1 (1992): 19–44. doi: 10.1215/08992363-5-1-19.

Bob, Clifford. *The Marketing of Rebellion: Insurgents, Media, and International Activism.* New York: Cambridge University Press, 2005.

Bolter, Jay, and Richard Grusin. *Remediation: Understanding New Media.* Cambridge, MA: MIT Press, 1998.

Boris, Eileen, and Jennifer Klein. *Caring for America: Home Health Workers in the Shadow of the Welfare State.* Oxford: Oxford University Press, 2012.

Brock, André. "From the Blackhand Side: Twitter as a Cultural Conversation." *Journal of Broadcasting & Electronic Media* 56, no. 4 (2012): 529–49. doi: 10.1080/08838151.2012.732147.

Brueck, Laura R. *Writing Resistance: The Rhetorical Imagination of Hindi Dalit Literature.* New York: Columbia University Press, 2014.

Bruns, A., & Burgess, J. (2015). Twitter hashtags from ad hoc to calculated publics. In N. Rambukkana (Ed.), Hashtag publics (pp. 13–28). New York: Peter Lang.

Chakraborty, Angshukanta. "Bhima Koregaon Violence: Why Indian Media Can't See Caste." *Daily O.* January 3, 2018. https://www.dailyo.in/politics/bhima-koregaon-dalits-media-tv-twitter-maharashtra-bjp-modi-brahmins/story/1/21524.html.

Chakravarti, Uma. "Whatever Happened to the Vedic Dasi? Orientalism, Nationalism, and a Script for the Past." In *Recasting Women: Essays in Colonial History*, edited by Kumkum Sangari and Sudesh Vaid, 27–87. New Brunswick, NJ: Rutgers, 1990.

———. *Gendering Caste: Through a Feminist Lens Theorizing Feminism.* India, Sage 2018.

Charmaz, Kathy. *Constructing Grounded Theory: A Practical Guide through Qualitative Analysis.* London: Sage, 2006.

Chatterjee, Partha. "History and the Domain of the Popular." *Seminar*, no. 522 (February 2003): n.p. http://www.india-seminar.com/2003/522.htm.

———. "Subaltern Studies: No Dalit Movement so No Dalit Question Part 1–4." By Javed Alam. YouTube video, 16:23, posted by Dalit Camera, June 30, 2012. https://www.youtube.com/watch?v=67m-UuI9268.

———. "The Nationalist Resolution of the Women's Question." In *Empire and Nation: Selected Essays*, 116–35. New York: Columbia University Press, 2010.

Chaudhuri, Maitrayee. *Refashioning India: Gender, Media and a Transformed Public Discourse.* Hyderabad: Orient Blackswan, 2017.

Chen, Gina Masullo. "Don't Call Me That: A Techno-Feminist Critique of the Term Mommy Blogger." *Mass Communication and Society* 16, no. 4 (2013): 510–32.

Chun, Wendy, and Sarah Friedland. "Habits of Leaking: Of Sluts and Network Cards." *Differences: A Journal of Feminist Cultural Studies* 26, no. 2 (2015): 1–28. doi 10.1215/10407391-3145937.

Clark, L. S. "'Participants on the Margins: #BlackLivesMatter and the Role That Shared Artifacts of Engagement Played among Minoritized Political Newcomers on Snapchat, Facebook, and Twitter.'" *International Journal of Communication* 10, no. 1 (2016): 235–53.

Coffey, Diane, and Dean Spears. *Where India Goes: Abandoned Toilets, Stunted Development, and the Costs of Caste.* Noida, UP, India: HarperCollins India, 2017.

Cooper, Brittney. *Eloquent Rage: A Black Feminist Discovers Her Superpower.* New York: St. Martin's Press, 2018.

Crenshaw, Kimberlé. "Mapping the Margins: Intersectionality, Identity Politics, and Violence against Women of Color." *Stanford Law Review* 43, no. 6 (July 1991): 1241–99. doi: 10.2307/1229039.

Curry, Tyler. "Gay Men, Lesbians and the Ocean between Us," The Blog, *Huffington Post,* January 30, 2014, last updated February 2, 2016, https://www.huffingtonpost. com/tyler-curry/gay-men-lesbians-and-the-_b_4688477.html.

Das, Devaleena. "Resisting Sexual Violence and Thinking beyond Due Process." Paper presented at National Women's Studies Association, Atlanta, GA, November 9, 2018.

Dasgupta, Rohit K., and Debanuj DasGupta. *Queering Digital India: Activisms, Identities, Subjectivies.* Edinburgh: Edinburgh University Press, 2018.

Dave, Naisargi N. *Queer Activism in India: A Story in the Anthropology of Ethics.* Durham, NC: Duke University Press, 2012.

Dean, Jodi. *Blog Theory: Feedback and Capture in the Circuits of Drive.* Malden, MA: Polity, 2010.

Deo, Nandini. *Mobilizing Religion and Gender in India: The Role of Activism.* New York: Routledge, 2015.

Dey, Adrija. *Nirbhaya, New Media and Digital Gender Activism.* Bingley, UK: Emerald Publishing Limited, 2018.

Dhanaraj, Christina Thomas. "MeToo and Savarna Feminism: Revolutions Cannot Start with the Privileged, Feminist Future Must Be Equal for All." *Firstpost,* November 18, 2018. https://www.firstpost.com/india/metoo-and-savarna-feminism-revolutions-cannot-start-with-the-privileged-feminist-future-must-be-equal-for-all-5534711. html.

———. "#MeToo, Violence against Migrants in Gujarat and More." *Reporters without Orders,* ep. 40, podcast audio, October 11, 2018. https://www.newslaundry.com/ 2018/10/11/reporters-without-orders-ep–40-metoo-migrants-gujarat-haryana-rohtak? fbclid=IwAR12lv6EmGy4Qrva4PEMWuCI9AVhunLNwMDvk-GuG53iuV5KtqP4wh0h870.

———. "Swipe Me Left, I'm Dalit." *GenderIT,* April 14, 2018. https://www.genderit. org/node/5082/.

Dublin, Thomas. *Women at Work: The Transformation of Work and Community in Lowell, Massachusetts, 1826–1860.* Second edition. New York: Columbia University Press, 1979.

Duncan, Nancy. *BodySpace: Destabilizing Geographies of Gender and Sexuality.* London and New York: Routledge, 1996.

Enteen, Jillana B. *Virtual English: Queer Internets and Digital Creolization.* New York and London: Routledge, 2010.

Federici, Silvia. *Revolution at Point Zero: Housework, Reproduction, and Feminist Struggle.* Oakland, CA: PM Press, 2012.

Fraser, Nancy. "Rethinking the Public Sphere: A Contribution to the Critique of Actually Existing Democracy," *Social Text,* nos. 25–26 (1990): 56–80.

Gairola, Rahul K. "Digital Closets: Post-millenial Representations of Queerness in *Kapoor & Sons* and *Aligarh.*" In *Queering Digital India: Activisms, Identities, Subjectivies,* edited by Rohit K. Dasgupta and Debanuj DasGupta, 54–71. Edinburgh: Edinburgh University Press, 2018.

Gajjala, Radhika. "An Interrupted Postcolonial/Feminist Cyberethnography: Complicity and Resistance in the 'Cyberfield.'" *Feminist Media Studies* 2, no. 2 (2002): 177–93. doi: 10.1080/14680770220150854.

———, ed. *Cyberculture and the Subaltern: Weavings of the Virtual and Real.* Lanham, MD: Lexington Books, 2012.

———. *Cyber Selves: Feminist Ethnographies of South Asian Women.* Walnut Creek, CA: AltaMira Press, 2004.

———. "GIAN Programme: Studying Gender, Digital Labor and Globalization: Theory and Method." Lecture, Savitribai Phule Pune University, Maharashtra India, July 2018. http://dmcs.unipune.ac.in/news-detail.php?id=16.

———. "Networked Affect in Online Philanthropy." With coauthors Jeanette Dillon and Anca Birzescu. In *Online Philanthropy in the Global North and South*, 73–104. Lanham, MD: Lexington, 2017.

———. *Online Philanthropy in the Global North and South: Connecting, Microfinancing, and Gaming for Change.* Lanham, MD: Lexington Books, 2017.

———. "Placing South Asian Digital Diasporas in Second Life." In *The Handbook of Critical Intercultural Communication*, edited by Thomas K. Nakayama and Rona Tamiko Halualani, 511–33. Hoboken, NJ: Wiley, 2011. doi: 10.1002/9781444390681.

———. "Studying Feminist E-spaces: Introducing Transnational/Postcolonial Concerns." In *Technospaces*, edited by Sally Munt, 113–26. London: Continuum International, 2001.

———. "The SAWnet Refusal: An Uninterrupted Cyberethnography." PhD diss, University of Pittsburgh, 1998. ProQuest (304446170).

———. "'Third World' Perspectives on Cyberfeminism," *Development in Practice* 9, no. 5 (1999): 616–19. http://www.jstor.org/stable/23317590.

———. "When an Indian Whisper Network Went Digital." *Communication, Culture and Critique* 11, no. 3 (September 2018): 489–93.https://doi.org/10.1093/ccc/tcy025.

Gajjala, Radhika., Dillon, Jeanette., & Anarbaeva, Samara. (2017). Prosumption. In Van Zoonen, L. (Ed.),International Encyclopedia of Media Effects. Hoboken, NJ: Wiley-Blackwell

Gajjala, Radhika, and Annapurna Mamidipudi. "Cyberfeminism, Technology, and International 'Development.'" *Gender and Development* 7, no. 2 (1999): 8–16. http://www.jstor.org/stable/4030445.

Gajjala, Radhika, and Sofia Ashraf. "Cyberfeminism and Content Creation." By Ian M. Cook. *Online Gods*, no. 6, podcast audio. March 2, 2018. https://www.stitcher.com/podcast/online-gods/e/53542877.

Gajjala, Radhika, and Tarishi Verma. "Whatsappified Diasporas and Transnational Circuits of Affect and Relationality." In *Appified: Culture in the Age of Apps*, edited by Jeremy Wade Morris and Sarah Murray, 205–18. Ann Arbor: University of Michigan Press, 2018.

Ganeshan, Balakrishna. "Rohith Vemula 2nd Death Anniversary: Prakash Ambedkar among Activists Invited to Speak." *News Minute*, January 15, 2018. https://www.thenewsminute.com/article/rohith-vemula-2nd-death-anniversary-prakash-ambedkar-among-activists-invited-speak-74766.

Goffman, Erving. *The Presentation of Self in Everyday Life.* New York: Doubleday, 1959.

Gopinathan, Sharanya ."Why People Are Freaking Out about the New Trans Bill," *The Ladies Finger!* (blog), December 7, 2017. http://theladiesfinger.com/trans-bill-2016/

.Gross, Lawrence. Foreword to *Queer Online: Media Technology and Sexuality*, edited by Kate O'Riordan and David J. Phillips, vii–x. New York: Peter Lang, 2007.

Gorringe, Hugo. 2005. *Untouchable citizens: Dalit movements and democratization in Tamil Nadu.* Thousand Oaks: Sage Publications.

Guha, Pallavi. "Mind the Gap: Connecting News and Information to Build an Agenda against Rape and Sexual Assault in India." PhD diss., University of Maryland, 2017.

Guru, Gopal. "Dalit Women Talk Differently." *Economic & Political Weekly* 30, nos. 41–42 (October 1995): 2548–50. https://www.jstor.org/stable/4403327.

Habermas, Jürgen. *The Structural Transformation of the Public Sphere: An Inquiry into a Category of Bourgeois Society* (Cambridge, MA: MIT Press, 1989).

Haraway, Donna. "A Cyborg Manifesto: Science, Technology, and Socialist-Feminism in the Late Twentieth Century." In *Simians, Cyborgs and Women: The Reinvention of Nature*, 149–81. New York: Routledge, 1991.

Harris-Perry, Melissa. *Sister Citizen: Shame, Stereotypes, and Black Women in America*. New Haven, CT: Yale University Press, 2013.

Hearn, Alison. "Commodification." In *Keywords for Media Studies*, edited by Laurie Oullette and Jonathan Gray, 43–46. New York: New York University Press, 2017.

Hegde, Radha Sarma. *Mediating Migration*. Global Media and Communication. Cambridge, UK: Polity, 2016.

Heinz, Bettina, Li Gu, Ako Inuzuka, and Roger Zender. "Under the Rainbow Flag: Webbing Global Gay Identities." *International Journal of Sexuality and Gender Studies* 7, nos. 2–3 (2002): 107–24.

hooks, bell. *Teaching to Transgress: Education as the Practice of Freedom*. New York: Routledge, 1994.

Jha, Sonora. "Gathering Online, Loitering Offline: Hashtag Activism and the Claim for Public Space by Women in India through the #whyloiter Campaign." In *New Feminisms in South Asian Social Media, Film, and Literature: Disrupting the Discourse*, edited by Sonora Jha and Alka Kurian, 63–84. New York: Routledge, 2018

Jha, Sonora, and Alka Kurian, eds. *New Feminisms in South Asian Social Media, Film, and Literature: Disrupting the Discourse*. New York: Routledge, 2018.

Kamat, Sangeeta, Ali Mir, and Biju Mathew. "Producing Hi-Tech: Globalization, the State and Migrant Subjects." *Globalisation, Societies and Education* 2, no. 1 (2004): 5–23. doi: 10.1080/1476772042000177023.

Kanagasabai, Nithila. "Possibilities of Transformation: Women's Studies in Tier II cities in Tamil Nadu, India." *Discourse: Studies in the Cultural Politics of Education* 39, no. 5 (2018): 1–15. doi: 10.1080/01596306.2018.1448702.

Kandukuri, Divya. "Outrage over Jack Dorsey Holding Smash Brahmanical Patriarchy Poster Shows Casteist Souls Can't Face Reality," *News 18*, last updated November 20, 2018. https://www.news18.com/news/opinion/outrage-over-jack-dorsey-holding-smash-brahmanical-patriarchy-poster-shows-casteist-souls-cant-face-reality-1945061.html?fbclid=IwAR3feMH4X_pX_ytOUtE5hbjy_H-d68WTrn2sTLwBACnBCKbiwLe-kmtvi10.

Karunakaran, Valliammal. "The Dalit-Bahujan Guide to Understanding Caste in Hindu Scripture." *Medium*, July 13, 2016, https://medium.com/@Bahujan_Power/the-dalit-bahujan-guide-to-understanding-caste-in-hindu-scripture-417db027fce6.

Kee, Jac sm, ed. *Erotics: Sex, Rights and the Internet: An Exploratory Research Study*. Johannesburg: Association for Progressive Communications, 2011. https://www.apc.org/sites/default/files/EROTICS.pdf.

Kergel, David, and Birte Heidkamp. Introduction, in *Precarity within the Digital Age: Media Change and Social Insecurity*, edited by Birte Heidkamp and David Kergel [Prekarisierung und soziale Entkopplung—transdisziplinäre Studien]. Wiesbaden: Springer Fachmedien, 2017), Kraidy, Marwan M. "The Body as Medium in the Digital Age: Challenges and Opportunities." *Communication and Critical/Cultural Studies* 10, nos. 2–3 (2013): 285–90. doi: 10.1080/14791420.2013.815526.

Krishnan, Kavita. "'It's Like Blackening Faces': Why I Am Uneasy with the Name and Shame List of Sexual Harassers." *Scroll.in*, October 25, 2017. https://scroll.in/article/

855399/its-like-blackening-faces-why-i-am-uneasy-with-the-name-and-shame-list-of-sexual-harassers.

Kumar, Vivek. "Understanding Dalit Diaspora." *Economic and Political Weekly* 39, no. 1 (2004): 114-16. http://www.jstor.org.ezproxy.bgsu.edu/stable/4414473.

Lakshmi, Rama "The new 140-character war on India's caste system," *The Washington Post*, May 12, 2016.

Lal, Vinay. "The Politics of History on the Internet: Cyber-diasporic Hinduism and the North American Hindu Diaspora." *Diaspora: A Journal of Transnational Studies* 8, no. 2 (1999): 137–72. doi: 10.1353/dsp.1999.0000.

Landes, Joan B., ed. *Feminism, the Public and the Private*. Oxford: Oxford University Press, 1998.

Loftus, Timothy. "Dalit Feminism as Postsecular Feminism." In *Postsecular Feminisms: Religion and Gender in Transnational Context*, edited by Nandini Deo. London: Bloomsbury Academic, 2018.

Losh, Elizabeth. "Hashtag Feminism and Twitter Activism in India." *Social Epistemology Review and Reply Collective* 3, no. 12 (2014): 10–22. http://wp.me/p1Bfg0–1Kx.

Mallapragada, Madhavi. "Home, Homeland, Homepage: Belonging and the Indian-American Web." *New Media & Society* 8, no. 2 (2006): 207–27. doi: 10.1177/1461444806061943.

———. "The Indian Diaspora in the USA and around the Web." In *Web Studies: Rewiring Media Studies for the Digital Age*, edited by David Gauntlett, 179–85. London: Arnold & Oxford University Press, 2000.

———. *Virtual Homelands: Indian Immigrants and Online Cultures in the United States*. Champaign: University of Illinois Press, 2014.

Martinez-Torres, Maria Elena. "Civil Society, the Internet, and the Zapatistas." *Peace Review* 13, no. 3 (2001): 347–55.

Matchar, Emily. *Homeward Bound: Why Women Are Embracing the New Domesticity*. New York: Simon & Schuster, 2013.

———. "Sorry, Etsy. That Handmade Scarf Won't Save the World," *New York Times*, Sunday Review, May 1, 2015. https://www.nytimes.com/2015/05/03/opinion/sunday/that-handmade-scarf-wont-save-the-world.html.

Menon, Nivedita. "In the Wake of the AUD Report." *kafila.online*, October 3, 2018. https://kafila.online/2018/03/10/in-the-wake-of-the-aud-report/#more–38051.

———. Is Feminism about 'Women'? A Critical View on Intersectionality from India." *Economic & Political Weekly* 1, no. 17 (April 25, 2015): 37–44.

Mitra-Kahn, Trishima. "Offline Issues, Online Lives? The Emerging Cyberlife of Feminist Politics in Urban India." In *New South Asian Feminisms: Paradoxes and Possibilities*, edited by Srila Roy, 108–30. London: Zed Books, 2012.

Miyake, Esperanza. "My, Is That Cyborg a Little Bit Queer?" *Journal of International Women's Studies* 5, no. 2 (2004): 53–61. http://vc.bridgew.edu/jiws/vol5/iss2/6/.

Morris, Jeremy Wade, and Sarah Murray. *Appified: Culture in the Age of Apps*. Ann Arbor: University of Michigan Press, 2018.

Mudliar, Preeti. "Public WiFi Is for Men and Mobile Internet Is for Women: Interrogating Politics of Space and Gender around WiFi Hotspots." *Proceedings of the ACM on Human-Computer Interaction* 2 (November 2018): 1–24. doi: 10.1145/3274395.

Murray, Padmini Ray. "Bringing up the Bodies: The Visceral, the Virtual, and the Visible." Keynote Presentation at Diginaka, Tata Institute of Social Sciences, Mumbai, January 6–8, 2016.

———. "Writing New *Sastras*: Notes towards Building an Indian Feminist Archive." In *New Feminisms in South Asian Media, Film, and Literature: Disrupting the Discourse*, edited by Sonora Jha and Alka Kurian, 105–17. New York: Routledge, 2018.

Nagar, Ila. "Digitally Untouched: Janana (In)Visibility and the Digital Divide." In *Queering Digital India: Activisms, Identities, Subjectivities*, edited by Rohit K. Dasgupta and Debanuj DasGupta, 97–111. Edinburgh: Edinburgh University Press, 2018.

Nagar, Richa. "Mujhe Jawab Do! (Answer Me!): Women's Grass-Roots Activism and Social Spaces in Chitrakoot (India)." *Gender, Place and Culture: A Journal of Feminist Geography* 7, no. 4 (2000): 341–62. doi: 10.1080/713668879.

Nayar, Pramod. "The Digital Dalit: Subalternity and Cyberspace." *Sri Lanka Journal of the Humanities* 37, no. 1–2 (2011): 69–74. doi: 10.4038/sljh.v37i1–2.7204.

Nilsen, Alf Gunvald, and Srila Roy. "Reconceptualizing Subaltern Politics in Contemporary India." In *New Subaltern Politics: Reconceptualizing Hegemony and Resistance in Contemporary India*, edited by Alf Gunvald Nilsen and Srila Roy, 1–31. Oxford: Oxford University Press, 2015.

Noelle-Neumann, Elisabeth. *The Spiral of Silence: Public Opinion—Our Social Skin.* Chicago: Chicago University Press, 1984.

Norman, Donald. "Affordances, Conventions, and Design." *Interactions* 6, no. 3 (1999): 38–43. doi: 10.1145/301153.301168.

Novoselova, Veronika, and Jennifer Jenson. "Authorship and Professional Digital Presence in Feminist Blogs." *Feminist Media Studies.* Published electronically February 23, 2018. doi: 10.1080/14680777.2018.1436083.

O'Riordan, Kate. "Queer Theories and Cybersubjects: Intersecting Figures." In *Queer Online: Media Technology and Sexuality*, edited by Kate O'Riordan and David J. Phillips, 13–30. New York: Peter Lang, 2007.

O'Riordan, Kate, and David J. Phillips, eds. *Queer Online: Media Technology and Sexuality.* New York: Peter Lang, 2007.

Paik, Shailaja. *Dalit Women's Education in Modern India: Double Discrimination.* New York: Routledge, 2014.

Pandey, Gyanendra. "The Subaltern as Subaltern Citizen." Introduction to *Subaltern Citizens and Their Histories: Investigations from India and the USA*, edited by Gyanendra Pandey, 1–12. London: Routledge, 2010.

Papacharissi, Zizi, and Maria de Fatima Oliveira. "Affective News and Networked Publics: The Rhythms of News Storytelling on #Egypt," *Journal of Communication* 62, no. 2 (2012): 266–82. doi:10.1111/j.1460–2466.2012.01630.x.

Penelope, Julia. *Speaking Freely: Unlearning the Lies of the Father's Tongues.* New York: Pergamon Press, 1990.

Phadke, Shilpa, Sameera Khan, and Shilpa Ranade. *Why Loiter? Women and Risk on Mumbai Streets.* New Delhi: Penguin Books, 2011.

Puar, Jasbir. *Terrorist Assemblages: Homonationalism in Queer Times.* Durham, NC: Duke University Press, 2007.

Rai, Amit S. "India On-line: Electronic Bulletin Boards and the Construction of a Diasporic Hindu Identity." *Diaspora: A Journal of Transnational Studies* 4, no. 1 (1995): 31–57. doi: 10.1353/dsp.1995.0021.

Rajan, Rajeswari Sunder. *The Scandal of the State: Women, Law, and Citizenship in Postcolonial India.* Durham, NC: Duke University Press, 2003.

Rawat, Ramnarayan S. and K. Satyanarayana, eds. *Dalit Studies.* Durham, NC: Duke University Press, 2016.

Ray, Raka, and Seemin Qayum. *Cultures of Servitude: Modernity, Domesticity, and Class in India.* Stanford, CA: Stanford University Press, 2009.

Rege, Sharmila. "Dalit Women Talk Differently: A Critique of 'Difference' and Towards a Dalit Feminist Standpoint Position." In *Feminism in India*, edited by Maitrayee Chaudhuri, 211–35. London: Zed Books, 2004.

———. *Writing Caste, Writing Gender: Narrating Dalit Women's Testimonials.* Delhi: Zubaan, 2006.

Riches, Harriet. "*Pix* and *Clicks*: Photography and the New 'Digital' Domesticity." *Oxford Art Journal* 40, no. 1 (2017): 185–98. doi: 10.1093/oxartj/kcx010.

Ross, Andrew. *Nice Work If You Can Get It: Life and Labor in Precarious Times.* NYU Series in Social and Cultural Analysis. New York: New York University Press, 2009.

Rowena, Jenny. "The 'Dirt' in *The Dirty Picture*: Caste, Gender and Silk Smitha." *Savari*, June 17, 2012. http://www.dalitweb.org/?p=736.

Roy, Srila. "Lesbian Existence and Marginalization in India. *OUPblog* (blog). Oxford University Press, June 25, 2015, https://blog.oup.com/2015/06/lesbian-marginalization-india/.

Roy, Srila. "#MeToo Is a Crucial Moment to Revisit the History of Indian Feminism." *Economic and Political Weekly* 53, no. 42 (October 20, 2018). https://www.epw.in/engage/article/metoo-crucial-moment-revisit-history-indian-feminism?fbclid=IwAR3RHHfal_dRESLmsDSUaYaA4dNl9V8zCs2dT3IhBr5M65ZGZ0g59RR_VMU.

———. "Women's Movements in the Global South: Towards a Scalar Analysis." *International Journal of Politics, Culture, and Society* 29, no. 3 (2016): 289–306. doi: 10.1007/S10767–016–9226–6.

Salo, Elaine. "South African Feminisms—Coming of Age?" In *Women's Movements in the Global Era: The Power of Local Feminisms*, edited by Amrita Basu, 29–56. Boulder, CO: Westview Press, 2010.

Samant, Mayuri. "Re-inventing 'Public' and 'Private' in Social Experience of Movements: A Case of Magowa Group." *Contributions to Indian Sociology* 50, no. 3 (2016): 415–35. doi: 10.1177/0069966716657467.

Sangari, Kumkum, and Sudesh Vaid, eds. *Recasting Women: Essays in Colonial History*. New Brunswick, NJ: Rutgers, 1990.

Sangtin Writers Collective and Richa Nagar. *Playing with Fire: Feminist Thought and Activism through Seven Lives in India*. Minneapolis: University of Minnesota Press, 2006.

Sarkar, Tanika. "The Woman as Communal Subject: Rashtrasevika Samiti and Ram Janmabhoomi Movement." *Economic and Political Weekly* 26, no. 35 (August 31, 1991): 2057–62.

Saunders, Kay, 1947- (1984). Indentured labour in the British Empire, 1834-1920. Croom Helm, London ; Canberra

Schiller, Dan. *Digital Capitalism: Networking the Global Market System*. Cambridge, MA: MIT Press, 1999.

Schmid, Katie, "Why Would Anyone Ever Want to Be a Wife," *The Establishment/Medium*, February 19, 2018. https://medium.com/the-establishment/why-would-anyone-ever-want-to-be-a-wife-b48d81d097c4.

Scholz, Trebor. "Why Does Digital Labor Matter Now?" Introduction to *Digital Labor: The Internet as Playground and Factory*, edited by Trebor Scholz, 1–9. New York: Routledge, 2013.

Sengupta, Somini. "Acquittal in Killing Unleashes Ire at India's Rich," *New York Times*, March 13, 2006. Accessed December 7, 2018. https://www.nytimes.com/2006/03/13/world/asia/acquittal-in-killing-unleashes-ire-at-indias-rich.html.

Shah, Nishant. "Thrice Invisible in Its Visibility: Queerness and User Generated 'Kand' Videos." *Ada: A Journal of Gender, New Media & Technology*, no. 8 (2015), doi: 10.7264/N3VD6WRR.

Shahani, Parmesh. *Gay Bombay: Globalization, Love and (Be)longing in Contemporary India*. New Delhi: Sage, 2008.

Sharma, Aradhana. *Logics of Empowerment: Development, Gender, and Governance in Neoliberal India*. Minneapolis: University of Minnesota Press, 2008.

Sharma Ursula (1980a) 'Purdah and Public Space,' in Alfred de Souza (ed.), *Women in Contemporary India and South Asia* (Delhi: Manohar), pp. 213–39.

Singh, Neha. *Why Loiter?* (blog). http://whyloiter.blogspot.com/.

Smith, Aaron. "African Americans and Technology Use: A Demographic Portrait." Pew Research Center, January 6, 2014. http://www.pewinternet.org/2014/01/06/african-americans-and-technology-use/.

Soundararajan, Thenmozhi, "Twitter's Caste Problem." *New York Times*, December 3, 2018. https://www.nytimes.com/2018/12/03/opinion/twitter-india-caste-trolls.html.

Spivak, Gayatri Chakravorty. "Can the Subaltern Speak?" In *Colonial Discourse and Post-Colonial Theory: A Reader*, edited by Patrick Williams and Laura Chrisman, 66–111. New York: Harvester/Wheatsheaf, 1994.

Srinivasan, Ramesh. "Bridges between Cultural and Digital Worlds in Revolutionary Egypt." *The Information Society* 29 (2013): 49–60. doi: 10.1080/01972243.2012.739594.

Stoler, Ann Laura. *Carnal Knowledge and Imperial Power: Race and the Intimate in Colonial Rule*. Berkeley: University of California Press, 2002.

Sturman, Rachel; Indian Indentured Labor and the History of International Rights Regimes, *The American Historical Review*, Volume 119, Issue 5, 1 December 2014, Pages 1439–1465,https://doi-org.ezproxy.bgsu.edu/10.1093/ahr/119.5.1439

Subramanian, Sujatha. "From the Streets to the Web: Looking at Feminist Activism on Social Media." Review of Women's Studies, *Economic & Political Weekly* 50, no. 17 (April 25, 2015): 71–78. https://www.genderit.org/sites/default/upload/from_the_streets_to_the_web.pdf.

Sundén, Jenny. *Material Virtualities: Approaching Online Textual Embodiment*. New York: Peter Lang, 2003.

Tagore, Rabindranath. *The Home and the World*. Edited by William Radice. Translated by Surendranath Tagore. London: Penguin Books, 1985.

Tarrow, Sidney. *The New Transnational Activism*. Cambridge Studies in Contentious Politics. Cambridge: Cambridge University Press, 2005.

ThePrint Team. "Twitter's Apology a Cop Out or Was CEO Jack Dorsey Wrong to Hold Brahmin-Patriarchy Poster?" *ThePrint*, November 20, 2018. https://theprint.in/talk-point/twitters-apology-a-cop-out-or-was-ceo-jack-dorsey-wrong-to-hold-brahmin-patriarchy-poster/152114/.

Tufekci, Zeynep, and Christopher Wilson. "Social Media and the Decision to Participate in Political Protest: Observations from Tahrir Square." *Journal of Communication* 62, no. 2 (2012): 363–79. doi:10.1111/j.1460–2466.2012.01629.x.

Udupa, Sahana. "*Gaali* Cultures: The Politics of Abusive Exchange on Social Media." *New Media & Society* 8, no. 2 (2017): 187–206doi: 10.1177/1461444817698776.

Uteng, Tanu Priya. "Rethinking 'Mobilities': Exploring the Linkages between Development Issues, Marginalized Groups, and Gender." In *Gender, Mobilities, and Livelihood Transformations: Comparing Indigenous Peoples in China, Inda, and Laos*, edited by Ragnhild Lund, Kyoko Kusakabe, Smita Mishra Panda, and Yunxian Wang, 21–42. London: Routledge, 2014.

Vanniyar, Smita. "To Mingle and Make Friends Online: Lesbians and Bisexual Women in India and the Internet as a Safe Space to Socialise." Master's thesis, Tata Institute of Social Sciences, 2015.

Vemuri, Ayesha. "After Nirbhaya: Anti-Sexual Violence Activism and the Politics of Transnational Social Media Campaigns." Master's thesis, McGill University, 2016. http://digitool.library.mcgill.ca/webclient/StreamGate? folder_id=0&dvs= 1521324901089~502.

Vicks India. "Vicks—Generations of Care #TouchOfCare." YouTube video, 3:37. March 29, 2017. https://www.youtube.com/watch?v=7zeeVEKaDLM&t=64s.

Wakeford, Nina. "Cyberqueer." In *Cybercultures Reader*, edited by David Bell and Barbara M. Kennedy, 403–15. New York: Routledge, 2002.

Walia, Shelly. "What Indian Lesbians Have to Say about an Advertisement Depicting Indian Lesbians" (includes commentary by Rituparna Borah). *Quartz India*. June 12,

2015. https://qz.com/425657/what-indian-lesbians-have-to-say-about-an-advertisement-depicting-indian-lesbians/.

Walsh-Haines, Grant. "The Egyptian Blogosphere: Policing Gender and Sexuality and the Consequences of Queer Emancipation." *Journal of Middle East Women's Studies* 8, no. 3 (2012): 41–62. doi: 10.2979/jmiddeastwomstud.8.3.41.

Warner, Michael. *Publics and Counterpublics.* Cambridge, MA: Zone Books, 2002.

———. "Publics and Counterpublics (abbreviated version)," *Quarterly Journal of Speech* 88, no. 4 (2002): 413–25.

Weise, Elizabeth Reba. "A Thousand Aunts with Modems." In *Wired Women: Gender and New Realities in Cyberspace*, edited by Lynn Cherny and Elizabeth Reba Weise, vii–xv. Seattle, WA: Seal Press, 1996.

Wolman, David. "Cairo Activists Use Facebook to Rattle Regime," *Wired*, October 20, 2018. Accessed December 7, 2018. https://www.wired.com/2008/10/ff-facebookegypt/.

Zwick-Maitreyi, Maari, Thenmozhi Soundararajan, Natasha Dar, Ralph F. Bheel, and Prathap Balakrishnan. *Caste in the United States: A Survey of Caste among South Asian Americans.* N.p.: Equality Labs, 2018.

Index

abuses, 42; online, 95
academia, 157; feminism and, 104, 199;
 #metooIndia and, 205; narrative
 and, 100; sexual harassment and,
 191
access, 2, 152; class and, 114;
 conditions on, 185; digital spaces
 and, 24; opportunities and, 172;
 representation and, 194;
 technologies and, 1; women and, 77,
 82, 87
accountability, 94
activism, 19–23; caste and, 196–197;
 cyber-activism, 92; Dalit and, 131;
 digital streets and, 179; dilution of,
 142, 143; empowerment and,
 133–135; exploration of, 106;
 hierarchies and, 180; initiation of,
 189; legitimacy and, 194;
 neoliberalization and, 117; privacy
 and, 36–37; privilege and, 118;
 Telegram and, 230; terminology of,
 169, 174. *See also* digital activism
Adivasi, 197
advocacy, 98; competition and, 116
affordances, 2, 172; perceptions and,
 45–46; tools and, 15

African Americans: Dalit and, 97, 129;
 feminism and, 129; Twitter and, 132
Alcoff, Linda, 27, 31n58
alcohol, 77
Ambedkar, B. R., 97, 132
Anderson, Benedict, 12, 154
anti-rape, 179; rural feminists and, 181
appified space, 229; formations in, 16
appropriation, 27
the Arab Spring, 115; scholars and, 123
archive, 36
Arendt, Hannah, 43
Association for Women's Rights in
 Development (AWID), 174
atrocities, 103
attention, 86
audience, 102; content for, 203; social
 media and, 120
authentication, 20
authenticity, 40
autonomy, 13, 45; expression of, 235;
 subaltern and, 134; women and, 114
awareness, 231
AWID. *See* Association for Women's
 Rights in Development
Ayyar, Varsha, 95–98; on Dalit-African
 American solidarity, 129

information, 121; engagement and, 182
information communication
technologies (ICTs), 133
information technology, 12
initial coin offering (ICO), 214
initiatives, 96
interactions, 144
International Institute of Information
Technology (IIIT), 228
the internet, 81; communities and, 196;
connection and, 11, 73; digital
activism and, 23–25; entrance into,–
151, 156; homosexuality and, 155;
performance and, 82; privilege and,
152; Scholz on, 85; search on, 232;
sociality on, 48, 156; trolling on,
173
internships, 201
intersectionality, 10; digital activism
and, 20; feminism and, 106;
inclusion and, 94; interpellation of,
66; issues and, 41; movements and,
105
interviews, 10, 232; comments from,
58; identities and, 11; issues and,
126; as semi-structured, 13; women
in, 66
involvement, 100
issues, 78; acknowledgment of, 186;
debates and, 99; interviews and,
126; labor and, 116
iterative dialogue process, 141
iterative engagement, 13–16
Iyer, Harish, 159, 165n23

Jha, Sonora, 127
jobs, 68

Kafila.online blog, 192
Kanagasabai, Nithila, 99–105
Kandukuri, Divya, 54, 105–108
Kaur, Sukhnidh, 91–94
knowledge production: hierarchies and,
131; ideology and, 183–184
Kraidy, Marwan, 115, 128

Kulshrestha, Chirag, 207
Kumar, Vivek, 8

labeling, 169
labor, 85; hashtags and, 116–117;
indentured labor, 8; issues and, 116;
Losh on, 127; migration and, 9
labor migration, 9
Ladies Finger website, 193
Lal, Jessica, 120
Landes, Joan, 42
language, 172; HTML, 122, 158; media
and, 102, 106; translation of, 184;
vernacular as, 57; violence and, 200
leadership, 132, 180, 201; Dalit
feminists and, 167–177
learning, 174
legitimacy, 142; activism and, 194
Leone, Sunny, 203
lesbians, 162–164
LGBTQ+, 91; safe space for, 189;
solidarity and, 93; visibility and, 94.
See also queer digital spaces
liberation, 153
listprocs, 7
LiveJournal, 122
loitering, 76–78
Losh, Elizabeth, 116–117; on labor,
127
#LoSHA, 124; dialogue on, 188–197;
discussions and, 125; visibility and,
22–23

maids, 75
marginalization, 101; castes and, 6;
centering and, 91–108; Savarna
movement and, 27; Western spaces
and, 130; women and, 27
marriage, 79; technology and, 229–230
Martinez-Torres, Maria Elena, 21
masculinity, 5
mass media, 12
Matchar, Emily, 48–49
media, 44; the Arab Spring and, 115;
local language and, 102, 106

mediation, 21; reflections on, 167–177
Menon, Nivedita, 192
messaging, 10
#metoo, 144; recognition of, 22
#metooIndia movement, 18; academia
and, 205
micro-aggressions, 173
micro-struggles, 87
micro-transformations, 84
migration,. *See also* labor; migration 8
Mitra-Kahn, Trishima, 126–127
mobile phones, 37; women and, 37
mobilization: connection and, 190; of
diaspora, 5
movements, 54, 232; content and, 116;
intersectionality and, 105; micro-
movements, 87; publics and, 146;
#whyloiter as, 81; women and, 135.
See also specific movements
moving, 68–70
Mudaliar, Preeti, 148

naming, 170
narrative, 2; academia and, 100;
experience as, 170, 199; social
media, 103
nationalism: connections to, 51. *See
also specific types of* nationalism
nation-state, 7
neoliberalization: activism and, 117;
globalization and, 57
new domesticity, 48
non-government organizations (NGO),
134–135; movements and, 135
nonprofit organizations, 207–212
normalization, 44
nostalgia, 4

Obama, Michelle, 172, 177n1
offline, 119; dilution of activism, 143;
ethnographics, 88; hierarchies, 46;
performance, 143
online, 143, 203; abuse, 95;
communities, 132, 144; corporate
platforms, 85; histories and

presence, 2–4; individualization, 49;
loitering, 82; performance, 40, 145;
texts, 1; women, 52–56
opinion, 195
opportunities, 67; access and, 172; class
and, 73
oppression, 131; history of, 131;
households and, 149. *See also* caste
oppression
Orkut, 96, 97
OUP. *See* Oxford University Press
outsourcing, 12
Oxford University Press (OUP), 93

Paik, Shailaja, 55
participants, 132; experience and, 101
participation, 120; forms of, 36; naming
of, 41
patriarchy, 95; in the home, 39
pedagogy: exercise in, 184; research on,
104
Pennu, Inji, 195–197
perceptions: affordances and, 45–46;
binary and, 58; of gender, 193; of
roles, 71
performance, 143, 153; gender and,
5–6; the internet and, 82; online, 40,
145; protest and, 84; of violence,
200
Perry, Melissa, 175
persona, 25
perspective, 100, 173; inclusion and,
171; opinion and, 195
Pew study, 132
physical space, 148
Pinjra Todd movement, 54
platforms, 95; for rural feminists, 181
plays, 84
poetry, 176
politics, 145; hashtags and, 87;
visibility politics as, 86
popularization, 89
population, 55, 157
praxis, 191
precarity, 24

Contributor Biographies

Sarada Nori Akella is the founder and artistic director of Layavinyasa school. She is a Kuchipudi dancer, Carnatic classical singer, and instructor at her dance and music school. As a computer science major she worked in the information technology industry for five years. She traveled to the United States in 2006 on behalf of her IT company to lead outsourced projects onsite. She is pursuing her master's in Kuchipudi currently and does freelance research work.

Varsha Ayyar, PhD, is assistant professor and chairperson of the Centre for Labour Studies, at Tata Institute of Social Sciences, India. Her teaching and research interests are situated at the intersection of Dalit and postcolonial feminist studies. Her recent writings cover topics such as Dalit feminism, caste and gender in Mumbai, sexual violence against women in India, and feminist epistemology in South Asia. She has also contributed to several book chapters on caste, color, and gender discrimination, caste and urbanity, and feminized labor in the export informal economy of India. Varsha is a cofounder of the first international Dalit Feminist Press based in California and is editing its inaugural series. Varsha is currently working with Prof. Sheldon Pollock and Group for Experimental Methods in the Humanistic Research based at Columbia University on "Ambedkar Papers."

Sohni Chakrabarti is a second-year PhD student in the School of English at the University of St. Andrews. Her thesis explores spatiality and temporality in contemporary diasporic women's writing of the United States, emphasizing the transcultural narrative spaces imagined by women writers across the diasporas. Her research aims to closely scrutinize the intersections of race, gender, class, and nationhood to critically locate diasporic women writers within the American literary canon. Her wider research interests include postcolonial studies, memory studies, contemporary fiction, women's writing of the twentieth and twenty-first centuries, literary theory, and feminist theory.

Arpita Chakraborty is a doctoral researcher at the Ireland India Institute, Dublin City University. She is also currently serving as the chair of the Sibeal Feminist and Gender Studies Network of Ireland and Northern Ireland. Her writings have been published in *Economic and Political Weekly*, *Religion and Gender*, and *Indian Express*.

Sriya Chattopadhyay (MA, Bowling Green State University) is a former journalist from India with over fourteen years of experience as a reporter, and later, senior editor with leading publications such as the *Times of India*, *Entrepreneur-India*, and *Hindustan Times*. A critical scholar, her research examines colorism and racism in India's matrimonial advertisements, and the role played by online matrimonial platforms in providing agency to women and other marginalized members within social groups. She also studies the role of digitization in mass media.

Christina Thomas Dhanaraj is a Christian Dalit woman from Chennai/Bangalore, India. She is a consultant for women and minority-led initiatives focusing on social justice, self-determination, and collaborative models of scholarship. She is actively involved in the #dalitwomenfight campaign and is the cofounder of #dalithistorymonth. She is currently working in Beijing, China.

Radhika Gajjala, PhD, is professor at Bowling Green State University.

Mirna Guha, PhD, is an acting senior lecturer in sociology at Anglia Ruskin University (Cambridge), where she is course leader for MA sociology and teaches on feminist theory and practice, sexuality and social control, and globalization and social policy. She holds a PhD in International Development from the University of East Anglia; her thesis explored the lives of women formerly and actively in sex work in Eastern India. She writes on gender-based violence, sex work, social injustice, and social development. Her research experience has included working with asylum seekers and ethnic minorities in the UK, and youth and women vulnerable to violence in South Asia. Mirna identifies as an intersectional feminist. She grew up in Kolkata, India, and currently lives in Cambridge, UK.

Pallavi Guha, PhD, is an assistant professor of journalism and new media at Towson University, where she studies anti-rape and sexual harassment activism on mass media and social media platforms; the role of gender in electoral campaign and media; and politics and social media. Guha has a PhD in journalism from the University of Maryland, and her academic background lies in the intersection of political science, international relations, communication, journalism, and women's studies. She has worked internationally for leading media organizations including BBC News and television in London and the *Times of India* in the UK, India, and the United States.

Nithila Kanagasabai is a doctoral candidate in women's studies at the Tata Institute of Social Sciences (TISS), Mumbai, India. Her areas of interest include feminist epistemology, gender and media, and digital media cultures. She has a master's degree in media and cultural studies from TISS, and a postgraduate diploma in broadcast journalism from Asian College of Journalism, Chennai. She has also worked as a journalist at NDTV and Times Now.

Divya Kandukuri is a freelance journalist whose work focuses the intersections of caste, gender and mental health. She is the founding member of Blue Dawn Mental Health Care group that is a support group exclusively for Bahujans and a facilitator of affordable mental health care services. She is also the co-founder of 'Everyday Casteism.'

Sukhnidh Kaur is a twenty-year-old activist, musician, and aspiring academic. She uses social media to explore the intersections of gender and pop culture and their impact on the lives of the LGBTQ+ community and other marginalized identities. Sukhnidh believes in the power of the internet and social media to democratize narratives and galvanize young Indians to be more socially conscious, inclusive citizens. She is currently in her final year of economics at St. Xavier's College, Mumbai.

Damini Kulkarni is a junior research fellow at the Department of Media and Communication Studies at Savitribai Phule Pune University. She is working on her PhD thesis—a study of Indian women's reception of commercially successful Hindi cinema. Her writing has previously appeared in publications such as *Film Criticism, Economic and Political Weekly*, and *Scroll.in*, among others.

Inji Pennu works as a technologist, moonlights as a digital journalist, advocates for digital rights, and is always in between deadlines.

Shilpa Phadke, PhD, is an associate professor at the School of Media and Cultural Studies, Tata Institute of Social Sciences, Mumbai. She is coauthor of *Why Loiter? Women and Risk on Mumbai Streets.* She has been ICCR chair professor in Indian studies at the University of Leipzig, Germany, in 2015 and Madeleine Haas Visiting Professor in South Asian Studies at Brandeis University during the spring semester 2018. She writes for academic journals and books as well as for popular media.

Debipreeta Rahut has been working as a lecturer at the Department of Journalism and Mass Communication, Surendranath College for Women, Kolkata, India, since 2015. She is pursuing her PhD from the Department of Journalism and Mass Communication, University of Calcutta, India.

Pallavi Rao is a PhD candidate at the Media School at Indiana University, Bloomington. Her research interests include caste, gender, and class in India's mainstream news media.

Raya Sarkar (Raya Steier) is a lawyer and South Asian women's rights activist.

Riddhima Sharma is currently a doctoral student at Bowling Green State University. She has completed her MA LLB from Mumbai University, India, and taught gender, law, and policy at the Research Centre for Women's Studies, SNDT Women's University, Mumbai, as a visiting professor. She is the founder of a digital feminist platform,

FemPositive, that works toward building a more informed feminist movement through online and offline campaigns. Her research interests lie at the intersections of digital media and contemporary feminist movements in India.

Puthiya Purayil Sneha works with the Centre for Internet and Society (CIS), Bangalore, India. Her training is in English literature, and she has previously worked in the field of higher education. Her work at CIS primarily engages with shifts in modes and practices of knowledge production in the humanities and arts with the digital turn. Her areas of interest include methodological concerns in arts and humanities, digital media and cultures, higher education and pedagogy, and access to knowledge. She has published a report on mapping initiatives in the field of Digital Humanities in India, and coedited a reader on digital activism efforts in Asia.

Shobha SV is an independent researcher with a combined cross-sectoral experience of more than thirteen years in journalism, research, and digital media for nonprofits. She is presently involved in a research project trying to study the impact of foreign direct investment in e-commerce and its impact on street vendors and small retailers in India. She has worked on one of the first research studies from India that tracked the hate women experience for being publicly online on social media networks. In the past she has worked in the nonprofit sector in varied capacities and also been a journalist with reputable news organizations in India.

Noopur Tiwari is an independent journalist and founder of the non-profit startup Smashboard based in Paris, France. She has taught journalism at the Sciences Po University in Paris and co-curates a feminist handle on Twitter called @genderlogindia. Cofounder of an Indian tech startup called Idea Chakki, Noopur has previously worked in New Delhi, India, as a senior television producer, reporter, and scriptwriter.

Smita Vanniyar is a queer feminist, currently working at Point of View, India, on gender, sexuality, and technology. They hold a master's degree in media and cultural studies from Tata Institute of Social Sciences, Mumbai. Their areas of interest include gender, queer studies, internet, technology, history, stories, popular culture, films, and TV shows, etcetera. Smita can be found wandering the cyberspace, or hunting for good coffee.

Ayesha Vemuri is a PhD student in communication studies at McGill University. Her research focuses on the intersections of feminist activism, social media platforms, and transnational feminist solidarity networks.

Tarishi Verma is a PhD student at the School of Media and Communication, Bowling Green State University, Ohio. She comes from a background of journalism and audiovisual production. She graduated in journalism from the University of Delhi, and completed her master's degree in media and cultural studies from the Tata Institute of Social Sciences in Mumbai, India. She has also worked as a journalist with the *Indian Express*. Her research interests lie in new/digital media and feminist activism online, gendered spaces, digital labor, and representations of gender.

Kaitlyn Wauthier is a doctoral candidate in the American Culture Studies program at Bowling Green State University, where she has taught courses in women's studies, ethnic studies, and American culture studies. Her research interests include questions of access and mobility as they relate to critical disability studies, tourism, and immigration.